The definitive guide to accessible London

WWW.OPENBRITAIN.NET

Foreword
by Sally Chatterjee, Visit London

Visit London supports the tourism industry in making our city open to all and ensuring every aspect of a visitor's stay is as accessible as possible – from step free access for attractions to adapted hotel rooms.

London's accessibility as a visitor destination and our welcome for disabled visitors has significantly improved in recent years and Visit London is fully behind the Mayor of London's vision of making the 2012 Olympic and Paralympic Games as inclusive and accessible as we possibly can.

The information within this guide will be updated regularly on the Visit London website - www.visitlondon.com, where you will be able to find the latest information on all accessible goods and services in addition to the latest events and special offers in London.

I wish you an enjoyable stay in our city.

S. L. Chatterjee

Sally Chatterjee
CEO
Visit London

I am delighted to welcome you to the OpenLondon guide which provides a comprehensive source of specialist information on accessible accommodation, attractions and places of interest in London.

Contents

Foreword

by Chris Holmes, Tourism for All UK Patron, Britain's most successful Paralympic swimmer

As we are all living longer, more and more of us are experiencing the need for facilities in order to take advantage of opportunities to travel and enjoy leisure facilities and activities.

There are over 10 million people in the UK with a disability, and over 87 million in Europe who are wanting to take part in travel and holidays.

This is a huge and growing market, and needs to be catered for not as a 'special group' but as a normal part of customer service.

Going the extra mile is what good customer service is all about. It's important for all those serving customers to have the right attitude, knowledge and training, and appropriate facilities. Communicating to the public is last and most vital part of the equation.

Disabled people often find it hard to know if, when and where they are going to be able to use a service. That is what OpenBritain is all about.

For providers of services, those included here have recognised the need to take those steps. And with an OpenBritain sticker to display, you can readily be identified. This guide will be the principal means for the traveller with access needs to find what he or she needs, backed up by the comprehensive new website, **www.openbritain.net**

I am delighted that this fresh new initiative has been launched at a time when we need to be joining forces to offer a welcome to all in the biggest visitor event Britain has ever hosted, the Olympics and Paralympics in 2012. The hosting of the Paralympics in the UK in 2012 represents the best opportunity to change attitudes to disability, once and for all, that we are ever likely to have.

I urge every reader to use the facilities offered, get involved, and give us feedback.

Chris Holmes

Welcome to the OpenLondon guide
to accessible places to stay and visit.

This exciting new guide has been produced as the first 'Open' guide to a major city, following the initiative to set up OpenBritain as a one stop shop to accessible tourism in the UK. This resulted from an historic collaboration between two major UK disability charities – Tourism for All UK (TFA) and RADAR – who previously published their own guides, the former in collaboration with the national tourism agencies. Both charities share a *raison d'etre* in seeking to influence the public sector and industry to attain the highest standards of accessibility – to take the 'disability' out of people's lives.

This guide includes all the London accommodation inspected under the National Accessible Scheme (NAS) operated by VisitEngland. It also includes hotels inspected by Direct Enquiries on behalf of VisitLondon. In addition, all the providers listed in the former RADAR guides have been invited to join OpenBritain and be subject to randomized checks of their facilities. This system is being applied to other self-referred providers such as attractions and restaurants. Readers should therefore be aware that there is a distinction between properties that have been officially inspected and those which are self-assessed but subject to a random check.

In addition, we have been provided with information by DisabledGo, who have undertaken inspections of over 549 restaurants in London.

OpenBritain cannot take responsibility for information which has been wrongly supplied to us. We are keen to include a wide range of choice for you, the traveller looking for accessible facilities, and as all the schemes in the UK are voluntary rather than statutory, there is no one comprehensive, reliable source. It is also evident that what will suit one person may not suit another.

We hope that you can help us build the level of information available by giving feedback that will help other travellers. This will provide yet a further source to help you in your decisions. You can do so via the OpenBritain website: **www.openbritain.net**

We also look forward to receiving your recommendations for new places to include in the future. We are conscious that at present we have very little information about restaurants. We are delighted to say that we have recently had agreement from the Good Food Guide to collect information about disabled access to provide to us, and hopefully from there we can build a more comprehensive picture of accessibility to the wonderful range of places to eat in the capital. The Restaurant Association has also offered to help collect information.

We are delighted to have been joined by so many partners – from Government Ministers in the Tourism, Culture, and Olympic Executive departments – to the Mayor and Deputy Mayor of London, the London Development Agency, especially Tourism Manager Deborah Evans, Visit London, and a whole range of industry associations including the British Hospitality Association, the AA, the Association of Train Operating Companies, the Historic Houses Association, the National Trust, English Heritage, and individual companies of all sizes.

We thank those charities that are helping to distribute this guide, especially the National Federation of ShopMobility.

Please play a part in taking this initiative forward – join our campaigns, and give us your feedback and your nominations for good providers. In this way, we can create a true legacy from 2012 for disabled citizens and visitors alike.

Thank you for your support

Jenifer Littman

Jenifer Littman, MBE
Chief Executive
Tourism for All UK

tourismforall

**Worried about finding the right place to stay?
Frustrated by not being able to identify what you need?**

Help is at hand...

Tourism for All UK is the UK's central source of holiday and travel information for people with access requirements. Our new guide and website **OpenBritain** is a vital resource in this objective. But you may find a human voice on the phone or someone who can answer your detailed enquiries by email is the only way to gain the level of assurance you need. Tourism for All UK operates the only free helpline and independent information service that provides this. With 30 years of expertise as an organisation, we hope to answer all your questions.

The free TFA helpline is funded by charitable support, along with fees from those who choose to join us as Friends. We invite all readers of this guide to consider joining TFA as a Friend. This not only helps us to secure the future of this vital service, but also provides you with a range of benefits:

Tourism for All Friends :

- Receive a newsletter packed with items about accessible tourism, from new developments, places to stay and visit, changes in the law, and much more

- Special offers, exclusive to our Friends, which include

  » an exclusive rate at the Copthorne Tara Hotel in Kensington, which has a number of fully adapted rooms, including two with hoists

  » a special rate from InterContinental hotels worldwide - which include Holiday Inn, Holiday Express, and Crowne Plaza hotels The Kensington Forum Holiday Inn also has rooms with hoists

  » Many other time-limited offers which are published in the newsletter and on the TFA website www.tourismforall.org.uk

- Free publications on specific topics, such as financial help for holidays, overseas travel, extra services such as care support (worth £3.00 - £6.00 each)

- Access to special members' only areas of the website including a members' forum

TOURISM FOR ALL SERVICES

Tourism for All Services is a wholly owned subsidiary of the charity that offers access audits, destination audits, and consultancy to business and public sector organisations seeking to improve their accessibility or comply with the Disability Discrimination Act.

Businesses advised by TFA Services have gone on to win Access Awards.

"I cannot thank Brian Seaman and Tourism for All enough for all their help and advice. Put simply, we could never have done it, or done it so well, without you".
Mortons House Hotel, Dorset

Brian also takes up campaigns for better access raised by visitors and Tourism for All individual members, and is a mine of information. Brian Seaman is on 01293 776225 or brian@tourismforall.org.uk

We can also offer assistance with staff training and access to our online training programme in welcoming guests with disabilities. The Access for All training has been developed with the help of people with impairments and industry professionals, and is endorsed by the Institute of Hospitality.

So if you like the idea of not just being a traveller, but working in the industry, this could be a way to get started. Contact timgardiner@tourismforall.org.uk

Tourism for All Services Limited donates 100% of all profits to the charity Tourism for All UK Registered Charity 279169

All this for only **£25.00** which you can save in a single hotel booking.

To join, or for information call: **0845 124 9971**

To make a reservation, call: **0845 124 9973**

email **info@tourismforall.org.uk**, join online on **www.tourismforall.org.uk/Membership.html**

Or write to us at: **Tourism for All UK, c/o Vitalise, Shap Road Ind. Est, Shap Road, Kendal LA9 6NZ**

Tourism for All UK is a registered charity No 279169 and a company limited by guarantee No 01466822

Over 2000 stations with accessible information

The improved Blue Badge map is just the ticket . . .

The new Blue Badge rail map contains information on accessible facilities for more than 2000 train stations.

We've searched the UK and also found information for you on accessible football stadiums, tube stations, airports, public toilets, beaches, petrol stations and much more.

www.direct.gov.uk/bluebadgemap

Directgov

Public services all in one place
www.direct.gov.uk

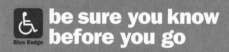

be sure you know before you go

Blue Badge

How to use this guide

The new OpenLondon guide is the definitive guide to London for visitors with access needs. The guide contains everything required to enjoy London to the full.

OpenLondon is packed with useful information on accommodation, places of interest, transport, theatres, restaurants and shopping. Clear, attractive entries present the reader with facts at their fingertips and useful maps help find locations.

Inspirational information about places to visit and practical advice on getting around the city makes this guide an invaluable holiday or business trip planning tool for anyone with access needs.

We've made the organisation of OpenLondon as intuitive as possible – but here are some useful tips to get you started and help you find the information you need more easily:

- Generally, we have restricted the entries in the guide to places within the M25

- Each postcode also has the name of the area it covers to help identify its location.

- We've given you the contact details so that you can find out more. These include phone and textphone numbers, email addresses and websites. The longer web addresses should take you directly to the pages which cover accessibility, which are not always easy to find. If you prefer to find these pages yourself, just use the shorter web address ending in .com, .co.uk or .org

- If you have access to the internet, we would recommend you use it to the full. Many of London's biggest attractions have impressive pages on their websites devoted to information for disabled visitors.

- Wherever possible, we have included the 2010 information. Where we were not able to obtain this information before going to press, we have listed the 2009 information – so do check with the attraction you want to visit before setting off.

- There is a key to the symbols used in the Where to Stay, Where to Eat and Accessible Sightseeing sections on the opening page of each section. Because of the different facilities at each of these three sections, we have used different symbols, which are for guidance only.

Key to symbols

Information about many of the facilities and services available at attractions, hotels/places to stay and restaurants is given in the form of symbols.

 Accessible to wheelchair user

 Fully wheelchair accessible

 Wheelchair user with assistance

 Mobility Impaired Walker

 Seat Available

WC WC Standard

 Adapted Changing Rooms

 Changing Places Facilities

 Contacting the venue

 Home Service

 Car Parking at Venue

 Blue Badge Parking Available

 Public Car Park (200m approx)

 Adapted Accommodation

 Sign Language used

 Disability Awareness Training

 Access trained staff

 Facilities for the visually impaired

 Induction Loop system

 Hearing facilities

abc Large print information

 Braille information

 Assistance dogs welcome

 Wheelchair accessible leisure facilities

Designated wheelchair accessible public toilet

 Wheelchair accessible dining area

 Wheelchair accessible ground floor

 Wheelchair accessible bedroom

 Children welcome

 Designated parking

 Ramped or level entrance

 Staff available to assist by arrangement

 Licensed bar

 Evening meal by arrangement

 Special diets by arrangement

 Accessible Lift

 Hoist available

 Garden/patio

 Bedroom(s) on ground floor

 Text phone/inductive coupler

 TV with subtitles

 Tea/coffee facilities in all bedrooms

 Accessible shower

 Seating in shower

 Toilet seat raiser

 Overnight holding area

 Motor home pitches reserved for day trips off-site

 Electrical hook-up points for caravans and tents

 Calor Gas/Camping Gaz purchase/exchange service

 Chemical toilet disposal point

 Motor home waste disposal point

 Showers

 Laundry facilities

 Caravans

 Motor caravans

 Tents

Britain's train companies working together to make rail travel easier

Stations made easy →

Check out the new 'Stations Made Easy' journey planning application at:

www.nationalrail.co.uk/stations_destinations

or call 08457 48 49 50 to arrange assistance for your journey

Disabled Persons Railcard

For more information on how to save money when you travel see **www.disabledpersons-railcard.co.uk**

Burlington Arcade, Piccadilly © Britainonview/Simon Winnall

Introduction to London

Hyde Park © Britainonview

"By seeing London, I have seen as much of life as the world can show"

Samuel Johnson English Poet, Critic & Writer (1709-1784)

There is always something new to see or do in London and this, combined with its fascinating history as the capital city of England and Britain, makes it such a fantastic and varied visit that delivers on so many levels. London is a vibrant, multi-cultural, twenty-four hour city for those looking for the 'buzz'! It also offers peace and quiet in superb parks, world-class galleries, museums, cathedrals and churches.

The following pages aim to give a taste of what is on offer to help you plan your visit and make sure you get the most from your trip. Most importantly, there are sources of reliable information on accessibility from both organisations and businesses.

There is an A-Z of useful addresses at the end of this section.

We've given you the contact details so that you can find out more. These include phone and textphone numbers, email addresses and websites. The longer web addresses should take you directly to the page that covers accessibility, which are not always easy to find. If you prefer to find these pages yourself, just use the shorter web address ending in .com, .co.uk, or .org

House of Parliament © Britainonview

Top Ten sightseeing areas in central London

A brief description of selected sightseeing areas in central London. This is to help you get your bearings, plan a visit and check on the map (page 136) to see how to make the most of your time.

Westminster (SW1)

Westminster is the starting point for sightseeing in London. Within a short distance, you can visit the Houses of Parliament and Big Ben, Westminster Abbey and the Cabinet War Rooms. Just across Westminster Bridge on the South Bank of the Thames are newer attractions, including Merlin Entertainments London Eye.

St James's (SW1)

St James's Park, one of London's most delightful parks, connects Westminster with a cluster of Royal sights: Buckingham Palace, The Queen's Gallery and The Royal Mews. Not surprisingly, the area around St James's is the place to enjoy the pageantry of London.

Piccadilly Circus/Leicester Square/Soho (WC2/W1)

The Circus, once considered the hub of the Empire, attracts a large crowd. Leicester Square is an entertainment area with cinemas, restaurants, attractions and theatres. Because it has so many cinemas, Leicester Square hosts lots of big movie premieres. Both areas act as the gateway to Soho, with its restaurants, shops and markets.

Trafalgar Square/The Strand (WC2)

Trafalgar Square is home to Nelson's Column, the famous stone lions, the infamous fourth plinth and,

visitlondonimages / Pawel Libera

lately fewer pigeons. It is also home to the National Gallery, the National Portrait Gallery and St Martin-in-the-Fields. Heading down the Strand, you will find The Royal Courts of Justice and Somerset House.

Covent Garden (WC2)

Covent Garden is a vibrant area with everything from speciality shops to a huge choice of bars, restaurants and cafés. It is home to the Apple Craft Market, street performers and, of course, the Royal Opera House. Everything is housed in and around the Market Building and Piazzas. A word of warning for wheelchair users: Covent Garden has more than its fair share of cobbles.

Holborn (WC1)

The four Inns (Lincoln's Inn, Gray's Inn, Inner and Middle Temple) form the Inns of Court. Step back in time to discover a haven of ancient buildings and well manicured gardens steeped in fascinating history. Temple Church, built by the Knights Templar in 1185, welcomes all visitors.

Knightsbridge/Kensington (SW3)

Kensington is one of London's wealthiest areas, but you don't need to be rich to visit, as some of London's best free museums are based in Kensington: the Science Museum, the Natural History Museum and the Victoria and Albert Museum (V&A). Kensington also boasts two Royal Parks, Kensington Palace, the Serpentine Gallery, and a great range of shops in High Street Kensington. And Knightsbridge, the home of Harrods, also offers plenty of chic shops.

The City (EC2, EC3, EC4)

The City of London is a small city within Greater London. It's the historic core of London around which the modern metropolis grew.

It's often referred to as just "the City" or as "the Square Mile". In, or close to, the City are some of London's most famous sights: St Paul's Cathedral and many other historic churches; the Barbican, the Museum of London and, further east, the Tower of London and Tower Bridge.

Southwark (SE1)

Home to one of London's great cultural icons the Southbank Centre, the Merlin Entertainments London Eye and the BFI Imax cinema. Check out the designer boutiques in the Oxo Tower and Gabriel's Wharf. Don't miss Shakespeare's Globe Theatre and the Tate Modern art gallery. Continue east to Southwark Cathedral and Borough Market with up to 70 stalls selling various gourmet foods - delicious!

Docklands (E14) – (outside Central London but easily accessible on the DLR)

Head to London Docklands in East London, and you'll find the informative Museum of London Docklands. London Docklands was once part of the historic Port of London, the busiest port in the world. The area around Canary Wharf is thoroughly 21st century and houses the newest of London's financial districts.

Buckingham Palace © Britainonview

Shaftesbury Theatre London © Britainonview/Pawel Libera

Theatre and nightlife

London offers some of the best theatre, music and nightlife in the world. As many of London's theatres are historic buildings with varying floor levels, staircases and narrow aisles, this section is designed to help you plan your visits. You'll find that newer venues like the Southbank Centre and the National Theatre tend to have good access for wheelchair users.

Access facilities

One of the best sources of information is the Society of London Theatres.
t: 020 7557 6700
email: enquiries@solttma.co.uk
web: www.officiallondontheatre.co.uk/access/

The website contains Venue Access Information on all the access options available in Theatreland. This includes wheelchair accessibility, adapted toilet and bar facilities, sound amplification systems, admission policy on guide dogs, public transport and parking. They also publish the Access London Theatre Guide. Published three times a year, the guide features complete listings of audio-described, captioned and signed performances in London theatres.

Assisted performances

The different types of assisted performances (audio-described, captioned and sign language-interpreted performances) usually consist of:-

Audio described performances

Audio description is a live description of the characters, their expressions, actions, costumes and the sets, which is relayed to patrons over personal headsets. This happens unobtrusively between the lines and offers patrons who cannot see the stage assistance in sharing the visual aspects of the programme. Touch tours are also sometimes available for people with visual impairments.

Captioned performances

At a captioned performance words are displayed on a screen at the same time as they are spoken or sung by an actor, thus enabling people with a hearing loss to understand everything. The process is similar to subtitling. It aims to offer deaf and hard-of-hearing people the same experience, as far as possible, as a hearing audience.

Sign language interpreted performances

A British Sign Language (BSL) theatre interpreter will stand on or at the side of the stage, in a place clearly visible to the audience, and interpret the spoken and heard aspects of the show for deaf and hard-of-hearing patrons who are British Sign Language users.

Other useful addresses

Artsline

Artsline provides an online and telephone information and advice service about all aspects of access to arts and entertainment activities. Its extensive database provides information to theatres, cinemas, music venues and all other places of entertainment.
t: 020 7388 2227
web: www.artsline.org.uk

DisabledGo

DisabledGo provides free detailed access information about a variety of entertainment venues. Its access guides have been specially designed to answer the everyday questions of disabled people, their assistants, carers, family and friends.
web: www.disabledgo.com

Shape Arts

Shape Arts offers a fully accessible ticket booking service, and organises Access Assistants for those who need help getting to and from the venue.
t: 0845 521 3457
Minicom: 020 7424 7368
web: www.tickets.shapearts.org.uk

Major venues

Apollo Victoria Theatre, 17 Wilton Road SW1V 1LL
t: 0844 826 8000 **txt:** 0870 145 1178
web: apollovictorialondon.org.uk

Barbican Centre, Silk Street EC2Y 8DS
t: 020 7638 8891 **web:** www.barbican.org.uk

Donmar Theatre, 41 Earlham Street WC2H 9LX
t: 0844 871 7642 **web:** www.donmarwarehouse.com

Hammersmith Apollo, Hammersmith W6 9QH
t: 020 8563 3800 **web:** venues.meanfiddler.com

National Theatre, South Bank SE1 9PX
t: 020 7452 3000
web: www.nationaltheatre.org.uk/accessibility

New London Theatre, Drury Lane WC2B 5PW
t: 0844 4124 648
web: www.reallyuseful.com

The O$_2$ Arena, Greenwich Peninsula SE10 0BB
t: 0870 600 6140 **typetext:** 18001 0870 600 6140
web: www.theo2.co.uk

Open Air Theatre, Regent's Park NW1 4NR
t: 0844 826 4242
web: openairtheatre.org/p6.html

Piccadilly Theatre, 16 Denman Street W1D 7DY
t: 0871 297 5477

Prince of Wales Theatre, Coventry Street W1D 4HS
t: 0871 716 7960
web: www.princeofwalestheatrelondon.com

Roundhouse, Chalk Farm Road NW1 8EH
t: 0844 482 8008
web: www.roundhouse.org.uk/your-visit/access

Royal Albert Hall, Kensington Gore SW7 2AP
t: 0845 401 5045 **web:** www.royalalberthall.com

Royal Opera House, Covent Garden WC2E 9DD
t: 020 7304 4000 **web:** www.roh.org.uk

Shaftesbury Theatre, Shaftesbury Ave. WC2H 8DP
t: 020 7379 5399 **web:** www.shaftesburytheatre.com

Shakespeare's Globe, Bankside SE1 9DT
t: 020 7401 9919 **web:** www.shakespeares-globe.org

Sadler's Wells Theatre, Rosebery Ave. EC1R 4TN
t: 0844 412 4300
web: www.sadlerswells.com/page/visitor-info

Southbank Centre, Belvedere Road SE1 8XX
t: 0844 875 0073 (select option 2)
web: www.southbankcentre.co.uk/visitor-info/access

Prince of Wales Theatre © Britainonview/Pawel Libera

What's On in London Theatres

Of course, London's calendar of theatre and cultural events is ever-changing. But here are some highlights of the 2010 season which are being staged in accessible venues:-

Mamma Mia! Prince of Wales Theatre till March 2011. The hit Abba musical continues its successful West End run with the story of a young woman and her mother on the eve of the daughter's wedding day.

Wicked Apollo Victoria Theatre till April 2011. The magical hit musical about two unlikely friends and how they become the Wicked Witch of the West and Glinda the Good.

Grease Piccadilly Theatre till 26 October 2010. Grease, the smash hit musical about high school love, returns to the West End to bring smiles to the faces of all wannabe T-Birds and Pink Ladies. Includes favourite songs *You're The One That I Want*, *Hopelessly Devoted* and *Summer Nights*.

King Lear Donmar Warehouse from 07 Sept 2010 to 05 Feb 2011. Derek Jacobi takes on one of Shakespeare's greatest roles, the aging king who sees his kingdom and life disappear before his eyes.

War Horse New London Theatre till February 2011. War Horse is set at the outbreak of World War I, when Joey, young Albert's beloved horse, is sold to the army. The National Theatre's epic production, War Horse is based on the celebrated children's novel. Actors working with striking life-sized puppets lead the audience on a gripping journey through history.

There is also a **Kings and Rogues** season at Shakespeare's Globe Theatre, featuring **Macbeth**, **Comedy of Errors** and other **classic Shakespeare plays** until October 2010. The National Theatre, the Barbican, the Open Air Theatre at Regent's Park and the Royal Opera House all offer excellent access, to see what's on and book your tickets in advance see their contact details below.

In all there are around 22 theatre venues in London which offer full wheelchair access. Please check the details of the theatre you hope to visit either directly with the Box Office, or online at **www.officiallondontheatre.co.uk/access**

National Theatre

The National Theatre is at the centre of the cultural life of the country, housing three auditoriums on London's South Bank presenting over 1,000 performances every year.

Visitors can also enjoy free exhibitions and live music, outdoor summer events and more. We aim to be accessible and welcoming to all and are committed to making your visit as easy and enjoyable as possible.

Backstage Tours

Go backstage at Britain's largest theatre complex and discover the secrets behind bringing our productions to the stage.

Eating & Drinking

Restaurants, cafés and bars can be found throughout the building, most with al fresco seating overlooking the vibrant South Bank.

For details of captioned and audio-described performances visit the website, or for access information call 020 7452 3400.

VISIT LONDON AWARDS 2008 — GOLD WINNER

enjoyEngland Awards for Excellence 2009 — SILVER WINNER

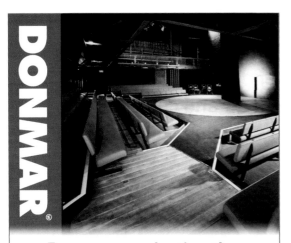

The National Theatre

Each year the National Theatre receives over 800,000 visitors through its doors. The building is home to three theatres – the Olivier, Lyttelton and Cottesloe – and presents an eclectic mix of new plays and classics from the world repertoire, with seven or eight productions in repertory at any one time.

With an extensive programme of Platform performances, backstage tours, foyer music, exhibitions, and free outdoor entertainment, the NT recognises that theatre doesn't begin and end with the rise and fall of the curtain.

Last year, the National delivered over 100 assisted performances at the South Bank and on tour, offering audio-description and touch tours for blind and visually-impaired people, and captioned performances for deaf and hard of hearing people.

All NT productions are audio described. Live commentary is given by experienced describers and relayed to audience members via a discreet headset. Fifteen minutes before curtain up, there is a short 'programme notes' section that aims to set the scene and capture the atmosphere, costumes, characters and action before a performance.

Touch tours are offered for each production ahead of an audio-described performance. They are free, friendly and informal (and it goes without saying that guide dogs are welcome too!). Members of the cast are on hand to take visitors up onto the stage where they can handle the various props and costumes. To find out more about how touch tours and audio-description works, there are three short films on the NT's BAFTA-nominated Discover website - **www.nationaltheatre.org.uk/discover**

The National Theatre at night
Image: Stephen Cummiskey

Working together with Stagetext, the NT also delivers captioned performances for all of its productions. In January 2010, 110 deaf and partially hearing people and their companions attended the captioned performance of Alan Bennett's new play, The Habit of Art – making it the most popular captioned performance ever held at the National.

An infra-red audio system is available in all theatres for every performance, and free headsets are available from the information desk. Last year, the NT issued 15,000 headsets and neck loops to its visitors. Contego wireless assisted listening devices are also available for partially hearing people who wish to enjoy backstage tours and outdoor performances.

The NT access mailing list is free to join and information on our productions and services is available in various formats, including Braille, large print, on CD, email and via our website. For further information, please email **access@nationaltheatre.org.uk** or call **020 7452 3400**.

Young people attend War Horse as part of Mousetrap Theatre Projects' Envision day in partnership with the National Theatre
Image: Signe Galschiot

Artsline – breaking down barriers to access for disabled people

Artsline is London's premier advice service for disabled people, their families and friends to the arts, entertainments and cultural activities in the Greater London region. We provide detailed access information on tourist attractions, theatres, cinemas, museums, galleries, music venues, hotels etc. In addition, we work with venues to improve disabled access from the planning stage for new developments to enhancing existing facilities.

Artsline has been the leading provider of access information for almost 30 years and in 2007 was awarded Gold for "Accessible Tourism" at the Visit London Awards.

The online database has expanded to well over 2,000 venues and includes a variety of events specifically tailored to the needs of disabled people. Typically, over 35,000 visitors (from over 80 countries) use this invaluable resource each month.

Artsline has always been proud of the quality of information it provides and recently conducted a survey of all its venues to ensure that the information is current. Carefully worded online questionnaires are designed by disabled people to maximize the quality of data. Not forgetting those users without internet access; all our access surveys can be printed and posted as well as accessed from our more traditional telephone hotline service.

t: 020 7388 2227
email: admin@artsline.org.uk
web: www.artsline.org.uk

Hayward Gallery

Southbank Centre

What is Southbank Centre?

Southbank Centre is positioned at the heart of London's thriving South Bank and welcomes visitors 364 days a year. Attend an event from our wide ranging artistic programme, relax with a glass of wine on Festival Terrace, wander through the Royal Festival Hall foyers, take part in any of our hundreds of free events, enjoy a meal from an array of cafes and restaurants, browse the shops and markets or visit one of Southbank Centre's iconic venues - **Royal Festival Hall**, **Queen Elizabeth Hall**, **Purcell Room**, **Hayward Gallery** and the **Saison Poetry Library**.

Southbank Centre is pleased to welcome visitors with any disability. Please join the free Access List, membership may include tickets at concessionary price, or bringing a companion for free who can assist you during your visit and to receive information in alternative formats.

Southbank Centre is able to provide:

- Accessible auditoria, cafes, restaurants and toilets.
- Infrared system in all auditoria.

- Accessible performances (speech-to-text reporting, captioning and audio described).
- Information in alternative formats (large print, MP3, photo maps).
- Full access to all restaurants, cafes and bars on site to all visitors.
- Assistance during your visit.

Parking

There is free parking available for Blue Badge holders attending ticketed events. Please take your parking ticket and event ticket to any Southbank Centre Ticket Office and exchange it for a free exit ticket.

General information:

t: 0844 847 9910
f: 020 7921 0607

email: accesslist@southbankcentre.co.uk
web: www.southbankcentre.co.uk
We also accept calls from
Text Relay: www.textrelay.org

Ronnie Scott's Soho © Britainonview

93 Feet East, 150 Brick Lane E1 6QL

t: 020 7247 3293
web: www.93feeteast.co.uk

O₂ Academy Brixton, 211 Stockwell Road SW9 9SL
t: 0207 787 3159
web: www.o2academybrixton.co.uk

Cargo, 83 Rivington Street, Shoreditch EC2A 3AY
t: 020 7739 3440
web: www.cargo-london.com

Dogstar, 389 Coldharbour Lane, Brixton SW9 8LQ
t: 020 7733 7515
web: www.antic-ltd.com/dogstar

Fabric, 77a Charterhouse Street, London EC1M 3HN
t: 0207 336 8898
web: www.fabriclondon.com

Herbal, 10-14 Kingsland Road, Shoreditch E2 8DA
t: 020 7613 4462
web: www.herbaluk.com

Jazz Café, 5 Parkway, Camden Town NW1 7PG
t: 020 7916 6060
web: www.jazzcafe.co.uk

Ministry of Sound, 103 Gaunt St, London SE1 6DP
t: 020 7378 6528
web: www.ministryofsound.com/club

Ronnie Scott's, 47 Frith Street, Soho W1D 4HT
t: 020 7439 0747
web: www.ronniescotts.co.uk

Shepherd's Bush Empire, Shepherd's Bush Green W12 8TT
t: 0870 7712000
web: www.o2shepherdsbushempire.co.uk

visitlondon.com pick of accessible night spots

In recent years, access to clubs and music venues has improved. The result is that disabled people are increasingly finding it easier to enjoy the many clubs and music venues London has to offer. However, not all venues are accessible and even at accessible venues, wheelchair access can be limited. We recommend calling in advance or notifying the venue of your access needs when making a booking.

This section includes a selection of accessible DJ clubs and live music venues in London to get you started on your night out. There are other accessible clubs and music venues not listed here and we encourage you to explore.

The following clubs and music venues are all wheelchair accessible and most have a accessible toilet. However, not all areas may be wheelchair accessible. At some venues, the main entrance is not wheelchair accessible. In these cases, there's an alternative entrance or a portable ramp. Assistance dogs are allowed at all venues, but restrictions may apply.

Cinemas

London is full of cinemas showing the latest blockbusters, arthouse, independent and world cinema. Many of the cinemas are wheelchair accessible. Some cinemas provide a range of facilities to meet individual needs, such as induction loops, audio-described screenings, or autism-friendly screenings. Artsline and DisabledGo have details of accessibility for many London cinemas.

The following cinema chains have many accessible locations across London.

Picturehouse Cinemas
web: www.picturehouses.co.uk/accessibility.aspx

Cineworld
web: www.cineworld.co.uk/accessibility

Odeon
web: www.odeon.co.uk/fanatic/accessibility

Vue
web: www.myvue.com/

Empire
web: www.empirecinemas.co.uk/index.php?page=home

Other useful sites

Barbican Cinema, Silk Street EC2Y 8DS
t: 020 7638 8891
web: www.barbican.org.uk

Curzon Mayfair, 38 Curzon St W1J 7TY and Curzon Soho, 99 Shaftesbury Avenue W1D 5DY
web: www.curzoncinemas.com

BFI IMAX, 1 Charlie Chaplin Walk, South Bank, Waterloo SE1 8XR
t: 020 7199 6000
web: www.bfi.org.uk/ /whatson/bfi_imax

BFI Southbank, Belvedere Road, South Bank SE1 8XT
t: 020 7928 3232
web: www.bfi.org.uk/whatson/bfi_southbank

Comedy Clubs

Access to comedy clubs has improved significantly in London making it easier for people with access needs to enjoy some of the UK's hottest comic talent. However, not all venues are accessible. We recommend calling in advance or notifying the venue of your access needs when making a booking. This section includes a selection of comedy clubs in London to get you started. There are other accessible comedy clubs not listed here and we encourage you to explore or see **www.visitlondon.com**.

The following clubs and music venues are all wheelchair accessible and most have an accessible toilet. Bear in mind that not all areas may be wheelchair accessible. Assistance dogs are allowed.

The Bedford, 77 Bedford Hill SW12 9HD
(entrance has one step, staff will assist)
t: 020 8682 8959 **web:** www.thebedford.co.uk/

The Chuckle Club, Surrey Street WC2R 2NS
t: 020 7476 1672 **web:** www.chuckleclub.com/

The Comedy Café, 66/68 Rivington Street EC2A 3AY
t: 020 7739 5706 **web:** www.comedycafe.co.uk/

The Comedy Store, 1a Oxendon Street SW1Y 4EE
(wheelchair users must be able to transfer into a chair lift)
t: 020 7930 2949 **web:** www.thecomedystore.co.uk/

Lee Hurst Backyard Comedy Club, 231 Cambridge Heath Road E2 0E4
t: 020 7739 3122 **web:** www.thefymfygbar.com/

BFI IMAX, Waterloo © Britainonview

The O₂ Arena

Access to The O₂

The O₂ is the world's most popular music venue with over 18 million visitors to date since it opened in June 2007 as a fully accessible venue. The 20,000 capacity arena is surrounded by Entertainment Avenue, an indoor site home to cafes, bars and restaurants, an 11 screen Vue cinema complex, matter nightclub and The O₂ bubble exhibition space – host to the British Music Experience, the UK's ultimate permanent interactive music museum. The O₂ also houses indigO₂, a smaller more intimate live music venue.

Wheelchair users or those with specific access requirements can access The O₂ easily. All buildings

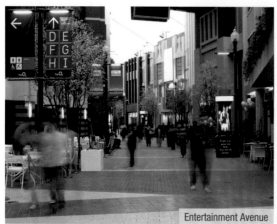

Entertainment Avenue

All images © O₂

within The O₂ are DDA compliant with wide entrances, and a spacious and smooth street runs the length of Entertainment Avenue. Toilet facilities, lifts and other public areas are designed for wheelchair use.

Staff at The O₂ receive specialist customer service training to enable them to provide appropriate assistance when required. The dedicated in-house disability booking line operated by The O₂ is manned by staff fully informed about the venue. In addition to this, across all events, venue wide, The O₂ offers a complimentary ticket to the personal assistant or companion of disabled visitors.

In terms of access to The O₂ itself, the venue is serviced by North Greenwich underground station (Jubilee Line) and bus station, and the Thames Clipper river boat service, all of which are accessible.

Metallica arena

An access forum was formed by The O₂ in order to advise on accessibility in all aspects of the visitor journey. Venue wide, improvements have been implemented on the basis of feedback received.

One visitor remarked that "staff [at The O₂] are well trained, and being mostly young are enthusiastic, friendly, observant, and very helpful. I do love The O₂ as a venue for food and concerts, and for the disabled person, the toilet facilities [and] the entry access etc [is] good"

A former Bronze award holder, The O₂ was awarded Gold for this year's M+IT Award for Access Excellence in acknowledgement of is dedication to provide all visitors the same high experiential standards. Neva Elliott, Senior Customer Service Manager at The O₂ commented that "accessibility is considered in every aspect of The

O₂'s venue and events. We believe that every individual should have access to a great day or night out."

More information on access at The O₂ as well as relevant contact details can be found at **http://www.theo2.co.uk/venue/venue-access.html.**

The O₂ Arena crowd

Harrods, Knightsbridge © Britainonview/Juliet White

Shopping

London is among the best places in the world for shopping. In recent years many of the stores, especially the bigger ones, have ensured that there is wheelchair access and that they provide a user friendly environment. Many of the major retailers employ personal shoppers who will help you shop and, in some cases, will take a brief and even do your shopping for you.

The result is that disabled people generally find it easier to enjoy shopping at London's famous department stores and on the high street. Also, newly built shopping centres around London provide exciting accessible shopping. London is also home to a wealth of covered and outdoor street markets. The most famous being Portobello Road market in West London which goes through trendy Notting Hill. Spitalfields Market in East London is famous for furnishings, fashion and food.

While access to shops and services has improved, not all stores are accessible. Smaller independent outlets often have restricted access, particularly those in older buildings. Large stores with multiple outlets (chain stores) are often accessible, but not always. If a particular outlet is not accessible, there may be an accessible one nearby.

Most large stores provide assistance for disabled people. For example, someone who is blind can get help reading labels and choosing items. Someone with a mobility impairment can get help reaching items and carrying them to the check-out. Disabled people can also use personal shoppers for personalised service. They will help if you need to update your wardrobe, choose an outfit for a special occasion or find the perfect gift. Personal shoppers do the hard work of shopping. They select a range of items to reflect your tastes and bring them to you. These services are often complimentary but some may require a minimum spend or extra charge.

Shopmobility

What is Shopmobility?

Shopmobility is a scheme which lends manual wheelchairs, powered wheelchairs and powered scooters to members of the public with limited mobility, to shop and to visit leisure and commercial facilities within a town, city or shopping centre. It aims to enable people with temporarily or permanently impaired mobility to engage or re-engage with their community and travel with confidence, thus enhancing their quality of life, and providing them and their carers with independence.

How much does it cost?

All schemes operate slightly differently; some provide Shopmobility as a free service while others make a charge. Most schemes welcome any donations you wish to make.

Who can use Shopmobility?

Shopmobility is for anyone, young or old, whether their disability is temporary or permanent. It is available for those with injuries, long or short-term disabilities – anyone who needs help with mobility. Shopmobility is about the freedom to get around. You do not need to be registered disabled to use it.

How do I use Shopmobility?

A member of staff or volunteer will give you all the information you need. Most schemes ask that you bring identification containing your name and address on your first visit; this is so that schemes can complete a registration form and keep a record of your details. Many schemes will issue you with a membership card, and on your next visit you can simply show this card. See page 32 for some London Shopmobility centres.
t: 0845 644 2446
email: info@shopmobilityuk.org
web: www.shopmobilityuk.org

Oxford Street © Britainonview/Ingrid Rasmussen

If it's shopping you want, you will never get bored in London with over 30,000 shops to choose from and a well-established reputation in the fashion world. Here is a small selection of London's most famous stores and shopping areas, chosen by **visitlondon.com** these stores are accessible and provide various services for disabled people. For specific details, contact the store directly. There are many more to visit.

Canary Wharf: The three shopping malls at Canary Wharf offer an accessible alternative to the high street, with many high street stores, as well as pubs and restaurants, in one location. The shopping centre is step-free and there are wheelchair-accessible toilets throughout. Individual store access varies but it is generally very good. There is Blue Badge parking on site and Canary Wharf underground station is accessible.
t: 020 7418 2000
web: www.mycanarywharf.com/

Fortnum & Mason is legendary for its traditional reputation and being the stockists of fine food. Step-free access to the store is through the entrance on Piccadilly. Lifts provide access to all floors and there are wheelchair-accessible toilets on the 2nd and 4th floors. There is step-free access to the St James's Restaurant. Ask a member of staff about alternative access to the Fountain Restaurant and the Patio Restaurant. Assistance is available upon request. Wheelchair hire is available, but it is recommended to call in advance to arrange.
t: 020 7734 8040
web: www.fortnumandmason.com/the-store.aspx

Foyles on Charing Cross Road has been supplying books for over 100 years and is home to Ray's Jazz at The Café. Audio books are available. The building is accessible throughout and there is a wheelchair-accessible toilet. Assistance is available upon request.
t: 020 7437 5660
web: www.foyles.co.uk/addtxtfeature07.asp?&

Hamley's is the world's largest toyshop and all 7 floors are accessible by lift. There is a wheelchair-accessible toilet on the 5th floor. Assistance is available upon request.
t: 020 7479 7319 **web:** www.hamleys.com

Harrods, the world-famous Knightsbridge department store, is largely accessible. There is step-free access to almost all areas of the store and wheelchair-accessible toilets are located throughout. A detailed store guide is available at entrances and from store staff. Wheelchairs are available for hire. As Harrods is organised as a series of concessions for specific brands and designers, there is limited central assistance available.
t: 020 7730 1234
web: www.harrods.com/harrodsstore

HMV is a large music store with several outlets in London. The Oxford Street store has step-free access throughout. There are no toilets. Assistance is available upon request.
t: 020 7631 3423
web: www.hmv.com

Carnaby Street, Soho © Britainonview/Pawel Libera

House of Fraser is a large department store with several branches in London. The Oxford Street branch has flat and ramped entrances. Lifts serve all floors and step-free eating places are available. There is a wheelchair-accessible toilet on the 5th floor. Assistance is available upon request.
t: 020 7631 3423
web: www.houseoffraser.co.uk

John Lewis is a large department store with several branches in London, which are generally accessible and offer a range of facilities. At the Oxford Street branch, the 7 floors are accessible by lift and there is a wheelchair-accessible toilet on the 4th floor. There is step-free access throughout and accessible fitting rooms are available. Services include hearing loops, large print, wheelchair hire, and free delivery to all local areas. If you require assistance, please ask any member of staff.
t: 020 7629 7711

Portobello Road, Notting Hill © Britainonview

textphone: 18001 + 020 7629 7711 (via Typetalk)
web: www.johnlewis.com/Shops

Marks & Spencer (M&S) is a large department store with many branches located throughout London. The biggest is the Marks & Spencer flagship store at Marble Arch, which is step-free via a lift. All floors of the M&S's Pantheon store on Oxford Street are also accessed by a lift and there is a wheelchair-accessible toilet on the ground floor. All staff have disability-awareness training and assistance is available if required.
t: 020 7935 7954 **web:** www.marksandspencer.com

Selfridges is one of London's largest department stores. The entrance on Edward Mews is flat with automatic doors. The floors are connected via central lifts and most areas have step-free access. There is a car park with step-free access to the store on the ground and 2nd floors, which is expensive to use. There are wheelchair-accessible toilets on the 3rd floor. It is possible to book wheelchairs at the information desk. As Selfridges is organised as a series of concessions for specific brands and designers, there is limited central assistance available.
t: 0800 123400
web: www.selfridges.com

Top Shop is a large trendy fashion retailer for women and men. The Oxford Street store has 4 floors, which are accessible by lift and escalator and there is a wheelchair-accessible toilet in the basement. This shop can get very busy on the weekends and during sales, making it difficult to navigate through the crowds. There is a hearing loop system. Assistance is available upon request.
t: 020 7636 7700 **web:** www.topshop.com

Waterstone's at Piccadilly offers a wide range of books, including a large selection of audio books. There is step-free access throughout the shop and a wheelchair-accessible toilet. Assistance is available upon request.
t: 020 7851 2400 **web:** http://www.waterstones.com

SHOP EASY THROUGH SHOPMOBILITY

Registered Charity Number 1079758 n   Company Limited by Guarantee Number 3689727

NATIONAL FEDERATION OF

Shopmobility

The National Federation of Shopmobility UK
PO Box 6641 Christchurch BH23 9DQ

info@shopmobilityuk.org   www.shopmobilityuk.org

T: 08456 442446
(24hr answerphone service)

"The sign of a quality service"

The Shopmobility word and symbol is a UK Registered Trademark No. 2185606

LONDON, MERTON, SOUTH WIMBLEDON
Scootability, High Park Resource Centre
63 High Path, South Wimbledon, London
SW19 2JY

Day: 020 3326 2524   **Fax:** 020 8648 9767
Open: Monday to Friday: 9.00am to 4.00pm
Notes: Service charge of £5 per day. Manual
wheelchairs are £2.50p per day. Delivery and
collection to home address within Merton is free
of charge.

ROMFORD (THE BREWERY)
Havering Shopmobility
1 The Brewery, Waterloo Road, Romford, Essex
RM1 1AU

Office: 01708 722570   **Fax:** 01708 722523
Email:: haveringshopmo@btconnect.com
Open: Monday to Saturday: 10.00am to 5.00pm
Notes: Membership fee £8 per year, plus £2.50 per day
for electric scooters £2 per day for electric wheelchairs
and £1.50p per day for manual wheelchairs. Equipment
available for hire. Please call for information.

ENFIELD
Enfield Shopmobility Centre
Enfield Civic Centre, Silver Street, Enfield, Middex,
EN1 3XY

Office: 020 8379 1190
Open: Monday to Friday: 9.30am to 5.00pm
Notes: Satellite at Edmonton Shopmobility Centre,
4 Monmouth Road, Edmonton, London, N9
Tel: 020 8379 1193 Open: Tuesday to Saturday:
9.30am to 5.00pm

ILFORD
Redbridge Disability Association
Exchange Car Park, The Exchange Mall, High Road,
Ilford, Essex, IG1 1RS

Office: 020 8478 6864
Open: Monday to Saturday: 10.00am to 4.00pm
Notes: Escorts available by appointment only.
Long term loan available on manual wheelchairs
only.

LONDON, WALTHAM FOREST
Live Ability Waltham Forest
45 Selborne Walk, Selborne Walk Shopping Centre,
Walthamstow, London, E17 7JR

Office: 020 8520 3366   **Fax:** 020 8520 6418
Email:: liveabilitywf@googlemail.com
Open: Tuesday to Saturday: 10.00am to 4.30pm
Notes: £3 charge for Life Membership and £2 per
day loan for a wheelchair or a scooter.

For a complete list of shopmobility centres go to www.shopmobilityuk.org

The balcony

Westfield southern entrance

Westfield services

Westfield London

At Westfield London, we don't just aim to provide the best shops in town, but also provide the best shopping experience for all our guests.

With a distinctive mix and match of designer and high street labels, Westfield London offers the ultimate shopping experience. As well as the best shops in town we also provide the best shopping experience for all our guests.

During the design process, Westfield London worked closely with the Human Engineering Limited, which advised with regard to inclusion and accessibility of public transport, including taxis, buses, coaches, trains, trams; London Underground step free programme; medical product design and instruction leaflets

Westfield London's shop mobility equipment, electric scooters and wheelchairs, are free of charge both within the centre and externally through the town centre footprint.

All concierge staff have been disability-awareness trained

by HAFAD (Hammersmith & Fulham Action on Disability.) and they can provide services such as hands-free shopping and home delivery. Our mall guides, which also come in Braille version, can be collected at the concierge desks.

All toilet facilities in the centre incorporate disabled cubicles and a special needs adult change facility with bespoke equipment including a height-adjustable bench and a hoist. Some parent and baby facilities in the centre have special facilities for wheelchair user parents and children.

Westfield sees every new development as an opportunity to improve the design and efficiency of its shopping centres and make them accessible and enjoyable for all. 2010 openings such as the GymBox and Vue's launch of its state-of-the-art cinema complex will add to the integrated offer spanning retail, leisure and food all under one roof.

web: www.uk.westfield.com/london

Open spaces

Hyde Park © Britainonview

London's parks are a delightful refuge from the crowded city streets. They are free and, in the main very accessible. Here is a selection including the nine Royal Parks (surprisingly, the Brompton Cemetery is a Royal Park) but there are more and all worth a visit. The websites offer even more details on accessibility with excellent information on special events held in the parks.

Greenwich Park © Britainonview/Simon Kreitem

Bushy Park

Hampton Court Road, Bushy Park, TW12 2EJ
t: 020 8979 1586
email: bushy@royalparks.gsi.gov.uk
web: www.royalparks.org.uk/parks/bushy_park/
web (accessibility): www.disabledgo.info/
AccessGuide.asp?BusinessID=51114&TownID=24

A large area of rural parkland, **Bushy Park** is home to many free-roaming deer. The famous mile-long Chestnut Avenue, conceived by Sir Christopher Wren, was the formal approach to Hampton Court Palace and is flanked on both sides by horse chestnuts and lime trees.

Richmond Park © Britainonview

Become a cyclist using a special cycle and aid of a 'pilot' (carer, friend or 'Companion Cycling' volunteer).
t: 07961 344 545 (leave a message)
web: www.companioncycling.org.uk

Try horse riding with The Horse Rangers Association riding school for disabled people.
email: rda@horserangers.com
web: www.horserangers.com

Greenwich Park

Charlton Way, Greenwich SE10 8QY
t: 020 8858 2608
email: greenwich@royalparks.gsi.gov.uk
web: www.royalparks.org.uk/greenwich/
web (accessibility): www.disabledgo.info/AccessGuide.asp?BusinessID=61181&TownID=54

Greenwich is the oldest Royal Park and home to a small herd of Fallow and Red deer. From the middle of the park, you can enjoy some of the best views of London across the River Thames to St Paul's Cathedral and beyond.

St. James Park © Britainonview

Kensington Gardens

Kensington W2 2UH
t: 020 7298 2000
email: kensington@royalparks.gsi.gov.uk
web: www.royalparks.org.uk/kensington/
web (accessibility): www.disabledgo.info/AccessGuide.asp?BusinessID=46524&TownID=76

Kensington Gardens is next to Hyde Park. The combination of elegant avenues, wide open spaces and fascinating monuments make Kensington Gardens a perfect park.

Richmond Park

Richmond Surrey TW10 5UH
t: 020 8332 2730
email: richmond@royalparks.gsi.gov.uk
web: www.royalparks.org.uk/richmond/
web (accessibility): www.disabledgo.info/AccessGuide.asp?BusinessID=32669&TownID=24

Richmond Park, with its famous herds of Red and Fallow deer, is only 10 miles from the central of London but feels as if it is in the heart of the countryside. Richmond is the largest and wildest of the Royal Park and is the biggest open space in London.

St James's Park

London SW1A 2BJ
t: 020 7930 1793
email: stjames@royalparks.gsi.gov.uk
web: www.royalparks.org.uk/stjamess/
web (accessibility): www.disabledgo.info/AccessGuide.asp?BusinessID=37805&TownID=54

St James's Park is one of the oldest Royal Parks and lies at the heart of ceremonial London. It is the setting for many ceremonial parades and events of national celebration. The flower beds and shrubberies can be enjoyed all year round. St James's Park is famous for its pelicans.

The Regent's Park

London NW1 4NR
t: 020 7486 7905
email: regents@royalparks.gsi.gov.uk
web: www.royalparks.org.uk/regents/
web (accessibility): www.disabledgo.info/AccessGuide.asp?BusinessID=38153&TownID=54

The Regent's Park was designed in 1811 by renowned architect John Nash and includes stunning rose gardens.

Green Park

London SW1
t: 020 7930 1793
email: stjames@royalparks.gsi.gov.uk
web: www.royalparks.org.uk/green/
web (accessibility): www.disabledgo.info/AccessGuide.asp?BusinessID=37806&TownID=54

Green Park is the smallest of the eight Royal Parks – but it has always been one of the most popular. The natural undulating landscape consists chiefly of grass and mature trees, making it an attractive and tranquil place to visit all year round.

Hyde Park

London W2 2UH
t: 020 7298 2000
email: hyde@royalparks.gsi.gov.uk
web: www.royalparks.org.uk/hyde/
web (accessibility): www.disabledgo.info/AccessGuide.asp?VenueID=52999&TownID=54

Hyde Park is an oasis of calm surrounded by some of central London's busiest roads. There's something for everyone: the unique Diana, Princess of Wales Memorial Fountain, over 4,000 trees, a lake, meadow, horse rides and more. **Liberty Drives** offers free rides for visitors with restricted mobility. **t:** +44 (0) 7767 498096

Brompton Cemetery

Fulham Road, SW10 9UG
t: 020 7352 1201
email: brompton@royalparks.gsi.gov.uk
web: www.royalparks.org.uk/brompton/

The **Brompton Cemetery**, located in the Royal Borough of Kensington and Chelsea, is regarded as one of the finest Victorian Metropolitan cemeteries in the country. It is the only Crown Cemetery.

Battersea Park

Battersea SW11 4NJ
t: 020 8871 7530
web: www.batterseapark.org

With its lake, riverside paths and Children's zoo, **Battersea Park** has much to offer – and it's just across the Thames from Victoria. Car parking, accessible toilets and easy paths make the park a delight to visit.
Battersea Park Children's Zoo: this small children's zoo is home to all sorts of animals - from farmyard favourites to monkeys, birds and reptiles. There is also a contact area where children can see the animals close up and stroke them. The zoo is fully accessible with signed events on request, Braille information sheets and disabled toilets.

Kensington Gardens © Britainonview

Hampstead Heath

Hampstead NW3
t: 020 7485 5757
web: www.cityoflondon.gov.uk

Hampstead Heath is one of London's most popular open spaces, situated just four miles from Trafalgar Square. An island of beautiful countryside, the magic of Hampstead Heath lies not only in its rich mosaic of flora and fauna and extensive recreational facilities, but also in its proximity and accessibility to millions of people. Accessible toilets, disabled parking and access to the mobile electric buggy scheme with prior booking.

Wimbledon Common

Wimbledon Parkside, SW19 5NR
t: 020 8788 7655
web: www.wpcc.org.uk

Wimbledon Common is an area of unspoilt countryside – mainly heathland, woods and pond – just a few miles from central London. The common is big (1,140 acres) and some of the paths are rough. Some 99 species of birds were seen on the Common in 2007. The Windmill

Spring in St James's Park © Britainonview

Nature Trail was created and opened in 2000. It is situated 200 metres east of the Windmill and its large car park. The trail was created to allow visitors with mobility handicaps the opportunity to enjoy a small but representative section of the Wimbledon Common and Putney Heath. A firm and level footpath winds its way around approximately 800 metres of trail. Trail markers and directional signs are placed throughout the trail.

**For details of more open spaces visit:
www.visitlondon.com/outdoors
or www.cityoflondon.gov.uk – select:
Forests, Parks & Gardens icon.**

Immerse yourself in natural beauty in the heart of London

DisabledGo guides are available on the website

The Royal Parks are: Bushy Park, The Green Park, Greenwich Park, Hyde Park, Kensington Gardens, The Regent's Park & Primrose Hill, Richmond Park, St James's Park

THE ROYAL PARKS

www.royalparks.org.uk

ENJOY GREEN LONDON

It's easy to get away from the crowds and relax in one of London's outdoor spaces. See new species of plants at the Royal Botanic Gardens at Kew, watch birds take flight at The London Wetland Centre or relax in one of the Royal Parks.

VISITLONDON.COM/ACCESS

St James's Park © VisitLondonImages/Pawel Libera

OPENBRITAIN.NET

The one-stop-shop for all your travel needs.

Go online and see how we can help you get in, out ...and about.

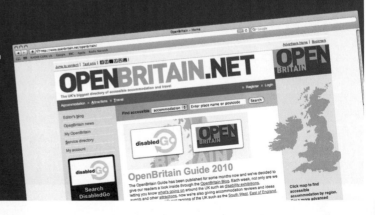

Walks with Wheelchairs

The site was founded by Marie Houlden in September 2007 and is the only UK website totally dedicated to providing free information on routes that are suitable for wheelchair users throughout the UK. The walks on our database have been tried and tested by wheelchair users, or those knowledgeable about accessible routes in the great outdoors. We currently have approximately 600 walks covering England, Northern Ireland, Scotland and Wales.

Walks with Wheelchairs will allow you to:

- Read reviews of the routes before trying any walks,
- Download walk directions and detailed, OS maps free of charge,
- Share your own routes for walking with wheelchairs,
- Add your own comments for others users to view.

Free resource

At **walkswithwheelchairs.com** we passionately believe that everyone has the right to get out into the fresh air and therefore there is no charge to use our website.

Why don't you try

Two of our favourite walks in London are Hyde Park (Knightsbridge) and the Regent's Park (Marylebone). Both are beautiful places to explore and are completely accessible to those with access challenges.

To find out more about these walks visit **walkswithwheelchairs.com**, choose Greater London as your region and then click on either Knightsbridge or Marylebone. You will then have a map and a walking description. We will look forward to receiving your review!

email: marie@walkswith.com
web: www.walkswithwheelchairs.com

Wimbledon © AELTC

Accessible Sporting Venues in London

From football, rugby, cricket and tennis, to more unusual sports on skates and skis, London is host to a wealth of sporting events and activities.

Access for spectators

Many of London's major sporting venues are accessible to disabled people, although facilities vary. Make sure you tell the venue about your access requirements when booking.

Wheelchair users

Many stadiums and arenas are wheelchair accessible. However, in some cases there are a restricted number of seats for wheelchair users. It's best to book in advance.

Hearing and visually impaired spectators

Most venues offer a live commentary via a headset for people with impaired vision and hearing. Sometimes hearing loops or infra-red systems are also available.

Assistance dogs

Stadiums and arenas generally allow assistance dogs, including guide dogs, hearing dogs and service dogs. It's usually against the law for service providers to refuse assistance dogs onto their premises.

Blue Badge parking

Most venues have blue badge parking onsite. In most cases, prior arrangement is necessary. Again, it's best to call in advance to enquire about any requirements or restrictions.

Stamford Bridge © Chelsea FC

The Rugby Stadium, Twickenham © Britainonview

Concessions for disabled people

Some teams and events offer concessions for people with access needs. Often, accompanying personal assistants or carers enter for free.

Accessible stadiums and arenas

Seven highly accessible sports venues are now being built for the London 2012 Olympic Games and Paralympic Games. The organisers are committed to ensuring that both Games will be fully inclusive for all participants and spectators. Test sporting events take place in 2011; meanwhile you can take a bus tour of the site in Stratford, East London.
t: 0300 2012001 (Tours).
See **www.london2012.com**.

The following venues are all wheelchair accessible and offer facilities for hearing and visually impaired spectators; many offer tours. This is not an exhaustive list - see Useful Addresses for more venues.

Arsenal Football Club
t: 020 7704 4504 (Stadium Tours) or 020 7704 4507 (Arsenal Museum).
web: www.arsenal.com/membership/buy-tickets

Ascot Racecourse
t: 08707 227 227
web: www.ascot.co.uk/aboasc/aboasc_acc.html

Chelsea Football Club
t: 0871 984 1955 (Tours)
email: tours@chelseafc.com
web: www.chelseafc.com/tours

Lord's Cricket Ground
t: 020 7616 8500
web: www.lords.org/tickets/spectators-with-disabilities/

The O$_2$ Arena
t: 0870 600 6140
typetext: 18001 0870 600 6140
email: access@theo2.co.uk
web: www.theo2.co.uk/venue/venue-access.html

The Oval
t: 08712 461100
email: enquiries@surreycricket.com
web: www.britoval.com/home/surrey-cricket

Tottenham Hotspur Football Club
t: 0208 365 5161
email: support@tottenhamhotspur.com
web: www.tottenhamhotspur.com/

The World Rugby Museum at Twickenham
t: 0208 831 6516
email: disabledaccess@therfu.com
web: www.rfu.com/TwickenhamStadium

Wembley Stadium
t: 0844 980 8001
email: accessforall@wembleystadium.com
web: www.wembleystadium.com/events/AccessForAll/

West Ham United Football Club
t: 0845 217 1332
email: disabledinfo@westhamunited.co.uk
web: www.whufc.com/page/SpecialNeeds/0,,12562,00.html

Wimbledon Tennis
t: 020 8971 2473
web: aeltc.wimbledon.org/en_GB/about/tickets/easyaccess.html

Liberty Festival

'Celebrating the contribution of deaf and disabled people to London's culture'

The Liberty Festival first took place at Trafalgar Square in September 2003 as a special event for European Year of Disabled People. Since then the event has taken place annually and has seen performances by upwards of 100 deaf and disabled artists, with presentations of both existing and newly commissioned work.

Liberty is organised as part of the Mayor of London's cultural event programme and is produced by Greenwich+Docklands festivals. Since 2006 it has received additional support each year from Arts Council England. The active involvement of deaf and disabled people has been central to making Liberty happen; the GLA works closely with an advisory group which in 2009 included Attitude is Everything, Artsline and Shape. Programming the event is undertaken in association with deaf and disabled artists and arts organisations, and in recent years has seen a wide variety of work in different creative zones. In 2009 these included over 30 performances by deaf and disabled with lots of new work specially produced for the occasion and covered music, street arts, children's arts, visual arts and comedy, cabaret and spoken word.

Liberty is promoted as being accessible and inclusive and to achieve this, the organisers have placed access at the heart of planning for the festival. A range of facilities and amenities are made available at the event, both for artists and audience. These include disability equality trained stewards and personal assistants, various interpretation services such as BSL, palantype and audio description, and free disabled parking near to the venue.

Liberty 2010 takes place on Saturday, 4 September. It is hoped that this exciting annual event will continue encouraging new creative work, which will lead to the participation of deaf and disabled artists in the Cultural Olympiad and in ceremonies and events for the Olympic Games and Paralympic Games in 2012

Events for London, Greater London Authority
web: www.london.gov.uk/gla/events

Greenwich+Docklands
International Festival

Greenwich+Docklands International Festival commissions and presents extraordinary arts events that transform lives. It is an annual event in Greenwich and East London committed to breaking new ground in outdoor arts and reaching out to new audiences and participants.

GDIF 2009 provided a "tour de force" showcase of UK and international outdoor arts at their very best. Audiences of 50,000 over four days were swept up in the GDIF experience, attending a series of mesmerising new commissions and premieres by a range of UK and international artists. It also launched an imaginative 4-year thematic programme with events drawing inspiration from "Water" in a variety of creative ways.

GDIF 2009 also saw the launch of "New Outdoor Horizons", an innovative programme of commissioned performances led by deaf and disabled artists. The programme featured London premieres from companies including Fittings Multimedia Arts (in collaboration with Sharmanka), Graeae Theatre Company (in collaboration with Strange Fruit), Extant (in collaboration with Braunarts), StopGAP Dance Company and Marc Brew Company.

GDIF has a dynamic and committed approach to building access into the heart of its events, and a wide range of access infrastructure and services were integrated into the fabric of the festival. In recognition of this GDIF 2009 was awarded two BT Visit London Awards in the categories of Accessible Tourism (Silver Award) and Consumer Event of the Year (Gold Award).

GDIF 2010 will run from 24 June – 4 July Save the dates! Full programme is listed at **www.festival.org**

Useful addresses

Where to find more information on accessible London:

Access in London

Access in London is a carefully researched guide, published in 2003, much of which is available online at www.accessinlondon.org

Artsline

Artsline provides an online and telephone information and advice service about all aspects of access to arts and entertainment activities. It also has an extensive database about access to clubs, theatres, cinemas, music venues, galleries, museums and hotels.
t: 020 7388 2227
web: www.artsline.org.uk/

Can Be Done

Can Be Done is a small-tour operator that organises tailor-made holidays and tours in London and elsewhere in the UK, for both groups and individuals. The director of Can Be Done is a wheelchair user and is aware of the travel requirements of disabled people.
t: 020 8907 2400
web: www.canbedone.co.uk

DIAL UK

DIAL UK is a national network of local disability information and advice line services (DIALs) run by and for disabled people. The DIAL UK information and advice services provide information and advice to disabled people and others on all aspects of living with a disability. It also publishes a fact sheet on holidays for disabled people.
web: www.dialuk.info

Direct Enquiries

The Nationwide Access Register was developed, in partnership with RADAR and Employers Forum on Disability and lists businesses throughout the UK with information about their accessibility.
t: 01344 360101
email: customerservices@directenquiries.com
web: www.directenquiries.com

Directgov

Directgov is a website produced by the Central Office of Information. It provides a wide range of information from across UK government departments on travel and holidays for disabled people.
web: www.direct.gov.uk/en/DisabledPeople/index.htm

Disability Now

Disability Now is a campaigning newspaper for disabled people, offering news and a wide range of information, including holidays.
web: www.disabilitynow.org.uk

DisabledGo

DisabledGo provides free detailed access information about goods, services and shops. Its access guides have been specially designed to answer the everyday questions of disabled people, their assistants, carers, family and friends.
web: www.disabledgo.com

Enabled London

Enabled London provides an online access guide to going out in London, including access maps and information on healthy living and venues in London. The site offers clear, easy-to-read information and a word bank to help people to understand difficult words and jargon.
t: 0207 749 4867
textphone: 07799 030 979
web: www.enabledlondon.com

Mencap

Mencap is a national learning disability charity working with people with a learning disability and their families and carers. Mencap publishes a holiday resource list, which provides information about holidays, for people with learning and other disabilities, including financial help towards the cost of a holiday, holidays for adults and children, and holiday information providers.
t: 020 7454 0454
web: www.mencap.org.uk

Mobilise

Mobilise aims to promote and protect the welfare of disabled people and to promote their personal mobility. It provides information and services for drivers with disabilities.
t: 01508 489449
web: www.dda.org.uk

Options Holidays

Options Holidays is a not-for-profit organisation that arranges holidays for people with learning disabilities. It runs holidays throughout the year in the UK, including London. Experienced and qualified carers take charge of the holidays, leading small groups of clients. These have a range of mild to moderate learning disabilities. Some also have physical disabilities.
t: 07000 790348 or 01285 740491,
web: www.optionsholidays.co.uk

RADAR

RADAR is a national network of disability organisations and disabled people. It offers a wide range of advice. RADAR also operates the National Key Scheme (see Getting Around London).
t: 020 7250 3222
Minicom: 020 7250 4119
email: radar@radar.org.uk
web: www.radar.org.uk

Royal National Institute of the Blind (RNIB)

RNIB is a national charity offering information, support and advice to people with sight problems in the UK. Its website is a good resource for blind and partially sighted people. In particular, it provides advice and information on leisure activities, events, specialist hotels and holiday schemes.

t: 0303 123 9999
web: www.rnib.org.uk

Royal National Institute for Deaf People (RNID)

RNID is a national charity offering information, support and advice to deaf and hard of hearing people in the UK. The RNID website is a good resource for deaf and hard of hearing people. In particular, it provides information about entertainment and activities.
t: 0808 808 0123
textphone: 0808 808 9000
web: www.rnid.org.uk

Society of London Theatres

An excellent source of information on London theatres, covering both what's on and information on the facilities of each venue.
t: 020 7557 6700
email: enquiries@solttma.co.uk
web: www.officiallondontheatre.co.uk/access/

Time Out

London events guide, based on the weekly magazine.
web: www.timeout.com

Transport for London

See Getting Around London section, page 47.
web: www.tfl.gov.uk

Tourism for All

Tourism for All provides information to people with disabilities and older people in relation to accessible accommodation and other tourism services. It publishes this guide and its sister guide OpenBritain which covers England, Scotland and Wales.
t: 0845 124 9971
web: www.tourismforall.org.uk

Visit London

Visit London is the official visitor organisation for London. The website is an excellent source of information about all aspects of London, as well as having an Accessible London section.
web: www.visitlondon.com/access

Wheelchair Travel

Wheelchair Travel provides a unique service, solving the private transport needs of disabled people either resident in, or visiting, the UK from overseas. Wheelchair Travel offers adapted vehicles on self-drive rental to either carry or be driven by a disabled person.
Full services including chauffeur and guide may also be provided if required.
t: 01483 233640
web: www.wheelchair-travel.co.uk

William Forrester

William Forrester is a Blue Badge Guide for London and a museum lecturer. He is a wheelchair user himself and offers tours in London for other wheelchair users and able-bodied individuals or groups. Including London attractions such as Big Ben, Houses of Parliament, Westminster Abbey and the British Museum; the tours use specially fitted taxis.
t: 01483 575401

Youreable

Youreable provides travel information for people with disabilities, including products, services, accommodation, attractions, equipment hire, specialist holiday companies and organisations, and more.
web: www.youreable.com

© Transport for London

Freedom of the City with
Oyster Card

Whether you're a regular visitor or making a one-off trip to London, using an Oyster card is the easiest way to access London's public transport network

Oyster is an electronic smartcard ticket. Simply touch the card on the yellow reader to get through the Tube gates or to board other London public transport services. It doesn't even need to be removed from its wallet. To ensure you pay the lowest fare you must always touch in on a yellow card reader at the start and end of every journey

A London Oyster card is the fastest, smartest and most cost-efficient way to pay for single journeys on the bus, Tube, DLR, tram, London Overground, Thames Clippers and most National Rail services.

Oyster Pay as You Go (Pre-pay Oyster) – the Sensible way to see London

Oyster cards are charged with the amount of credit of your choice.

Make as many journeys as you like in a 24 Hour period (4.30 am-4.30 am) You will be charged less than you would pay for a paper ticket

If you make lots of journeys, the Oyster card will automatically cap the day's charges at the price of an equivalent Day Travelcard or One Day Bus Pass

Visitors buy your card in advance

Save time by buying your Oyster card online before you travel to London The card comes charged and ready for use.

There is an initial fee for the card but thereafter you can 'top it up' once you are in London, with the amount of credit of your choice, at Tube stations, London Travel Information centres and participating shops.

Visit: **www.tfl.gov.uk/oyster** for further details

© Transport for London   © ATOC

Getting Around London

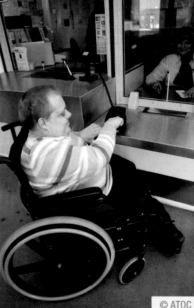

© ATOC

The accessibility of London's transport network has improved greatly in recent years, though it can still be a challenge, especially in peak times.

In this section we explain how to use all the different types of public transport available, and how they have been adapted to take access needs into account.

Getting Around London covers arriving in London and travelling around by both public and private transport once you are there. There is a wealth of online information available (some of it reproduced here) and a number of telephone helplines.

Key to travelling in London is: plan in advance, try to avoid the rush hour and on the day check that everything is running to plan.

Using online Journey Planners:
Both Direct.Gov and Transport for London have excellent online journey planners, which suggest the best way to get from A to B. The Transport for London Journey Planner enables you to put in various mobility restrictions (for example, 'I can't use the stairs') and then plans you a route taking this into account.

www.journeyplanner.tfl.gov.uk

web: www.direct.gov.uk/en/TravelAndTransport/PlanningYourJourney/DG_10036717

London is one of the world's largest and most historic cities. This means that it's a great place to visit, but it can also be a daunting experience to travel around, especially for disabled people.

Much has been done in recent years to make travelling around London more accessible. Getting Around London is designed to help you make the right preparation and to find the right information to get to London and to travel around once you are there. With careful planning, you will find that you can access many of the pleasures that a trip to London has to offer.

There is insufficient space in here to supply all the specific journey information for travelling around London, but key websites and phone numbers are given to help you plan your journey.

Essential Advice

© ATOC

1. Plan, plan and plan your journey ahead. If you have access to the internet, take full advantage of this. There is much more advice available online on all aspects of accessibility and at a level of detail that you may not find elsewhere. Always phone ahead and make sure that your journey is possible and practical, even if you've already checked it online.

2. Avoid peak travel times if your mobility is impaired. That means avoiding the rush hour in London and avoiding peak periods at airports.

3. There are various facilities for disabled travellers on all types of public transport in London. All visitors are encouraged to use public transport whenever possible, and to save money by using an Oyster card.

Good Sources of Information

Transport for London

TfL is the integrated body responsible for the Capital's transport system, and the main source of information for disabled travellers wanting to use London's transport system.

web: www.tfl.gov.uk/traveltools

Travel Information Centre:

t: 020 7222 1234. Plus: **Getting around London guide (a downloadable PDF)** describes all the accessibility features on the Tube, bus, DLR and tram.

Direct.Gov Journey Planner

Journey planner helps you find the quickest, easiest and cheapest route door to door to anywhere in Great Britain and provides full directions, live travel information and maps.

web: www.direct.gov.uk/en/TravelAndTransport/PlanningYourJourney/DG_10036717

National Rail Enquiries

For all overground railway enquiries, including specific information and plans on station accessibility.

t: 0845 748 49 50 **textphone:** 0845 605 0600
web: www.nationalrail.co.uk

National Express

For information on travelling to London by accessible coach.

web: www.nationalexpress.com/coach/OurService/disabled.cfm

National Express Disabled Persons Travel Helpline
t: 08717 818179 **textphone:** 0121 455 0086

Transport for All

Transport for All has been championing the cause of accessible transport in the capital for two decades.

web: www.transportforall.org.uk/londonwide/
t: 020 7737 2339

Blue Badge Parking Map

This can be used to find Blue Badge and Red Route parking bays throughout London.

web: www.direct.gov.uk/bluebadgemap

Direct Enquiries

Access guide to all London's underground stations and other useful information about accessible businesses

web: www.directenquiries.com
t: 01344 360101

Traveline

Traveline is a partnership of transport operators and local authorities formed to provide impartial and comprehensive information about public transport.

web: www.traveline.org.uk
t: 0871 200 2233

The Disabled Persons Transport Advisory Committee's (DPTAC)

Useful practical advice on travelling from the body responsible for advising the government on disabled travel.

web: dptac.independent.gov.uk/
t: 020 7944 8011
email: dptac@dft.gsi.gov.uk

© Transport for London

Travelling by Air to London

Top Tips

Top Tips from DPTAC for travelling by air

- Under European Law, if you are disabled or have difficulty moving around, you can pre-book to receive assistance when you fly to and from Europe, including within the United Kingdom (UK).

- It is advised that you ask for assistance at least 48 hours in advance to be sure of getting it.

- Airports will provide special assistance to get you to and from your flight free of charge, including checking in and getting through security, providing accessible flight information, reaching connecting flights and getting to the next part of your onward journey.

- All major airports in the UK have help points when arriving or departing, including at train stations, car parks, taxi ranks and bus stops.

- All front line staff should have Disability and Equality Awareness Training to ensure a smoother journey for you.

- Airport and airline staff may help you get to the toilet; however, they are not required to provide personal assistance in bathrooms.

- Assistance dogs are permitted on the flight free of charge, subject to Pet Passport Regulations. For the UK please refer to Defra at: www.defra.gov.uk/wildlife-pets/pets/travel/pets/index.htm.

- You are permitted to check two items of large mobility equipment free of charge (e.g. electric wheelchair and manual wheelchair).

- Wheelchair users may be able to stay in their own chair to the departure gate, depending on the impact of disability and whether the chair can be loaded from the gate.

- You will generally be the first person boarded on the plane and the last person to leave the plane, unless you request otherwise.

As a general rule, it is worth checking with different airlines before you book your tickets to find out what facilities and services they offer. Again, before you book, confirm which London airport offers the most suitable facilities for your own needs.

Safety and Security

Airlines have to ensure that passengers understand the emergency instructions given at take-off. Accompanied passengers with sensory impairments or learning disabilities are asked to make themselves known, although they may consider that they do not need any particular assistance. Airlines may choose not to provide any particular safety instruction services, such as large print information or subtitled videos.

Security Enhancements

- Anyone leaving a vehicle unattended outside a terminal should expect it to be removed.

- At some airports disabled people are helped into the building by a short free parking period at the nearest car park.

- Wheelchair users/other disabled people obviously cannot go through the regular metal detectors and can ask to be searched in private.

- Security staff are instructed to take particular care in re-packaging any luggage belonging to visually impaired people whom they search.

- A form of certification, such as a passport or driving licence is required for domestic flights.

Medicine and Injections

- Any medicines should be carried in hand luggage and kept in their original packaging.

- It is advisable to have a note saying what these medicines are, both to satisfy security personnel and to obtain further supplies if anything goes wrong.

- Despite the general ban on sharp objects, people who require injections must have a letter explaining the medical need for it, usually from their doctor.

Heightened Security

- At times of heightened security, additional restrictions may be imposed, relating to the use of private cars and even taxis in the area around airport terminals and on what may be taken onto aircraft.

London's Airports – A Quick Guide

London Heathrow is located 32 km (20 miles) to the west of Central London and there are excellent transport links by train (Heathrow Express is the fastest approx 15 minutes with dedicated areas for passengers using wheelchairs). Tube (approx 50 mins to Piccadilly Circus). Coach (between 40 mins and 1.5 hours)

London Gatwick is 45 km (28 miles) south of London. The Gatwick Express is the fastest way to central London (Victoria Station) and takes about 30 mins. Thameslink trains to London Bridge, Blackfriars and St Pancras take 40 mins upwards. National Express coach takes approx 1.5 hours.

London City is 9.5 km (6 miles) east of Central London and can be accessed by taxi, bus or Underground/ Docklands Light Railway (the UK's first fully-accessible railways for wheelchair users)

London Stansted is 64 km (40 miles) north-east of London. Stansted Express is quickest at approx 45 mins into London Liverpool Street station. easyBus non-stop to Baker Street approx 1hr 15 min.

London Luton is 51 km (32 miles) north-west of London. Regular First Capital Connect trains operate King's Cross, Farringdon and London Bridge to Luton Parkway station (approx 50 mins). A regular shuttle bus links Parkway to airport (8 mins)

All Airports have taxis available. Only use a black cab or reputable mini-cab. Ask the driver how much the journey will cost beforehand.

The websites for Heathrow, Gatwick and Stansted have a Special Assistance section which will give you detailed information on:

- Planning your journey

- Before leaving home

- Parking

- Public transport

- Help bus

- Help points

- In the Terminal

- Useful links

For Luton, there is a Disability Information page on the website under In the Terminal. For London City, there is a Special Needs page under the Airport Information section.

London City Airport
City Airport, Royal Docks, London E16 2PX
t: 020 7646 0088 email: CSC1@londoncityairport.com
web: www.londoncityairport.com

London Gatwick Airport
Gatwick, West Sussex RH6 0NP
t: 0844 335 1802 textphone: 01293 513179
web: www.gatwickairport.com

London Heathrow Airport
234 Bath Road, Hayes, UB3 5AP
t: 0844 335 1801 textphone: 020 8745 7950
web: www.heathrowairport.com

London Luton Airport
Navigation House, Airport Way, Luton LU2 9LY
t: 01582 405100 email: disabledfacilities@ltn.aero
web: www.london-luton.com

London Luton Airport
First Capital Connect Trains
t: + (0)800 058 2844

London Stansted Airport
Enterprise House, Bassingbourne Road, Stansted, Essex CM24 1QW
t: 0844 335 1803 textphone: 01279 663725
web: www.stanstedairport.com

© ATOC

Travelling by Rail to London

All London's mainline stations and many smaller ones are accessible by lifts and ramps. Much is being done under the auspices of the Department for Transport's £370 million Access for All Scheme with Europe's busiest station, Clapham Junction, finally getting lifts to all platforms by mid-2010.

Most trains serving London are new or have been refurbished and now have provision for disabled people. However, some services on extremely busy inner-London suburban services have facilities but do not have guards. Ramps for getting on/off trains are available at most accessible stations. Remember to travel by train is a potential solution not just to arriving in London but, in many cases, to travelling around Greater London.

The most important preparation you can do, whether you are arriving in London by train or using the train to travel within London, is to make sure that you have checked out the accessibility of the station and found out where to call ahead for assistance, particularly if you need to use a ramp to get on and off the train.

National Rail Enquiries
t: 0845 748 49 50 **textphone:** 0845 605 0600
web: www.nationalrail.co.uk

National Rail Enquiries is the first point for all information on accessible rail travel. It provides up-to-date information on train timetables, fares, disruptions to services and also has information on the accessibility of individual stations. To check the accessibility of the stations you will be using go to the "Stations and Destinations" page, click on "Stations Facilities Search", type in the name of the station and then click on "Stations Made Easy". You will be able to enter your travel preferences (for example, whether or not you can use stairs) and a route through the station will be generated. There are also maps of every station and photographs of all public areas (including baby change and toilet facilities) to enable you to plan. Train companies also produce their own information about accessibility of their stations as well as details of their policies concerning disabled and elderly people, so be sure to check their websites before travelling.

Assistance

Train companies can provide you with help using their services. When you plan your journey, you should make your needs known to rail staff. They are trained to give you help. So, if you are likely to require help getting on and off trains or receiving information, tell them. This will help them to help you if disruption affects your journey. There are limits to the amount of assistance they can provide. They cannot escort customers throughout their whole journey, neither can they provide personal care (for example, help with eating and drinking, taking medication or using the toilet) or carry heavy luggage.

If you need assistance they recommend that you book it at least 24 hours in advance of travel. Booking in advance enables train companies to check the accessibility of the stations you will be using, help you plan the journey best suited to your needs, and if necessary, arrange alternative transport to the nearest accessible station.

The 24-hour notice period also gives them time to relocate staff to assist you, or, if this is not possible, to arrange a taxi to take you to a station where assistance is available. This is important if you are going to travel at a time when a station is usually unstaffed.

UK Train Operators

Contacts for enquires about your journey:

Chiltern Railways
t: 08456 005165
textphone: 08457 078051
web: www.chilternrailways.co.uk/travelling-with-us/
disabled-travellers-info/using-our-trains-and-stations/

CrossCountry Trains
t: 0844 811 0125
textphone: 0844 811 0126
web: www.crosscountrytrains.co.uk/YourJourney/
AssistedTravel.aspx

East Coast
t: 08457 225 225
textphone: 08451 202 067
web: www.eastcoast.co.uk/On-Board-Our-Trains/
General-Information-Assisted-Travel/Your-journey-with-us/

European Passenger Services (for Eurostar)
t: 08705 186186

web: www.eurostar.com/UK/uk/leisure/travel_information/
before_you_go/special_travel_needs.jsp

First Capital Connect
t: 0800 058 2844
textphone: 0800 975 1052
web: www.firstcapitalconnect.co.uk/Main.
php?iCmsPageId=83

© ATOC

First Great Western
t: 0800 197 1329
textphone: 0800 294 9209
web: www.firstgreatwestern.co.uk

First Scotrail
t: 0800 912 2901
typetalk: 18001 0800 912 2 901
web: www.firstgroup.com/scotrail/content/specialneeds/index.php

Gatwick Express Ltd
t: 08458 501530
web: www.gatwickexpress.com

Grand Central
t: 0844 811 0072
textphone: 0845 305 6815
web: www.grandcentralrail.co.uk/travel-assistance.html

Heathrow Connect
t: 0845 678 6975
textphone: 08453 303729
web: www.heathrowconnect.com

Heathrow Express
t: 0845 600 1515
textphone: 08453 303729
web: www.heathrowexpress.com

© Transport for London

London Midland
t: 0800 092 4260
textphone: 0844 811 0134
Fax: 0845 051 8359
web: www.londonmidland.com/p/accessibility/

London Overground
t: 0845 601 4867
web: www.tfl.gov.uk/gettingaround/
transportaccessibility/1175.aspx

National Express
web: www.nationalexpress.com

National Express East Anglia
t: 0800 028 2878
textphone: 08456 067245
web: www.nationalexpresseastanglia.com/services/
journey_assistance

Northern Rail
t: 08081 561606 (freephone)
textphone: 0845 604 5608
web: www.northernrail.org/passenger/disabilities.asp

Southern Trains
t: 0800 138 1016
textphone: 0800 138 1018
fax: 0800 138 1017
web: www.southernrailway.com/your-journey/customer-
services/assistance-and-information/

Southeastern Railway
t: 0800 783 4524 or 01732 77 00 99
textphone: 0800 783 4548
web: www.southeasternrailway.co.uk/index.php/cms/
pages/view/135

South West Trains
t: 0800 528 2100
textphone: 0800 692 0792
fax: 023 8072 8187
web: www.southwesttrains.co.uk/SWTrains/
TravelInformation/Passengersrequiringassistance/

Stansted Express
t: 0845 600 7245
web: www.stanstedexpress.com

Transport For London
web: www.tfl.gov.uk
24-hour information: =44 (0)20 7222 1234

Virgin Trains
t: 08457 443366

textphone: 08457 443367
web: www.virgintrains.co.uk/travelling_with_us/journey_
assistance/default.aspx

Travelling with a wheelchair

Most trains can accommodate wheelchairs that are within the dimensions prescribed in government regulations covering public transport (700mm wide, 1200mm long). There are a small number of older trains that can only currently carry wheelchairs that have a maximum width of 670mm.

The maximum combined weight of a person and their wheelchair that can be conveyed is limited by: the capabilities of the individual member of staff assisting the passenger and the stated maximum safe-working load of the ramp (between 230kg and 300kg).

Powered scooters

Because scooters come in a wide variety of shapes and sizes, many have problems on trains, including: tipping backwards on ramps; being heavier than the ramp's safe working load; or being the wrong shape to manoeuvre safely inside a carriage.

These problems mean that some companies have trains that cannot carry scooters. So if you are a scooter-user who wants to travel by rail, you should contact the train company to check they can safely accommodate your scooter. Following several accidents involving scooters, some train operators only carry folded scooters or require the users to obtain a special pass. Train companies keep this aspect of their policy under review and as train fleets change, and refurbishments take place scooter policies have changed as well. If you want to travel with your scooter please check with the train company with whom you are travelling or check the National Rail Enquiries website.

Disabled person's railcard

Many disabled people are eligible for the Disabled Person's Railcard, which gives a third-off most rail fares for the cardholder and an adult companion.

For more information on the Railcard and how to apply see www.disabledpersons-railcard.co.uk or phone **0845 605 0525** (textphone/minicom: **0845 601 0132**)

Get 1/3 off rail fares for you...

and a companion...

Disabled Persons Railcard

£18 For a one-year Railcard

Only £48 For a three-year Railcard

You qualify if you meet any one of the criteria below:

- ✓ You receive Attendance Allowance
- ✓ You receive Disability Living Allowance (at either the higher or lower rate for getting around or the higher or middle rate for personal care)
- ✓ You are registered as having a visual impairment
- ✓ You have epilepsy and have repeated attacks or are currently prohibited from driving because of epilepsy

- ✓ You are registered as deaf or use a hearing aid
- ✓ You receive severe disablement allowance
- ✓ You receive War Pensioner's Mobility Supplement for 80% or more disability
- ✓ You are buying or leasing a vehicle through the Motability scheme

To find out how to apply see the leaflet 'Rail Travel Made Easy' (available at stations) or contact us:

 Web
www.disabledpersons-railcard.co.uk

 Email
disability@atoc.org

 Telephone
0845 605 0525

 Textphone
0845 601 0132

Motability
The leading car scheme for disabled people

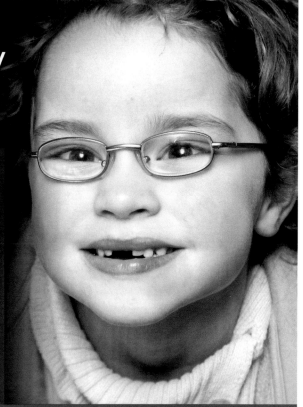

it changed our lives!

"The use of a reliable car is vital for our day-to-day routine. As the servicing, breakdown cover, tax and insurance are all included it saves me money as well as time. The car is comfortable and the peace of mind I have now is invaluable."

Emma, Charley's mum

where will yours take you?

use your mobility allowance to get mobile...

Simply exchange it for an all-inclusive worry-free mobility package, including:

- New car, powered wheelchair or scooter
- Insurance
- Servicing and repairs
- Tyres
- Breakdown cover

freephone 0800 093 1000

or visit www.motability.co.uk for further details

© National Express

Travelling by Coach to London

Contact your local coach operator for details of accessibility on the service you want to take to London. National Express are introducing a new generation of more accessible coaches on some routes which are opening up some new opportunities.

National Express Disabled Persons Travel Helpline
t: 08717 818179 **textphone:** 0121 455 0086
web: www.nationalexpress.com/coach/OurService/disabled.cm

The following information applies to National Express Coach Services to London or London's airports:

Concessionary Fares

The concessionary fare applies to all passengers who qualify as disabled. The scheme applies equally to both UK residents and overseas visitors. Check with National Express contact details above.

Wheelchair Accessibility

Accessible coaches

National Express is introducing a new generation of coaches onto the UK network that feature a wheelchair lift incorporated into the passenger entrance.

The easy access coach features a wider entrance and a completely flat floor throughout the coach to aid mobility for all. A streamlined NX Magic Floor Lift is incorporated into the passenger entrance and when deployed, the wheelchair is locked in place and the customer, safely and securely, uses the same standard three-point seat belt as other customers. Other features include reclining leather seats, air conditioning and a large toilet.

A programme of routes is currently being planned to roll-out the accessible coach across the network, with the whole network being fully accessible by 2012.

Routes with accessible coaches

The following services are already operating with easy

access vehicles. The majority of locations along these routes can be used by the easy access coach and wheelchair users, but please contact the National Express Disabled Persons' Travel Helpline for further information before travelling.

- 240 Leeds - Sheffield - Coventry - Heathrow Airport - Gatwick Airport
- 403 Bath - Swindon - Chippenham - Heathrow - London (side-entry passenger lift)
- 560 Barnsley - Sheffield - London (not including night or seasonal services)
- 562 Hull - Doncaster - London
- 591 Edinburgh - Newcastle - London (not including night or seasonal services)

To ensure that you can travel at your required time, and to make the most of the dedicated and experienced travel helpline staff, we highly recommend that you make a reservation.

Although it is not currently possible to reserve through the website, the Disabled Persons' Travel Helpline team will be pleased to make sure that your booking is made and that the drivers are fully aware of when you are travelling.

To make a reservation, contact the Disabled Persons Travel Helpline on **08717 818179**. A textphone is provided for customers who are deaf or hard of hearing on **0121 455 0086**

Megabus.com also offer a number of accessible bus services into London Victoria Coach Station. For passengers with walking difficulties, the driver will assist you to climb a few steps into the bus and help you into your seat. You should purchase your ticket on megabus. com in the usual way.

However, if you normally use a wheelchair and you need to remain in it for your trip on megabus, please **DO NOT PURCHASE** your ticket on the website. Fully accessible vehicles are being introduced across the megabus network, at present the following services offer accessible vehicles:

Service M7	Cardiff to London
Service M10	Bristol to London
Service M6	Plymouth to London via Exeter
Service M20	Edinburgh to London via Newcastle, Scotch Corner, Wakefield and Sheffield

If your service is listed and you wish to check availability on a specific journey and book travel for yourself or a wheelchair user please call **0141 332 9841**

It is very important that you make your reservation as early as possible, but no less than 48 hours before the intended date of travel.

Additional routes are being added on an ongoing basis, please check the website (megabus.com) for regular updates. For further information, contact **megabus.com**

© Stagecoach Group

Journeys within London by coach and/or other modes of transport can also be planned on-line using the TfL Journey Planner. If you do not have access to the internet, up-to-date information about coach routes, timetables and fares is available by calling Travelline on **0871 200 22 33**.

Some key points to consider from DPTAC:

- Check that both the departure and arrival coach stations, and any other stops along the way, are accessible.

- Check if there is a toilet on board. However, even if there is, space inside will be limited and access to it may be down steep steps, so it is always worth checking if there will be "comfort stops" along the journey.

- Some coaches have an 'at seat' trolley service where you can get sandwiches or snacks, but this service is usually limited and the choice can be small. You should check with the coach company if there will be stops along the way where you can get food. However if you have a special diet or will need food regularly during the journey it is advisable for you to take food with you on the coach.

- Carry medication, food, money and valuables with you on the coach.

- It may be possible to reserve special seats with more leg-room when you book your ticket, you will need to check with the operator.

- If you need oxygen and the equipment you use is portable and small you may be able to take it with you, but always check with the coach company.

Mobility Assistance at Victoria Coach Station

Transport for London does not operate coach services, but it does operate Victoria Coach Station (VCS), which is the main point of departure and arrival for coach services in and out of London. VCS comprises two buildings, one for departures and one for arrivals. VCS is a predominantly step-free environment.

A plan of Victoria Coach station is provided on in the TfL Getting Around London PDF.

There are other coach set down/pick up points in addition to VCS throughout London, including:

- Heathrow Airport

- Golders Green

- Stratford

- Coach stops in central London.

If you have a mobility impairment, you can pre-book Mobility Assistance at Victoria Coach Station by either phoning the Mobility Lounge on **020 7027 2520** or by completing the Mobility Assistance on-line request form on the TfL website tfl.gov.uk/vcs. Please ensure that this form is submitted at least 24 hours prior to your departure time. The Mobility Assistance service is free of charge, but please note that a small charge may be payable if you also require the service of a porter. Customers can arrange to be set down or picked up by a taxi, licensed minicab or private car at the Mobility Lounge. If you are arriving by coach and intending to continue your journey by other means, you should notify your coach driver, who will then request that Mobility Assistance is provided for you on arrival at VCS. If you are departing from one of the Green Line coach stops in Bulleid Way on a specific coach service, VCS staff will assist you in reaching the departure stop. As with coaches arriving at VCS, if you are arriving at one of the Green Line stops and need help in continuing to your next point of departure, help can be requested by calling the Mobility Lounge once you have arrived.

© National Express

© Transport for London

© ATOC

© Transport for London

Planning your journey within London

Key aids available from Transport for London to help you to plan a journey on London's Transport Network:

www.journeyplanner.tfl.gov.uk is TfL's online Journey Planner. You can plan any point to point journey in London and, with My Mobility Requirements, you can tick any of these four options:

✓ I cannot use stairs

✓ I cannot use escalators

✓ I cannot use lifts

✓ I use wheelchair accessible vehicles

You can opt for a Large Text version of the Journey Planner. As well as how to get around, the TfL website has details of fares, including concessions, and timetables.

Other TfL Guides that will Help You Plan:

The Interactive Journey Map gives the following information about stations on the Tube and Docklands Light Railway:

- Station facilities, including toilets, cash machines, car park and pay phones
- The type of access that there is to the station's Ticket Hall and platforms, and to trains themselves
- Train timetables (Tube stations only)
- A map of the local area (Tube stations only)
- A list of destinations that can be reached by bus from stops near the station, and the bus route numbers
- Links to the relevant bus timetables
- A list of destinations that can be reached by National Rail from the station (rail interchange stations only)

- Links to riverboat information where relevant

- The location and opening hours of the Travel Information Centre, if the station has one. If there is a bus spider map for the local area, this is also included. Bus spider maps are diagrams that clearly illustrate all bus routes serving a given area.

Accessible Tube maps include details of stations with step-free access. You can also call TfL Customer Service Centre for a large print (colour or black and white) or an audio version of the Tube map.

Describe online: audible descriptions of a number of stations. You can also find detailed information on access to individual stations, including walking distances between platforms, at Direct Enquiries.

Step-free tube guide: London Underground currently has 58 stations which are step-free from street to platform. This guide covers the Tube and DLR network showing stations that are step-free between the street and platform, plus information about the step and gap between the platform and train. It also shows where you can change, step-free, between different Tube lines, and between Tube lines with National Rail services. You can order it by calling **020 7222 1234** or going online to **tfl.gov.uk/accessguides**

Tube toilet map: Shows the location of toilets and baby changing facilities on the Tube network, including which toilets are suitable for wheelchair users or those with mobility impairments. Available online.

Customer Service Centre: Occasionally, a lift may be out of service. You can check this before you travel by using Journey Planner or calling **0845 330 9880**. Alternatively, you can sign up for free TfL Travel alerts and get travel news sent to your mobile phone.

Travel Information Centre: Call 24-hour (**020 7222 1234**) or Minicom (**020 7918 3015**) for help and advice. You do not need to book assistance in advance.

Direct Enquiries: http://www.directenquiries.com This website contains detailed access information about every Tube station including the number of steps and the length of walking routes to the platform and at interchanges.

Guides for People with Learning Difficulties

The '**Out and about in London**' series helps people with learning difficulties travel independently:

'**Out and about in London: My guide**' will help you travel independently, and covers different ways of travelling, including bus, cab, Tube, train, Docklands Light Railway and tram. It helps you keep yourself and your belongings safe, and shows you what to do if things go wrong. The guide has space for writing down or drawing details about your journey, and comes in an easy-to-use ringbinder.

'**Out and about in London: My guide for listening**' is the CD version of 'My guide' and includes sound effects.

'**Out and about in London: Supporting independent travel**' is for people supporting someone with learning difficulties. It is mainly for non-professionals, such as parents and carers, but will also help professionals. It offers travel training tips to help the learner get the most out of 'My guide'.

The guides can be ordered from London Travel Information on **020 7222 1234** or via the TfL website **tfl.gov.uk/gettingaround.**

TfL also provides a range of standard information products, in various accessible formats such as large print, black and white and audio maps. For more details on London Underground Accessibility maps and guides go online to **tfl.gov.uk/gettingaround**.

© ATOC

Help point

Emergency exit

© Transport for London

Travelling by Tube

Much of the London Underground system was planned and originally built in the last century – the challenge facing the Underground now is to introduce facilities which make it more accessible. A major investment programme is underway to deliver improved access across the Tube network. Here are some of the improvements now under way:

- Tactile strips on staircases and platforms
- More help points
- More seating on platforms
- Induction loops at all ticket offices
- Clearer priority seating signs on trains
- Platform humps in some locations, to reduce the step up from platform to train.
- New trains, coming into use over the next few years, will have easier access with lower floors and improved audio/visual customer information. There will also be more 'multi-purpose' open areas for wheelchairs, pushchairs and luggage.
- Better access between the train and the platform. By 2010, 25% of Tube stations will have step-free access between the street and the platform.
- By 2017, Crossrail will provide a number of new step-free stations, in particular in central London.

Travelling on the Underground – some important things to know:

- Most tube stations are accessed via steps and escalators, so if you are unable to use these you should check before you travel using the resources in the previous section, especially the Step-Free Tube Map, to ensure your route is suitable.
- If you need help buying a ticket, you can ask at the ticket office or ask a member of staff to help.
- All ticket offices are equipped with induction loops, which you can use by switching your hearing aid to the 'T' position.

- A number of stations now have wide aisle automatic gates. These work in the same way as standard ticket gates but are wider, so they can be used independently by customers using wheelchairs and customers travelling with assistance dogs or pushchairs.

- If you need assistance getting to the platform, ask a member of staff for help. They will escort you to your train and arrange for you to be met at your destination if necessary.

- For your safety and that of others, if you are a wheelchair user, you will not be allowed to travel on escalators whilst in your wheelchair. Please ask a member of staff for help.

- All staff receive regular training and will be able to help if it's safe to do so.

- If you have a guide dog, staff will help you avoid escalators or stop them to allow you and your dog to walk. However, at busy times it may not be possible to stop escalators immediately, as it may cause overcrowding. If you feel able, you may carry your dog on the escalator. From 2010, assistance dogs can be trained to use moving escalators safely. Assistance dogs that have been specifically trained will be permitted to travel on moving escalators. The training will be carried out by the organisation "Guide Dogs", and you can contact them for more information.

- Toilet facilities are available at some tube stations and may be located in the ticket hall or at platform level. A Tube toilet map will provide all necessary information but if you want to know the exact toilet location check with station staff.

- If you need to use the toilet whilst travelling but find it locked, please ask a member of staff for assistance.

- When boarding the train, be aware that with the exception of stations east of Westminster on the Jubilee line, there may be a gap between the platform and the train, and a step up or down onto the train. You may want to check the Step-Free Tube Guide for station specific information.

- If requested, a member of staff will help you onto the train and, if necessary, help you find a seat. They will then call ahead to your destination or interchange stations and arrange for a member of staff to meet and assist you there too.

- At some stations there are platform humps which raise sections of the platform to the same level as the train.

These are currently available at Brixton, Tottenham Hale, Kings Cross (Victoria line only), London Bridge and the Waterloo & City line. Please note that only a few doors of the train will have level access on these platforms.

- All train carriages have clearly marked seats which are designated for customers who are less able to stand. These are identified by notices and should be kept free or vacated for disabled passengers, pregnant women, older people, those travelling with children and anyone less able to stand. If you need a seat and no one offers, feel free to ask the people occupying the priority seats.

- With the exception of the Metropolitan line, all trains have audio announcements which state the train destination, the next station and any interchanges available. The District, Jubilee, Northern and Piccadilly lines also have visual information displays in the train.

- In the event of an emergency, you may be asked to evacuate a station or train. Staff will provide you with instructions and extra assistance if you so require.

- If you need help while travelling on the Tube, please ask a member of London Underground staff and they will do their best to assist you. They can be contacted via a Help Point if you can't see them on the platform or in the ticket hall.

- The last Underground trains leave central London at around 0030.

- All car parks operated by London Underground have accessible spaces, free for use by Blue Badge holders. See http://www.tfl.gov.uk/roadusers/ tubestationcarparks/default.aspx

- Tactile warning surfaces are being installed on platforms as stations are refurbished.

© Transport for London

© Transport for London

Docklands Light Railway (DLR)

Docklands Light Railway (DLR) links the City from Bank or Tower Gateway stations with a variety of destinations in east London: Beckton, Canary Wharf, Stratford, Lewisham and Woolwich Arsenal in south-east London. A map of Docklands Light Railway is included in the Tube map.

All details are on the Tfl website or by phoning the Information Centre (see Planning Your Journey)

DLR was the first fully accessible railway in the UK, making access much easier for people using wheelchairs, or who have other mobility impairments.

Lifts and Ramps

All DLR stations have a lift or ramp access to the platforms, with level access onto the trains. All lifts have alarms enabled, which allow you to talk directly with a member of DLR staff should you experience any problems.

Getting On and Off

The gap between the platform edge and the train is approximately 7.5cm wide and the step up or down from the platform to the train is approximately 5cm high. These levels allow easier access for most passengers. Most wheelchair users find getting on and off smoothest with the largest wheel first; this may mean reversing as appropriate.

© Transport for London

Buses

Buses are a highly accessible way to travel around London. All of London's 8,000 buses on normal routes are now low-floor, wheelchair accessible vehicles. The ramps on all buses must be in full working order at all times. Any bus with a defective ramp is taken out of service, so you are assured of full accessibility at all times.

London's buses are now fitted with iBus, the on-board **"next stop"** announcements. The system means passengers know exactly where their bus is and what the next stop and final destination will be.

Wheelchair users are entitled to free travel on buses, as are Freedom Pass holders.

Use the same planning tools listed under Planning Your Journey, plus Bus spider maps (these diagrammatic maps illustrate the full range of bus routes that serve areas throughout London).

Using Buses

- All buses are low-floor vehicles (excluding Heritage buses covering parts of routes 9 and 15), which means that the doorways are close to pavement level when the bus stops and the doors open.

- This enables all customers, including people using wheelchairs, people with buggies, people with assistance dogs, and people with other mobility impairments, to get on and off buses easily*.

- Every bus also has a retractable ramp, which connects the floor of the bus directly with the pavement, making access possible for wheelchair users.

- If you're unable to board a bus because of a broken ramp, please wait for the next one, and tell Customer Services as soon as possible on **0845 300 7000**.

* The wheelchair space on buses cannot take a wheelchair bigger than 70cm in width and 120cm in length

© Transport for London

© Transport for London

Passengers Using Wheelchairs

- On all buses, there is room for one person using a wheelchair. Wheelchairs can be accommodated up to a size of 70cm wide by 120cm long with a maximum weight of 300Kg.

- On most buses you'll be boarding at the centre doors, where the ramp is located, so you might find it easier to position yourself a little way along the pavement, before the stop, to allow the driver to see you sooner.

- When boarding the bus, the front doors will stay closed so passengers getting on don't obstruct you as you board. The centre doors will open so passengers can get off. The centre doors will then be closed and the wheelchair ramp extended.

- Once the centre doors are opened, it's safe for you to board the bus. It's best to board forward as it makes it easier to position yourself once on board.

- Once on board, position yourself in the wheelchair space, with your back against the backrest and your

brake on, to make sure your chair doesn't move when the bus does.

- To leave the bus, press the button with the wheelchair symbol on it, next to the wheelchair space, shortly before your stop.

- This button has a distinct sound and a light will appear on the driver's dashboard to let him know yours is the next stop. The bus will pull in close to the kerb. The front doors will stay closed to give you time to get off.

- The centre doors will open so other passengers can get off. The centre doors will close and the driver will extend the ramp. The centre doors will reopen so you can leave the bus. If, however, the ramp goes out of service after you have boarded, it is the responsibility of the bus operator to ensure that you can leave the bus safely.

- Wheelchair users have priority over everyone else for use of the wheelchair space, since this is the only place in which they can travel safely.

Passengers with Assistance Dogs

There is no limit on the number of assistance dogs the bus driver can allow on the bus, as long as there is space. London Buses welcome all assistance dogs, including guide dogs, hearing dogs, fetch and carry dogs, mental health companion dogs, and dogs that can sense when their owner is about to have an epileptic fit. All they ask is that your dog doesn't block the gangway.

© Transport for London

Tramlink

London Tramlink Comprises Three Routes:

1. Elmers End to Croydon.

2. Beckenham Junction to Croydon.

3. New Addington to Wimbledon.

A Tramlink map is available online clearly illustrating the three routes in operation. All trams on these routes are fully accessible.

Use the same planning tools listed under Planning Your Journey.

© Transport for London

River

On a fine day, this is the perfect way to combine sightseeing with getting from A to B. Many riverboats are accessible.

Using Riverboats

All piers are wheelchair accessible. Most river cruises last between 45 minutes and 1 hour 30 minutes.

Most riverboats are accessible, and most newer river craft have dedicated wheelchair spaces. You should check with individual service operators about the level of accessibility on their boats. Staff are always on hand to offer help in boarding and disembarking from river craft. However, it is advisable for people with mobility impairments who are travelling as a group to provide advance notice to the operator concerned, to ensure a smooth journey.

Riverboats – Useful Information

- Riverboat services call at over 20 piers on the River Thames in London.

- There are two commuter services, and a wide range of leisure services.

- Many operators offer 50% off the normal advertised adult fare on production of a valid Freedom Pass at the time of travel.

Many operators offer a third off normal advertised adult and child fares on production of a valid Travelcard or Oyster card loaded with a valid Travelcard, when buying a ticket. Some restrictions apply. Oyster cards with pre-pay are not accepted. Users of Oyster Pay As You Go get a 10% discount on Thames Clippers' normal fares.

- The Woolwich ferry is a free service operating between Woolwich and North Woolwich. This service is accessible to wheelchair users and powered buggy users.

Guide to Piers

Information for each operational pier on the River Thames in London:

- Type of access from the street

- Destinations served

- Interchanges with other transport modes

Can be found on the TfL website or by calling the Riverboat Information Line on **020 7941 2400**.

Riverboat Operators

Thames Clippers
0870 81 5149
www.thamesclippers.com

Crown River Services
020 7936 2033
www.crownriver.com

Thames Executive Charter
01342 820605
www.thamesrivertaxi.com

City Cruises
020 7740 0400
www.citycruises.com

Thames River Service
020 7930 4097
www.thamesriverservices.co.uk

Bateaux London
020 7695 1800
www.bateauxlondon.com

Road Users - Information for Disabled Drivers

A car or minibus that is already adapted to your needs is in many ways the most flexible option open to you. However, it is public policy in London to encourage both visitors and residents to use public transport whenever possible. The two biggest challenges you will face are parking and the 'big city' driving style of your fellow drivers in London. We can't help with the other drivers – except to say try to stay calm, don't try to drive like them unless it's your normal style and avoid the rush hour if you can.

But here is some useful advice on parking and other aspects of motoring in London.

The Blue Badge Parking Scheme

The Blue badge scheme provides a range of parking benefits for eligible disabled people. The scheme operates throughout the UK. In London, the following boroughs operate schemes that vary from the national scheme: City of Westminster, Royal Borough of Kensington & Chelsea, City of London and part of the London Borough of Camden. These concessions only apply to on-street parking and include free use of parking meters and pay-and-display bays.

Badge-holders may also be exempt from limits on parking times imposed on others and can park for up to three hours on yellow lines (except where there is a ban on loading or unloading or other restrictions). Your local authority is responsible for issuing Blue Badge parking permits. Please contact them directly for more information.

© Britainonview/Damir Fabijanic

If you have access to the internet, you can visit **direct.gov. uk/disabled people** for further information on the Blue Badge scheme. On this website you can enter your town or postcode, which will take you to your local authority website, where you can find out more and/or apply online. An interactive map showing parking bays for Blue Badge holders in over 100 towns and cities and spaces on Red Routes in London as well as parking rules for all councils in the UK is at **www.direct.gov.uk/bluebadgemap**.

There are a limited number of marked parking spaces for Blue Badge holders and the badge may also be recognised for reserved bays in car parks. The location of Blue Badge spaces, car parks other useful information is shown in "Blue Badge Parking Guide" price £4.99 from bookshops or the publishers on:
t: 020 7952 0456
web: www.thepieguide.com

Other Places to Park:

The car parks in central London that are operated by the London boroughs are relatively easy to find out about. The commercially-operated car parks are more difficult.

The best list is probably at **http://www.accessproject-phsp.org/london/parking.php** although it has not been updated since 2003.

Congestion Charge

Blue Badge holders are eligible to register for a 100% discount from the Congestion Charge, which means that once they have successfully registered with Transport for London they will not have to pay the £8 daily charge. You must first register with Transport for London before travelling. Please allow a minimum of 10 working days for your application to be processed. Call for information on how to register.

If you have access to the internet, you can download an application form.

t: 0845 900 1234 **textphone:** 020 7649 9123
web: cclondon.com

Disabled passenger-carrying vehicles, and vehicles used by disabled people that are exempt from Vehicle Excise Duty (road tax) are automatically exempt from the Congestion Charge and do not need to register with Transport for London.

Red Routes

To help pedestrians with mobility impairments, many crossings on the red routes are level with the pavement. This makes it easier to cross and has the added benefit of slowing down traffic. For those with visual impairments, tactile paving helps guide pedestrians safely to crossing points on the red route.

Ramps have been introduced to improve access and many footbridges are being widened, replaced or upgraded. Rest levels also allow you to take a break while crossing footbridges. A number of bus stops along the red route have raised kerbs, allowing bus ramps to be used more easily.

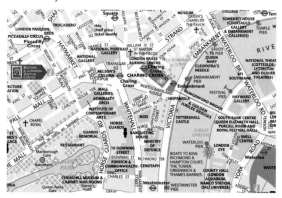

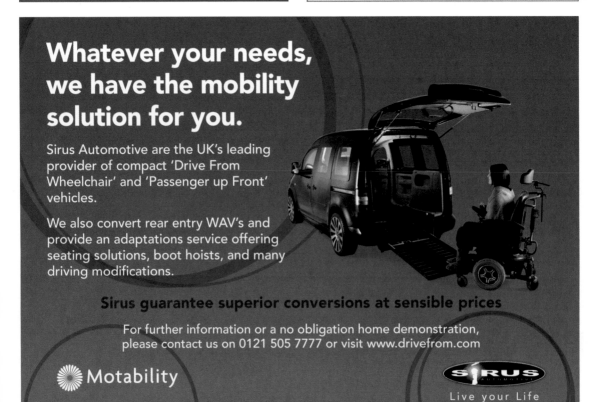

© Transport for London

London Taxis, Private-Hire Vehicles and Minicabs

Taxis and Private Hire

Transport for London licenses taxi and private hire (PHV also called minicabs) companies, drivers and vehicles in London and recognises that travelling by taxi or PHV is one of the most flexible ways to get around. Services operate across London, 24 hours a day, 365 days a year subject to local availability.

Taxis

Often referred to as 'black cabs', taxis can be hailed in the street or at designated ranks situated in prominent places, including many mainline rail, Tube and bus stations. They can also be booked by telephone by contacting one of the radio circa providers or by telephoning One-Number taxi bookings on **0871 871 8710** or you could **visit tfl.gov.uk/cabs** for more numbers.

All of London's taxis have space to carry a passenger in a wheelchair, both manual and powered. However, please note that there may not be space for passengers who use larger wheelchairs so check with the driver or the operator when you make a telephone booking.

All taxis have a ramp to make access easier and many also have a swivel seat and an extra intermediate step to make entering and exiting the vehicle easier. Other features include a hearing loop, colour contrasted sight patches and grab handles for visually impaired passengers. All taxis carry assistance dogs at no extra charge.

Fares are shown on the meter and the fare payable will be displayed on the meter at the end of the journey. There are no extra charges for additional passengers or luggage but charges do apply when booking by telephone or paying by credit or debit card. Up-to-date fares information for licensed taxis is provided on the Transport for London website, at **tfl.gov.uk/findaride**.

Licensed Private-Hire Services

Private hire covers a wide range of services, including minicabs. Unlike taxis, journeys must be booked through a licensed private hire operator and vehicles cannot be hailed or approached on the street. Fares are at the discretion of the operator but most have set fares including a minimum fare per journey.

© Transport for London

You should ask the operator for a quote or estimate before you start your journey. All licensed private hire, including minicab, drivers must wear their licence ID badge with a photo of them on it. Licensed private hire vehicles are generally saloon cars and you should check with the licensed operator on whether their vehicles meet your own accessibility requirements.

To get the numbers for minicab operators text 'CAB' to 60835 who will use GPS to send the numbers for two local licensed minicab operators direct to your mobile phone. Customers on the 3 network can also access the Cabwise service by texting their location (street name and partial postcode e.g. Victoria St, SW1) to the number **07797 800 000**. Visit **tfl.gov.uk/cabwise** for more information and terms and conditions.

You can search for licensed private hire operators online by visiting **tfl.gov.uk/findaride**. You can search for licensed operators by type of service, area served and also whether they can provide wheelchair accessible vehicles (although varying amounts of advanced notice may be required for booking these). Call TfL's 24 hour travel information

helpline on **020 7222 1234**, for further information on taxis and private hire vehicles.

Safer Travel at Night

If you are travelling home late at night, you should always use a licensed minicab, taxi or night bus. It is illegal for a taxi or minicab driver to approach you offering a journey for payment. Remember any minicab journey not booked with a licensed operator is illegal, unlicensed, uninsured and unsafe. Know what you're getting into.

- To get telephone numbers of licensed minicab operators in your area sent direct to your mobile phone, **text 'CAB' to 60835.**

- Visit **tfl.gov.uk/findaride** to search for licensed private hire operators by the service offered and area served

- To book a taxi at any time of day or night, call One Number Bookings, on **0871 871 8710**.

- Call TfL's 24 hour travel information helpline **020 7222 1234,** for further information on taxis and private hire vehicles.

© Transport for London

Assisted Travel

Dial-a-Ride

Assisted transport is intended to provide older and disabled people for whom public transport is not always accessible, with the freedom to travel around London. Dial-a-Ride offers a service to visitors to London.

To be eligible for Dial-a-Ride membership you must have a permanent or long-term disability which means you cannot use buses, trains or the Tube services some or all of the time.

You are automatically eligible for Dial-a-Ride membership if you are:

- Aged 85 or over
- A current member of Taxicard
- Registered blind

- Receiving Higher Rate Mobility Component of Disability Living Allowance
- Receiving Higher Rate Attendance Allowance
- In receipt of a War pension Mobility Supplement

To use Dial-a-Ride services while visiting London, you can apply for temporary membership and will need to complete the application form at: tfl.gov.uk/gettingaround/1187.aspx You will be asked to download and print the application form, complete and return it to Dial-a-Ride. Alternatively you can call: 0845 999 1 999 to request an application form. As a visitor you will need to give dates of your visit and where you are staying.

Dial-a-Ride

Progress House, 5 Mandela Way, London SE1 5SS

Accessible Toilets

There are thousands of public toilets in the capital that are accessible to disabled people. Many are accessible through the National Key Scheme (NKS.) The principle of the NKS is that if local authorities and other organisations decide to lock toilets in order to prevent misuse, they should use a standard lock.

There are 900 toilets in the NKS in Greater London. The Royal Association for Disability and Rehabilition (RADAR) maintain a list of toilets in the scheme, this is published annually in the National Key Scheme Guide. Keys and copies of the guide are available from RADAR; there is a small charge (£3.50) for a key. For further information visit: **www.radar.org.uk t:** 020 7250 4119. The guide is also updated on: **www.directenquiries.com t:** 01344 360101

Accessible toilets can be found in most mainline rail stations in London. For visitors travelling around the capital by tube, Transport for London have a comprehensive map which shows which underground stations have toilets and what facilities are available at each one. Ask for a map at any underground station or visit:
www.tfl.gov.uk/assets/downloads/toilets-map.pdf

In response to his commitment to improve the quality of life in London, the Mayor launched the Open London scheme in 2009. The scheme set out to increase access to toilets across London by asking businesses to open up their toilets for public use. A number of major retailers, **Asda**, **John Lewis**, **Marks & Spencer**, **Sainsbury's** and **Tesco** agreed to let people use their customer toilets without having to make a purchase. Other accessible toilets can be found in places such as Tourist Information Centres, fast food restaurants, some pubs and restaurants and many of London's major tourist attractions.

The City of Westminster has launched an innovative new service 'Sat Lav' to help locate the nearest public convenience in the borough 24 hours a day, 7 days a week. Simply text the word "TOILET" to 80097 and you will receive a return text with the location and opening hours of the nearest public toilet. Texts cost 25 pence plus your network standard rate. This service is only available in Central London.

There is also a website that gives locations and general information about public toilets throughout all of London, called **www.bluebadge.direct.gov.uk** You can use this service to specify whether you need any public toilet, a RADAR NKS toilet, or a Changing Places toilet which offers facilities for disabled people requiring assistance from a carer. This information is very useful in helping you plan your day out in advance, knowing that the facilities you need will be available nearby.

Dulwich Picture Gallery

Accessible Sightseeing

The majority of the attractions have been chosen from the list supplied by **Visit London** of the most requested places on their website **visitlondon.com** Not all are completely accessible so do take advantage of the additional phone and web contact details to find further information to help you plan your visit.

If you have access to the internet, we recommend that you use it to the full. Many of London's attractions have impressive pages on their websites devoted to information for disabled visitors.

If you are registered disabled, you can often take advantage of discounted admission prices for yourself and free admission for your carer.

The attractions are arranged by postcode in Inner London and then alphabetically within each postcode. The area names appear alongside the postcode (e.g SW7 Knightsbridge/South Kensington).

In Outer London, the attractions are arranged clockwise by area – North, East, South and West and by postcode within these areas.

See page 136 for map and listing giving general locations of attractions.

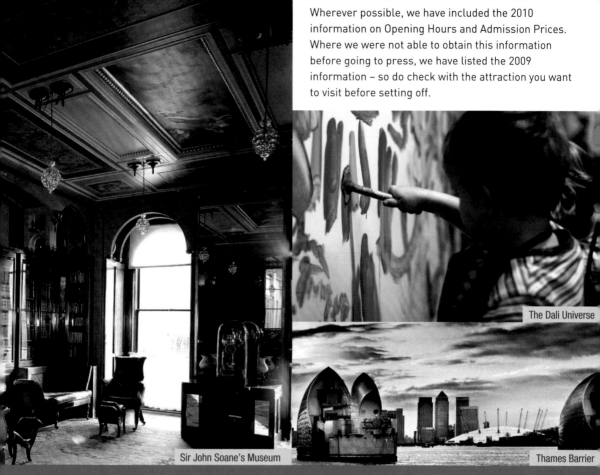

Wherever possible, we have included the 2010 information on Opening Hours and Admission Prices. Where we were not able to obtain this information before going to press, we have listed the 2009 information – so do check with the attraction you want to visit before setting off.

The Dali Universe

Sir John Soane's Museum

Thames Barrier

Key to symbols

Important note: the following symbols are designed to help you identify easily what facilities are available at London's attractions. The symbols are for guidance only. The description for each attraction has an 'Access' section, which gives more details about accessibility – use this as a guide but then please visit the attraction's own website and use the information telephone, teletext and email contact details to make absolutely sure that you have all the information you need in advance.

P Designated disabled parking

Accessible to wheelchair user

Designated wheelchair accessible public toilet

Assistance dogs welcome

abc Large print information

Braille information

 Sign language used

W1 Marylebone | Mayfair | Piccadilly | Soho | West End

Handel House Museum

Museum

25 Brook Street W1K 4HB

t: 020 7495 1685 **f:** 020 7495 1759
e: mail@handelhouse.org

www.handelhouse.org

Open: Tues, Wed, Fri, Sat: 10.00-18.00.
Thurs: 10.00 -20.00. Sun: 12.00-18.00
Closed Mon including Bank Hols. **Admission:** Adult £5.00.
Child (5-16) £2.00 (Free Sat/Sun). Under-5 free.
Concessions (disabled/senior citizens/students) £4.50.
Access: The museum contains original 18th-century floors
which can be uneven. Access by lift to all floors.
Description: Handel House Museum was home to
George Frideric Handel from 1723 until his death in 1759.
It was here that Handel composed 'Messiah', 'Zadok the Priest'
and 'Music for the Royal Fireworks'. The museum, with
its restored Georgian interiors, is the perfect place to learn
about Handel's life.

Royal Academy of Arts

Gallery

Burlington House, Piccadilly W1J 0BD
t: 020 7300 8000. 020 7300 5732 for accessible information
f: 020 7300 8001 **e:** access@royalacademy.org.uk
www.royalacademy.org.uk
Open: Daily except Fri: 10.00-18.00. Last admission to
galleries 5.30pm. Fri: 10.00-22.00. Last admission to galleries
21.30. **Admission:** Ticket prices vary for each exhibition.
Access: Ground and 1st floor accessible by lift.
Description: The Royal Academy of Arts, founded in 1768,
is the oldest fine arts institution in Britain. It is universally
renowned for hosting some of the capital's finest temporary and
touring exhibitions, including the annual Summer Exhibition.

The Museum at the Royal Institution

Museum

21 Albemarle Street W1S 4BS
t: 020 7409 2992 **f:** 020 7629 3569 **e:** ri@ri.ac.uk
www.rigb.org

Royal Academy of Arts © Britainonview

Open: Mon-Fri: 09.00-21.00. **Admission:** Free.
Access: Wheelchair access to all public areas.
Description: The small but entertaining exhibition explores the illustrious history of the RI, and uses animations and comedy to explain some of the groundbreaking concepts and equipment on show.

Wallace Collection

Gallery

Hertford House, Manchester Square W1U 3BN
t: 020 7563 9516. 020 7563 9524 for accessible information
f: 020 7224 2155 **e:** access@wallacecollection.org
www.wallacecollection.org
Open: Daily: 10.00-17.00. Closed 24, 25, 26 Dec
Admission: Free including temporary exhibitions.
Access: Access at entrance by ramps. All areas accessible.
Description: The Wallace Collection is a national museum, displaying superb works of art in an historic London town house. The 28 rooms present collections of French 18th century painting, furniture and porcelain together with paintings by Titian, Canaletto, Rembrandt and Gainsborough.

WC1 Bloomsbury

British Museum

Museum

Great Russell Street WC1B 3DG
t: 020 7323 8299 **f:** 020 7323 8616
e: information@britishmuseum.org
www.britishmuseum.org
Open: Daily: 10.00-17.30. Late closing Thurs and Fri: 20.30
Admission: Free but with charges for exhibitions.
Access: Lifts at main entrance … lifts throughout the Museum for access to most galleries. All special exhibitions are fully accessible. **Description:** The British Museum is one of the great museums of the world, showing the works of man from prehistoric to modern times with collections drawn throughout the world. Famous objects include the Rosetta Stone, sculptures from the Parthenon, the Sutton Hoo and Mildenhall treasures and the Portland Vase. There is also a programme of special exhibitions and daily gallery tours, talks and guided tours.

Brunei Gallery Soas

Gallery

Thornhaugh Street, Russell Square WC1H 0XG
t: 020 7898 4915 **f:** 020 7898 4259 **e:** gallery@soas.ac.uk
www.soas.ac.uk/gallery/
Open: Tues-Sat: 10.30-17.00. Closed: Sun, Mon and Bank Hols. **Admission:** Free. **Access:** Ramp at entrance. All areas accessible to wheelchairs. All floors accessible by lift.
Description: The Brunei Gallery is dedicated to showing historical and contemporary works of and from Asia and Africa. This is as part of the gallery's aim to present and promote cultures from these regions.

Charles Dickens Museum

Museum

48 Doughty Street WC1N 2LX
t: 020 7405 2127 **f:** 020 7831 5175
www.dickensmuseum.com
Open: Mon-Sat: 10.00-17.00. Sun: 11.00-17.00.
Admission: Adults: £5.00. Child £3.00. Students/seniors £4.00. Families:(2xA, 5xC) £14.00. **Access:** Wheelchair ramp currently being fitted and other facilities being improved. Check online photographic tour for suitability - ground floor only accessible. **Description:** Charles Dickens' home from 1837-1839, the house contains displays of letters, pictures, first editions, furniture, memorabilia and restored rooms. There are usually two temporary exhibitions per year.

Foundling Museum

Museum

40 Brunswick Square WC1N 1AZ
t: 020 7841 3600 **e:** enquiries@foundlingmuseum.org.uk
www.foundlingmuseum.org.uk
Open: Tues-Sat: 10.00-17.00. Sun: 11.00-17.00. Closed Mons. **Admission:** Adult £5.00. Child (under 16) free. Concessions £4.00. Art Fund members free. **Access:** Access ramp into the museum, lift facilitating wheelchairs to all floors.
Description: The Foundling Museum tells the story of the Foundling Hospital, London's first home for abandoned babies established by Royal Charter in 1739. The museum includes a contemporary social history gallery telling the story of the foundling children and the hospital's fine art collection.

St Bartholomew's Hospital Museum

St Bartholomew's, or Barts as it is popularly known, is one of the oldest and most distinguished hospitals in the world.

It was founded in 1123 by the monk Rahere and granted by Henry VIII to the City of London in 1546.

The Museum has a permanent exhibition of original archives and objects.

It includes works of art, surgical instruments and medical equipment used in the hospital.

Two vast and spectacular paintings by William Hogarth are also visible from the Museum.

Open Tuesday – Friday, 10am-4pm. (closed over Christmas and New Year, Easter and public holidays). Admission is free. Small groups welcome but should telephone 020 7601 8152 in advance to discuss requirements as space is limited. Wheelchair access by arrangement. An induction loop is available.

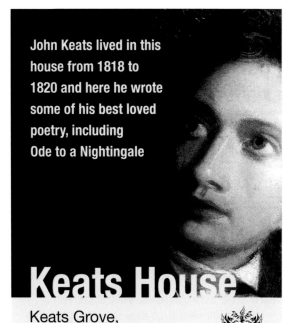

Enlightenment Gallery

The British Museum
A Museum for the World

The British Museum is the most popular visitor attraction in the UK, with over 5.56 million visitors in 2009 alone - the year that celebrated the Museum being open to the public for 250 years.

Mummy Gallery

Not only does it aim to be a collection for the 'learned and curious' but also 'for the benefit of the general public'. Indeed it is a collection preserved and held for the benefit of all the world, present and future, a forum for the expression of many different cultural perspectives and a place where the UK's diverse population and tourists from across the globe can explore their common inheritances.[1]

With diversity and inclusiveness being at the heart of the Museum, intellectual, physical and sensory services for disabled visitors are an important priority. Examples of Access services at the British Museum include large print information and tactile and Braille books in all of the Museum's popular exhibitions as well as some of the

Great Court

more recently refurbished galleries. Handling sessions for blind and partially sighted audiences are also programmed and a touch tour in the Egyptian sculpture gallery permits disabled audiences only to feel a variety of vast and ancient exhibits. All audio guides for popular exhibitions include audio description and fold up portable stools make the overall visitor experience more comfortable.

Blind and deaf audiences can also use free of charge the Museum's multi-media guide - a state-of-the-art means for audiences to learn about the Museum's unparalleled collections. The guide includes audio description for blind visitors and signed videos for deaf audiences. This superb provision allows visually impaired and hearing impaired audiences to walk off the street into the Museum and immediately access over 220 objects from the Museum's world collection.

These are but a few of the resources available for disabled visitors to the British Museum. The Museum is the greatest collection of human cultural achievement, ancient and modern in the world and as such aims to ensure that as many audiences as possible can benefit from and enjoy this awe inspiring collection.[2]

Jane Samuels, Access Manager, the British Museum

www.britishmuseum.org

[1] The British Museum Review, 2008 - 2009
[2] The British Museum Review, 2008 - 2009

Petrie Museum of Egyptian Archaeology

Petrie Museum of Egyptian Archaeology
`Museum`

University College London, Malet Place WC1E 6BT
t: 020 7679 2884 **f:** 020 7679 2886
e: petrie.museum@ucl.ac.uk
www.petrie.ucl.ac.uk/
Open: Tues-Fri: 13.00-17.00. Sat: 11.00-14.00. Closed
Christmas (approx 24 Dec- 5 Jan) and Easter.
Admission: Free. **Access:** Contact in advance for parking
information. Lift to museum and accessible toilets. Lift to 2nd
gallery. **Description:** The Petrie Museum is one of the largest
and most fascinating collections of Egyptian archaeology
anywhere in the world. There are over 80,000 artefacts
showing the development of Egyptian culture, technology and
daily life from prehistoric to Roman times.

Political Cartoon Gallery
`Gallery`

32 Store Street WC1E 7BS
t: 020 7580 1114
www.politicalcartoon.co.uk/html/contactus.html
Open: Mon-Fri: 09.00-17.30. Sat: 11.30-17.30.
Admission: Free. **Access:** Wheelchair access to some public
areas. Check for information. **Description:** The Political
Cartoon Gallery is the world's only centre dedicated to Political
Cartoons and Caricature. Only at the Political Cartoon Gallery
can you purchase the finest original cartoons by leading political
cartoonists from both the past and the present.

The Donmar Warehouse
`Theatre/Concert Hall`

41 Earlham Street WC2H 9XL
t: 0844 871 7677 for access booking. To book for a specific
assisted performance please contact 020 7845 5822.
e: access@donmarwarehouse.com
www.donmarwarehouse.com
Open: Check performance times online or by phone.
Admission: Check prices by phone or online.
Access: The Donmar is wheelchair accessible. For every
production a Captioned by Stagetext and Sign Language
interpreted performance for deaf and hearing impaired patrons
and an audio-described performance for blind and partially
sighted patrons led by Vocaleyes is offered.
Description: The Donmar Warehouse is a 250-seat subsidised
(not for profit) theatre located in the heart of London's West End
with a reputation as one of the UK's leading producing theatres.

Freemasons' Hall, Museum and Library
`Museum`

60 Great Queen Street, Holborn WC2B 5AZ
t: 020 7831 9811 **f:** 020 7404 7418
www.ugle.org.uk/freemasons-hall/
Open: Mon-Fri: 10.00-17.00. **Admission:** Free. **Access:** The
main entrance into Freemasons' Hall is in Great Queen Street.
It has automatic doors leading into the building. Accessible
lifts to all floors. **Description:** Freemasons' Hall has been the
centre of English Freemasonry for 230 years. The interior of the
building is richly decorated. The Library and Museum organises
free tours of the Grand Temple and ceremonial areas.

Hunterian Museum (Royal College of Surgeons)
`Museum`

35-43 Lincolns Inn Fields WC2A 3PE
t: 020 7869 6560. Textphone/typetalk
users: 18001 020 7869 6560
f: 020 7869 6564 **e:** museums@rcseng.ac.uk
www.rcseng.ac.uk/museums

Open: Tues-Sat: 10.00-17.00. **Admission:** Free.
Access: Wheelchair access at Nuffield entrance via lift. The College is happy to provide disabled visitors with a 'buddy' to accompany them during their visit. **Description:** The Hunterian Museum displays the collection of pioneering surgeon John Hunter (1728-93). There are plenty of pickled creatures in jars here. More contemporary exhibits explore contemporary and future surgery – not for the squeamish!

London Transport Museum © Britainonview

London Transport Museum
Museum

39 Wellington Street, Covent Garden WC2E 7BB
t: 020 7565 7292 **f:** 020 7565 7253
e: bookings@ltmuseum.co.uk
www.ltmuseum.co.uk/default.aspx
Open: Mon-Thurs, Sat, Sun: 10.00-18.00 (last admission 17.15). Fri:11.00-18.00 (last admission 17.15). Check for 'Friday lates'. **Admission:** Adult £10.00. Child (under 16 - accompanied) free. Senior citizens £8.00. Students £6.00.
Access: The museum is accessible for wheelchair users with level access at the Ticket Desk, and lifts to all floors. There are ramps in some areas. Not all of the vehicles are accessible.
Description: The museum explores the link between transport and the growth of modern London, its culture and society since 1800. The collection contains a wealth of heritage vehicles, posters, artworks, photographs, film and video footage, engineering drawings, uniforms, station signs and tickets.

National Gallery
Gallery

Trafalgar Square WC2N 5DN
t: 020 7747 2885. Access Officer on 020 7747 5855
f: 020 7747 2423 **e:** information@ng-london.org.uk
nationalgallery.org.uk
Open: Daily: 10.00-18.00. Fri 10.00-21.00. Closed 24, 25, 26 Dec, 1 Jan. **Admission:** Free. **Access:** Four entrances with level access but not main entrance. Access to all areas.
Description: London's National Galley is one of the world's great art galleries, with displays of Western European painting from about 1250-1900, including work by Botticelli, Leonardo da Vinci, Rembrandt, Gainsborough, Turner, Renoir, Cezanne and Van Gogh.

National Portrait Gallery
Gallery

St Martins Place WC2H 0HE
t: 020 7306 0055 dial ext 116 for accessible information
f: 020 7306 0056 **e:** dsaywell@npg.org.uk www.npg.org.uk
Open: Daily: 10.00-18.00 (21.00 Thurs-Fri). Closed 24, 25, 26 Dec. **Admission:** Free except for temporary exhibitions.
Access: Access to the Gallery for wheelchair users is via the Orange Street ramp entrance and the Gift shop entrance. Fully accessible inside. **Description:** The National Portrait Gallery houses the world's largest collection of personalities and faces, from the late Middle Ages to the present day. Visitors come face to face with the people who have shaped British history from kings and queens to musicians and film stars.

Donmar Warehouse © Britainonview/Pawel Libera

© John Walmsley, Education Photos, 2008

National Portrait Gallery

The National Portrait Gallery is home to the largest collection of portraiture in the world, with over 1000 portraits on display, from Elizabeth I to The Beatles.

The Gallery welcomes all visitors. Our building is fully accessible and we run a year-round programme of activities and events including Picture Description sessions for blind and partially sighted visitors and BSL tours.

For more information, including maps, facility details, exhibitions and events visit www.npg.org.uk or call 020 7306 0055, Typetalk 18001.

Admission is free. Concessionary entry fee is charged for some temporary exhibitions, which enables a disabled visitor to bring one free guest.

**Opening hours 10.00 – 18.00,
Thursdays and Fridays until 21.00
Nearest tube: Leicester Square**

Ripley's Believe It or Not! London located in the heart of London's West End at No. 1 Piccadilly Circus consists of over 500 unique, original, and unbelievable artefacts collected from all over the world. It is a must-see entertainment attraction for all visitors to the capital.

Ripley's Believe It or Not! London is proud of its ability to cater for the disabled community. It has lift facilities available so wheelchair users and the mobility impaired are easily able to access everything at their own pace.

There are facilities for those with service dogs and designated wheelchair accessible public bathrooms. The staff are trained in disability awareness and guided tours around the venue are available.

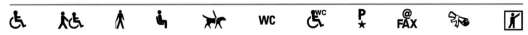

1 Piccadilly Circus, London, W1J 0DA - www.ripleyslondon.com

Several key works were lowered to enhance access for wheelchair users

The National Gallery

Be inspired and try something exciting at the National Gallery today, where you can experience iconic works by artists from Michelangelo to Monet.

The Gallery is committed to inclusion and access for all visitors. You'll find interpretation in alternative formats, an inspiring learning programme which appeals to different learning styles, and lifts and level entrances to enable physical access. If you are a disabled visitor, you can get a discount on exhibition tickets and you can bring an escort free of charge. Entrance to the permanent collection of paintings is free.

New resources have been produced for blind and partially sighted visitors including raised line drawings with Braille interpretation

All images © The National Gallery, London

At the Gallery, you can see paintings come to life as costumed characters step out of the frame; you can draw, discuss books relating to the paintings or enjoy movement-based activities. Popular paintings are occasionally lowered to enable visitors using wheelchairs to examine the paintings at close distance.

For blind and partially sighted visitors

The National Gallery runs monthly 'Art Through Words' verbal description sessions for blind and partially sighted visitors. These relaxed, interactive sessions can often include multi-sensory elements to appeal to a range of learning styles. For example, you might hear a detailed description of Holbein's Ambassadors, and then listen to a music historian and a lute player perform traditional songs from the Tudor court and tavern. Information about the sessions is available in alternative formats including Braille and large print.

You can request private tours of exhibitions or of the permanent collection, or try an audio tour such as Sounds of the Gallery, which features specially created sound art pieces. You may wish to try the Favourite Paintings guidebooks, which include tactile images, colour reproductions of details within the

Musical historians perform music and song to enhance interpretation of the collection

paintings, Braille interpretation and detailed painting descriptions in large print, to further enhance enjoyment for you and your companions visiting the Gallery. Large-print labels are also available within the permanent collection and for temporary exhibitions.

British Sign Language programme for deaf and hard of hearing visitors

As a deaf visitor, you may wish to participate in the vibrant British Sign Language (BSL) programme. Regular talks are given by deaf lecturers in BSL or are delivered in spoken English with BSL interpretation. The BSL programme offers a wide range of events including evening private views and social events as well as lectures. There is now a dedicated National Gallery BSL Facebook site and BSL introductions to exhibitions can be viewed on the Gallery website. Ten-minute talks and tours are sometimes lip-speaking supported for hard of hearing visitors, and induction loops are provided in key locations around the Gallery.

The National Gallery's Access Programme is generously supported by The BAND Trust.

For more information ask at the Information Desks in the Gallery, visit www.nationalgallery.org.uk/access, call **020 7747 2885** or email information@ng-london.org.uk

Art for All

The National Gallery, Trafalgar Square, London WC2N 5DN www.nationalgallery.org.uk

Sir John Soane Museum

Museum

P& &ʷᶜ 🐕 abc •: ✋

13 Lincoln's Inn Fields WC2A 3BP
t: 020 7405 2107. Accessibility information: 020 7440 4263
f: 020 7831 3957 **e:** sbhatti@soane.org.uk www.soane.org
Open: Tues-Sat: 10.00-17.00 (last Admission 16.30). Also on
the first Tues eve of each month: 18.00-21.00. Closed 24 Dec
and Bank Hols. **Admission:** Free. **Access:** Disabled Parking (4
bays - Camden Green Badge holders only); 8 steps at entrance
(assistance available). Two narrow wheelchairs available,
making most of Ground floor and basement accessible but not
first floor. **Description:** Former residence of Sir John Soane
(1753-1837), architect of the Bank of England. Soane designed
this house to live in, but also as a setting for his antiquities
and works of art. More than 20,000 architectural drawings,
antiquities and works by Hogarth, Turner, Canaletto
and Piranesi.

Somerset House/ Courtauld Gallery

Historic Attraction/Gallery

P& & &ʷᶜ 🐕 abc •:

South Building, Somerset House WC2R 1LA
t: 020 7845 4600. Access information line: 020 7845 4671
f: 020 7845 4637 **e:** info@somersethouse.org.uk
www.somersethouse.org.uk
Open: Daily: 10.00-18.00. Embankment Galleries 10.00-21.00
Thurs-Fri. **Admission:** Embankment Galleries: Adult £5.00.
Child (12-17) £4.00. Concession (OAPs/students/ES40 holders)
£4 00. Courtauld Gallery: Adult £5.00. Child (under 18) free.
Concession £4.00. Students, ES40 free. **Access:** Somerset
House and the Courtauld Gallery are accessible to wheelchair
users. **Description:** The Courtauld Gallery has iconic
Impressionist and Post-Impressionist masterpieces and other
important paintings from the Renaissance through to the 20th
century. The new Embankment Galleries stages exhibitions,
focusing on a broad range of contemporary arts.

St Clement Danes

Place of Worship

Strand WC2R 1DH
t: 020 7242 8282 **f:** 020 7404 2129
e: stclementdanes1@btconnect.com
www.raf.mod.uk/stclementdanes/
Open: Daily: 09.00-16.00. **Admission:** Free.

Sir John Soane Museum

Access: Check for details. One step at entrance otherwise
ground level accessible. **Description:** This is the 'Oranges and
Lemons' church and features include a Grinling Gibbons pulpit
and Samuel Johnson statue. Rebuilt by Sir Christopher Wren
in 1681 and burnt out during World War II. Now the Central
church of the Royal Air Force.

St Martin-in-the-Fields

Place of Worship

& &ʷᶜ 🐕 abc •: ✋

Trafalgar Square, 6 St Martin's Place WC2N 4JJ
t: 020 7766 1100 **f:** 020 7839 5163 **e:** info@smitf.org
www2.stmartin-in-the-fields.org/page/home/home.html
Open: Check concert times. **Admission:** Free. Check for
concerts. Carers free. **Access:** Accessible entrance via signed
ramp on north side. A lift is available between crypt and
church and from street to crypt level. The concert area is fully
accessible. **Description:** St Martin-in-the-Fields is not only
renowned as one of London's liveliest and best-loved churches,
but also has a reputation as a superb arts venue with more than
350 concerts every year.

NW1 Camden | King's Cross | Regent's Park

British Library
Museum

96 Euston Road NW1 2DB
t: 020 7412 7332. Textphone: 020 7387 0626
f: 020 7412 7807 **e:** visitor-services@bl.uk
www.bl.uk/whatson/planyourvisit/index.html
Open: Mon, Wed-Fri: 09.00-18.00. Tues: 09.30-20.00. Sat: 09.30-17.00. Sun and Bank Hols: 11.30-17.00.
Admission: Permanent galleries free. Check charges for exhibitions. **Access:** Access to all areas by lifts and ramps - for details, use website www.bl.uk/whatson/planyourvisit/disabled/index.html or phone. **Description:** The British Library is home to the UK's national library and to exhibition galleries. On display are some of the world's most famous written and printed items including: Magna Carta (1215), Shakespeare's First Folio (1623) and displays on calligraphy, bookbinding, printing, stamps and sound recording.

Madame Tussauds
Attraction

Marylebone Road NW1 5LR
t: 0870 4003000. 0871 894 3000 to book wheelchair visits
f: 0870 4003006 **e:** guest.services@madame-tussauds.com
www.madametussauds.com/London/
Open: Peak: (weekends, UK school holidays, public holidays): First admission 09.00, last admission 18.00. Off Peak: First 09.30. Last 17.30. Late Summer opening 09.30-9.00 (approx 25 July-30 Aug). **Admission:** Adult £25.00 (online £22.50). Child £21.00 (£18.50). Disabled visitors £12.50. Family (incl.

St Martin-in-the-Fields

free guidebook) £87.00 (£78.00). Carers free. Off-peak late-saver tickets £12.50. **Access:** All areas accessible except Spirit of London exhibit. Only 3 wheelchair users at one time so booking essential. Lifts to all floors. **Description:** Mingle and interact with the world's most famous figures at Madame Tussauds and attend an A-List party, go to a star-studded film premiere, challenge your sporting heroes, take to the stage with music's megastars, be knighted by the Queen or address the world's leaders.

Wellcome Collection
Museum

183 Euston Road NW1 2BE
t: 020 7611 2222 **f:** 020 7611 2211
e: info@wellcomecollection.org
www.wellcomecollection.org
Open: Tues-Sun: 10.00-18.00 (Sun 11.00), Thurs: 10.00-22.00. Closed Mon and Bank Hols. **Admission:** Free but charges apply to some exhibitions. **Access:** Access to all areas by ramps and lifts. Guided visits bookable. **Description:** Wellcome Collection is a free destination for the incurably curious. Explore what it means to be human through a unique mix of galleries, events and meeting, reading and eating places.

ZSL-London Zoo
Attraction

Regent's Park NW1 4RY
t: 020 7722 3333. 020 7449 6576 to book wheelchairs
f: 020 7483 4436 **e:** marketing@zsl.org
www.zsl.org/zsl-london-zoo
Open: Daily opens 10.00. Closes between 16.00-18.00 depending on season. Last admission is one hour before advertised closing time. Closed Dec 25. **Admission:** Adult £16.80. Child (3-15) £13.30. Under-3 free. Concession (student/60+/disabled) £15.30. Saver Ticket (2xA, 2xC or 1xA, 3xC) £53.70. Visitors can opt to make an additional £1.70 donation. **Access:** Most of the zoo is accessible for wheelchair users. Paths are generally tarmac. Level or ramped access to most buildings. No direct access to the Aquarium - ask for a volunteer to take you into the Aquarium via level access at the rear. **Description:** London Zoo has over 12,000 amazing animals to discover. With incredible animal displays and fascinating trails to follow, the zoo is the perfect day out. Come face-to-face with some of the hairiest, scariest, tallest and smallest animals on the planet - right in the heart of the capital.

Belmont New Window

St Martin-in-the-Fields

St Martin-in-the-Fields, Trafalgar Square, is renowned throughout the world for its music, architecture, hospitality and a forward-thinking approach to supporting people in need. From London's first free lending library, to pioneering work with homeless people, and the first religious radio broadcast, St Martin's continues to break new ground in defining what it means to be a church.

The latest milestone in the church's history is the Renewal of St Martin-in-the-Fields. This £36million project has restored old spaces and created new ones to serve the community, visitors and those in need, ensuring the life and sustainability of St Martin's. Natural light now floods into the church and crypt and both spaces are fully accessible for the first time. This work has been recognised at the 2009 Visit

London Awards when St Martin-in-the-Fields was awarded Gold in the Accessible Tourism Category.

With over 20 church services and 6 concerts per week, the award-winning Café in the Crypt, Brass Rubbing, Shop and new spaces available to hire for events and meetings – there is something for everyone at St Martin's. For music-lovers, a visit to St Martin's is a must. Since 1726 St Martin's has played host to

some of the greatest musicians including Handel and Mozart and the Academy of St Martin in the Fields, was founded here by Sir Neville Marriner in 1959. Its atmospheric candlelit concerts, every Thursday-Saturday at 7.30pm, offer a varied musical programme featuring internationally renowned orchestras, chamber groups, instrumental soloists and choirs. The Lunchtime Concerts Series on Mondays, Tuesdays and Fridays at 1.00pm has been running for over 50 years, and offers a performance platform for music students and young performers just starting their careers. For Jazz lovers, Jazz Nights in the Cafe in the Crypt are every Wednesday at 8pm.

The Café in the Crypt at St Martin's is well known to Londoners and visitors alike for its warm welcome, dramatic setting, and value-for money menu prepared freshly on site. It is open Monday-Saturday for breakfast, lunch, afternoon tea and dinner and Sunday for lunch, afternoon tea and dinner. Whilst in the crypt you can also try your hand at traditional brass rubbing. St Martin's has an extensive collection of replica brasses including simple dragons and knights for children, to more complicated images for the more dedicated artists. Visit the Shop at St Martin's for a range of gifts, music and books and pick up an audio guide to guide you around the church above. St Martin's also hosts art exhibitions in the Gallery in the Crypt.

Further information on regular and special events, opening times and help on planning your visit can be found on the St Martin-in-the-Fields website www.smitf.org Concert tickets can also be booked online, in person or via box office telephone number 020 766 1100.

Photographs: Phil Ashley

W2 Bayswater | Hyde Park | Paddington

Serpentine Gallery

Gallery

P& & &wc abc •:

Kensington Gardens W2 3XA
t: 020 7402 6075 **f:** 020 7402 4103
e: information@serpentinegallery.org
www.serpentinegallery.org/
Open: Daily: 10.00-18.00. **Admission:** Free. **Access:** Level
access throughout. **Description:** One of London's best-loved
contemporary art galleries, with a programme of modern
and contemporary art exhibitions from Andy Warhol to Piero
Manzoni, Cindy Sherman and Chris Ofili.

SW1 Pimlico | Victoria | Westminster

Banqueting House

Historic Attraction

& abc •:

Whitehall Palace, Whitehall SW1A 2ER
t: 020 3166 6152 **f:** 020 3166 6310
e: banquetinghouse@hrp.org.uk
www.hrp.org.uk/BanquetingHouse/
Open: Mon-Sat: 10.00-17.00. Closed: Suns, Bank Hols and
24 Dec-1 Jan, also for functions - phone to check
Admission: Adult £4.80. Child (under 16) free. Concession
(students/60+) £4.00. Carers free. **Access:** The Main Hall of
the Banqueting House is accessible via a lift in an adjoining
property. Portable or standard-size wheelchair is required.
Ramp down to The Undercroft. **Description:** Created by
Inigo Jones, Banqueting House was the first in England to
be designed in a Palladian style. Intended for the splendour
and exuberance of court masques, the Banqueting House is
probably most famous for one real-life drama: the execution
of Charles I.

Churchill Museum and Cabinet War Rooms

Buckingham Palace (State Rooms)

Historic Attraction

P& & &wc abc •:

Buckingham Palace Road SW1A 1AA
t: 020 7766 7300 **f:** 020 7930 9625
e: bookinginfo@royalcollection.org.uk
www.royalcollection.org.uk
Open: 27 July-29 Sept 2010: 09.45-18.00 (last admission
15.45). **Admission:** Adult £16.50. Child (under 17) £9.50.
Under-5 free. Concession (student/60+) £15.00. Family
(2xA, 3xC) £44.00. **Access:** Wheelchair-users book through
the Information Office by telephoning (+44) (0)20 7766
7324 - website has full details. An alternative Access Route
with step-free access is available for visitors with mobility
difficulties. Lifts. **Description:** Buckingham Palace serves
as both the office and London residence of Her Majesty The
Queen. It is one of the few working royal palaces remaining
in the world today. During the summer, visitors can tour the
19 State Rooms, which form the heart of the Palace. These
magnificent rooms are decorated with some of the greatest
treasures from the Royal Collection.

Churchill Museum and Cabinet War Rooms

Museum

& &wc abc •:

Clive Steps, King Charles Street SW1A 2AQ
t: 0207 930 6961 Textphone: 020 7839 4906
f: 020 7930 5897 **e:** cwr@iwm.org.uk
cwr.iwm.org.uk
Open: Daily: 09.30-18.00 (last admission 17.00) Closed 24,
25, 26 Dec. **Admission:** Adult £12.95. Child (under 16) free.
Senior citizens/students £10.40. Disabled £7.75. Carers
free. **Access:** The Churchill Museum and Cabinet War Rooms
(CM&CWR) is fully accessible to mobility impaired users. There
is a lift to the basement level. The entire site is without stairs.
The historic nature of the site means that there are some
narrow points within the corridors and doorways.
Description: The highly interactive and innovative Churchill
Museum is the world's first major museum dedicated to the
life of the 'greatest Briton'. Step back in time and discover the
secret underground headquarters that were the nerve centre
of Britain's war effort. Visitors can view this complex of historic
rooms left as they were in 1945.

Clarence House

Historic Attraction

The Mall SW1A 1BA
t: 020 7766 7303 **f:** 020 7930 9625
e: bookinginfo@royalcollection.org.uk
www.royalcollection.org.uk
Open: 31 July-1 Sept 2010: 10.00-16.00. Last admission
15.00. **Admission:** Adult £8.00. Child (5-17) £4.00. Under-5
free. Student/60+ £8.00. **Access:** Three steps at the entrance
to the house. The remainder of the route has level access. A
platform stair-lift provides step-free access into the building.
The lift measures 130cm in depth by 80cm in width. There
are no lavatories at Clarence House. The nearest accessible
lavatories are in St James's Park. **Description:** Clarence House
is the official residence of the Prince of Wales and the Duchess
of Cornwall. From 1953-2002 it was the home of HM Elizabeth
the Queen Mother. During the summer, visitors are guided
around the ground-floor rooms where the Prince and Duchess
undertake official engagements.

Guards Museum

Museum

Wellington Barracks, Birdcage Walk SW1E 6HQ
t: 020 7414 3271 **f:** 020 7414 3429
e: guardsmuseum@aol.com
www.theguardsmuseum.com
Open: Daily: 10.00-16.00 (last admission at 15.30).
Admission: Adult £3.00. Child (under 17) free. Senior
Citizens/students £2.00. Serving Military Personnel £1.00.
Access: Accessible throughout. Entrance accessible by lift.
Description: Spanning over 300 years of history, the museum
contains a wealth of information and artefacts relating to the
five regiments of Foot Guards namely Grenadier, Coldstream,
Scots, Irish and Welsh Guards.

Household Cavalry Museum

Museum

Horseguards, Whitehall SW1A 2AX
t: 020 7766 7330 **f:** 020 7414 2212
e: museum@householdcavalry.co.uk
www.householdcavalrymuseum.co.uk
Open: Mar-Sept, Daily: 10.00-18.00.Oct-Feb, Daily: 10.00-

Serpentine Gallery © John Offenbach

17.00. Closed 24, 25, 26 Dec. **Admission:** Adult £6.00. Child
(5-16) £4.00. Concessions £4.00. Family ticket (2 xA, 3xC)
£15.00. **Access:** The Household Cavalry Museum is accessible
to all visitors. Call for specific enquiries. **Description:** The
museum's outstanding collection of treasures represents over
300 years of military history and each item on display has its
own compelling story to tell. Plus, children's dressing-up area,
trails and interactive displays.

Houses of Parliament

Historic Attraction

2 Abbey Gardens, House of Commons SW1P 3SE
t: 0844 847 1672 **e:** mcdonaldm@parliament.uk
www.parliament.uk
Open: Tours: Aug: Mon(except Bank Hol), Tues, Fri, Sat:
09.15-16.30; Wed, Thurs: 13.15-16.30. Sept: Mon, Fri,
Sat: 09.15-16.30; Tues, Wed, Thurs: 13.15-16.30. Oct 2,
3: 09.15-16.30. Check 2010 dates. **Admission:** Adult from
£12.00. Children (5-15) from £5.00. Students/seniors from
£8.00. **Access:** Parliament is open and accessible to all visitors
with disabilities. All tours are accessible by wheelchair users.
Description: Houses of Parliament is one of London's most
famous landmarks and has been the home of Parliament since
1265. Also known as the Palace of Westminster, the Houses of
Parliament are home to the House of Commons and the House
of Lords and the famous clock tower Big Ben.

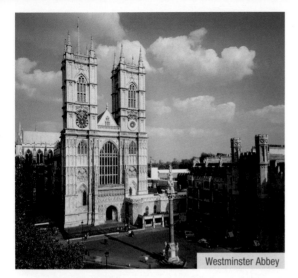
Westminster Abbey

Institute of Contemporary Arts

Gallery

Nash House, The Mall SW1Y 5AH
t: 020 7930 3647 Textphone: 020 7839 0737
f: 020 7873 0051 **e:** james@ica.org.uk
www.ica.org.uk
Open: Mon-Wed: 12.00-23.00. Thurs-Sat: 12.00-01.00.
Sun: 12.00-21.00. Galleries open daily 12.00-19.00 (21.00
on Thurs) during exhibitions. **Admission:** Free entry but check
for individual events and exhibitions. Concessionary rates
for disabled visitors. Carers free. **Access:** Level access to
entrance. Access by lift to cinemas and lower gallery. Restricted
lift access to upper gallery, Nash and Brandon rooms.
Description: The centre for international contemporary arts
in Britain with 3 galleries (exhibitions changing approximately
every 8 weeks). The ICA has cinema, theatre, live music,
restaurant, lectures and live music events, bookshop and late
bar and café.

Queen's Gallery

Gallery

Buckingham Palace, Buckingham Palace Road SW1A 1AA
t: 020 7766 7301. 020 7766 7324 for accessible information.
f: 020 7799 2331 **e:** bookinginfo@royalcollection.org.uk
www.royalcollection.org.uk
Open: Daily: 10:00-17:30 (last admission 16:30). Closed 25,
26 Dec, 15 Feb-18 Mar, 2 April, 1 Nov 2010-14 April 2011.

Admission: Adult £8.50. Child (5-16) £4.25. Under-5 free.
Concessions (60+/student) £7.50. Under-5 free. Family (2
xA, 3xC) £21.50. **Access:** Access by lift to exhibition area.
Description: The Queen's Gallery at Buckingham Palace
provides a year-round display space for works of art from
the Royal Collection. In addition to the Treasures of the Royal
Collection there are temporary exhibitions themed around
pieces within the collection.

Royal Mews

Historic Attraction

Buckingham Palace SW1A 1AA
t: 020 7766 7321. 020 7766 7324 for accessible information
f: 020 7799 2331 **e:** bookinginfo@royalcollection.org.uk
www.royalcollection.org.uk/
Open: 20 Mar-31 Oct: Daily, except Fri 11.00-16.00 (last
admission 15.15). Except 27 July-29 Sept: Daily, 10.00-17.00
(last admission 16.15). Closed during State visits.
Admission: Adult £7.50. Child (under 17) £4.80. Under-5
free. Concessions (60+/student) £6.75. Family (2xA, 3xC)
£20.00. **Access:** All areas of the Royal Mews have level
access. The Royal Mews is an historic building the floors are
uneven and cobbled in places. **Description:** One of the finest
working stables in existence, the Royal Mews at Buckingham
Palace is home to the royal collection of historic coaches and
carriages. The most dazzling of all the coaches on display
is the Gold State Coach, used as part of the Golden Jubilee
celebrations in 2002.

Tate Britain

Gallery

Millbank SW1P 4RG
t: 020 7887 8888. Minicom 020 7887 8687
e: information@tate.org.uk
www.tate.org.uk/
Open: Daily: 10.00-17.50 (22.00 on the first Fri of each
month). Closed 24, 25, 26 Dec. **Admission:** Free except
for major exhibitions (carers free). **Access:** Three accessible
entrances. Lift to main gallery and access to all areas.
Description: Tate Britain holds the largest collection of British
art in the world. The gallery shows work from the last five
centuries, with masterpieces by British artists such as Hogarth,
Gainsborough, Constable, Whistler, Sickert, Hepworth and
Bacon. The work of JMW Turner can be seen in the
Clore Gallery.

Westminster Abbey

Place of Worship

20 Dean's Yard, Chapter Office SW1P 3PA
t: 020 7222 5152 **f:** 020 7654 4891
e: info@westminster-abbey.org
www.westminster-abbey.org
Open: Mon, Tues, Thurs-Fri: 09.30-16.30 (last admission: 15.30). Wed: 09.30-19.00 (last admission: 18.00). Sat: 09.30-14.30 (last admission 13.30). Closed except for worship Sundays, Christmas Day, Good Friday. **Admission:** Adults £15.00. Child (11-18) £6.00. Under-11 free. Concessions (60+/students 18+) £12.00. Family tickets available. Free to wheelchair visitors and carers. **Access:** Accessible entry North Door via ramp. Not all of the Abbey accessible. Much of the Abbey floor and steps are uneven. Pre-booked guided tour available (020 7654 4823). **Description:** Kings, queens, statesmen and soldiers; poets, priests, heroes and villains - the Abbey is a must-see living pageant of British history. Every year Westminster Abbey welcomes over one million visitors who want to explore this wonderful 700-year-old building which is the coronation church of England.

Westminster Cathedral

Place of Worship

Victoria Street SW1P 1QW
t: 020 7798 9055 **f:** 020 7798 9090
www.westminstercathedral.org.uk/vinfo/vinfo_home.html
Open: Approx 08.00-19.00 (17.30 Public Holidays).
Admission: Free. **Access:** Accessible entrance from the

piazza. Side chapels are 2 steps up. The gift shop is down 3 very steep steps. The refectory is up 2 steep steps then down 19 steep steps. British Sign Language Mass first Sunday each month 16.30. **Description:** Westminster Cathedral is the mother-church of the Roman Catholic Archdiocese of Westminster It was begun in 1895 and was completed in 1903. Brick built the vast domed interior has the widest and highest nave in England and is decorated with mosaics plus 125 varieties of marble.

SW3 Chelsea | Knightsbridge

Chelsea Physic Garden

Garden

66 Royal Hospital Road SW3 4HS
t: 020 7352 5646 **f:** 020 7376 3910
e: enquiries@chelseaphysicgarden.co.uk
www.chelseaphysicgarden.co.uk
Open: Wed-Fri: 12.00-17.00. Sun, Bank Hol Mons: 12.00-18.00. Jul-Aug: Wed: Garden open until 22.00 (last admission at 20.30). **Admission:** Adults £8.00. Child (5-15) £5.00. Concessions (students/unemployed) £5.00. Free for Friends of the Garden. **Access:** Access is through the foyer at 66 Royal Hospital Road (open on public days only). No other steps in the garden and access is via gravel or grass paths. The West Gate may be opened by prior arrangement with the office. **Description:** Three and a half-acre garden with one of the oldest rock gardens in Europe, herb garden with culinary and medicinal plants, botanical order beds, glasshouses, rare plants and tender species.

National Army Museum

Museum

Royal Hospital Road SW3 4HT
t: 020 7730 0717 dial ext 2235 for accessible information.
f: 020 7823 6573 **e:** info@national-army-museum.ac.uk
www.national-army-museum.ac.uk
Open: Daily: 10.00-17.30. Closed 24, 25, 26 Dec, 1 Jan, Good Friday and early May Bank Hol. **Admission:** Free.
Access: All the museum galleries are accessible to wheelchair users. **Description:** Find out how Britain's past has shaped our present and future. Discover the impact the Army has had on the story of Britain, Europe and the world, and see how the actions of a few can affect the futures of many.

Chelsea Physic Garden

The Natural History Museum

Mention the Natural History Museum and most people will probably think about the ever-popular Dinosaurs Gallery.

However, frequent visitors to the Natural History Museum are aware that the Museum is also home to the nation's finest collection of natural history specimens. It is one of the UK's top visitor attractions, with more than four million people every year enjoying exhibitions, events and education programmes.

Every single visitor to the Museum has specific requirements to get the most out of their visit and the Museum aims to provide a friendly, accessible environment, to all our buildings, exhibitions and collections. Access is one of these key requirements, and can refer to accessing a building, information, learning, or self discovery.

There are distinct challenges in making a grade one listed building fully accessible, however access to most of the public spaces has been improved. A new lift has been installed in the lobby by the Museum's accessible entrance on Exhibition Road, alongside two accessible toilets and baby changing facilities. The accessible entrance anticipates the exciting Exhibition Road Project which is

The Natural History Museum

All images © Natural History Museum

Diplodocus skeleton in the Central Hall

likely to bring larger numbers of visitors to the Museum, especially during Olympics and Paralympics 2012.

The Museum has recently introduced new reception and information desks with built-in induction loops. Also, new to the Museum is our first audio descriptor/guide for the Veolia Environnement Wildlife Photographer of the Year 2009 exhibition, which is free for those who are visually impaired or blind. The Museum hopes to continue improving access for our blind and visually impaired visitors.

Listening to visitors is key to anticipating barriers that may inhibit access. Through greater engagement,

the Museum is learning to recognise those barriers and over the past four years has implemented a more inclusive approach to maximising access for a wider range of people. Real accessible provision comes through awareness and accordingly, the Museum has a programme of disability and diversity training for its staff.

The Museum has introduced Visit Planners, to ensure a rewarding and easy-going visit. More information can be found in the 'Access guide' found at **www.nhm.ac.uk**.

If you have specific access requirements, please phone Customer Services on **020 7942 5511** or email **customerservices@nhm.ac.uk**.

Royal Hospital Chelsea
Historic Attraction

Royal Hospital Road, Chelsea SW3 4SR
t: 020 7881 5204 **f:** 020 7881 5463
www.chelsea-pensioners.co.uk/about/visits
Open: Daily 10.00-12.00 and 14.00-16.00. Closed Sundays
from Oct-Mar. Grounds closed May/June for Chelsea Flower
Show. **Admission:** Free. **Access:** Wheelchair access to some
public areas. Check for more details. **Description:** Built by Sir
Christopher Wren, this is the home of the Chelsea Pensioners.
The Chapel, Great Hall and Figure Court are of particular
interest and the grounds are attractive. The Royal Hospital site
contains a small but interesting Museum.

Saatchi Gallery
Gallery

Duke of Yorks's Building, Kings Road SW3 4SQ
t: 020 7823 2363. 0207 811 3085 for accessible information.
www.saatchi-gallery.co.uk/
Open: Daily: 10.00-18.00. Last admission: 17.30.
Admission: Free. **Access:** Assisted or ramp access is
available at the main entrance. All floors have lifts. Level access
between the galleries on each floor. **Description:** The Saatchi
Gallery aims to provide an innovative forum for contemporary
art, presenting work by largely unseen young artists or by
international artists whose work has been rarely or never
exhibited in the UK.

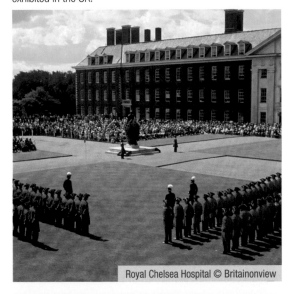

Royal Chelsea Hospital © Britainonview

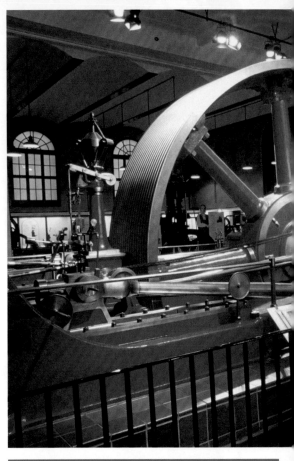

SW7 Knightsbridge | South Kensington

Natural History Museum
Museum

Cromwell Road SW7 5BD
t: 020 7942 5000. Typetalk: 18001 020 942 5000
f: 020 7942 9066 **e:** info@nhm.ac.uk
www.nhm.ac.uk
Open: Daily: 10.00-17.50 (last admission 17.30). Closed Dec
24, 25, 26. **Admission:** Free except for temporary exhibitions
Access: Exhibition Road entrance accessible. All floors of
the Blue, Green and Red zones and the Darwin Centre are
accessible by lift. There is currently no step-free access to Earth
Lab. **Description:** Hundreds of exciting, interactive exhibits.
Highlights include 'Dinosaurs', the ultimate dinosaur exhibition;
'Creepy-Crawlies', guaranteed to have you scratching in
minutes; 'Human Biology', the must-see exhibition about
ourselves; 'Ecology' and 'Mammals', with its unforgettable
blue whale.

The Science Museum © Britainonview

Science Museum
Museum

P♿ ♿ ♿wc ✕🐕 abc ••

Exhibition Road SW7 2DD
t: 020 7942 4000 **f:** 020 7938 8118
e: sciencemuseum@nmsi.ac.uk
www.sciencemuseum.org.uk/
Open: Daily: 10.00-18.00. Closed 24, 25, 26 Dec.
Admission: Free but charges apply for the IMAX 3D Cinema, simulators and for some of special exhibitions.
Access: Access to most areas by ramps and lifts. The Museum map is available online and on entry to the Museum from the information and ticket desks. The Map provides information about the location of stairs, lifts, ramps, eating areas and toilets
Description: The place to find life-changing objects from Stephenson's Rocket to the Apollo 10 command module, to catch an immersive 3D movie and enjoy the thrills of a special effects simulator. Science is interactive fun as you encounter the past, present and future of technology in seven floors of galleries.

Victoria and Albert Museum
Museum

P♿ ♿ ♿wc ✕🐕 abc •• 🤚

South Kensington, Cromwell Road SW7 2RL
t: 020 7942 2000.Disability Officer: 020 7942 2766.
Textphone: 020 7942 2002
f: 020 7942 2092 **e:** vanda@vam.ac.uk
www.vam.ac.uk
Open: Daily: 10.00-17.45, except Fri 10.00-22.00 . Selected galleries remain open after 18.00. Closed 24, 25, 26 Dec.
Admission: Free but charges apply for exhibitions. Check for prices and details. Exhibitions free to disabled visitors and up to 2 friends. **Access:** Access at entrance by ramps. Most galleries accessible by lifts and ramps. Escorts available (pre-book).
Description: Where can you see ceramics, furniture, fashion, glass, jewellery, metalwork, photographs, sculpture, textiles and paintings? The V&A is the one of the world's greatest museums of art and design, and home to 3000 years' worth of amazing artefacts from many of the world's richest cultures.

W8 Kensington

Kensington Palace
Historic Attraction

P♿ ♿wc abc •• 🤚

Kensington Palace State Apartments,
Kensington Gardens W8 4PX
t: 0844 482 7777. Outside UK: +44 (0)20 3166 6000.
Textphone: (18001) 0844 482 7777 **f:** 020 3166 6310
e: kensingtonpalace@hrp.org.uk
www.hrp.org.uk/KensingtonPalace
Open: 1 Mar-31 Oct, Daily: 10.00-18.00 (last admission 17.00). 1 Nov-28 Feb, Daily:10.00-17.00 (last admission 16.00). Closed 24-26 Dec. **Admission:** Adult £12.50 (£11.50 online). Child (5-16) £6.25 (£5.75). Concessions (disabled/students/60+) £11.00 (£10.00). Family (2xA, 3xC) £34.00 (£31.00). Carers free. **Access:** The State Apartments at Kensington Palace are on the first floor and there is no lift available. Most areas of the Royal Ceremonial Dress Collection are on a level access. **Description:** The palace first became a royal residence for William III and Mary II in 1689 and has magnificent State Apartments. The palace is home to an exquisite collection of English court dress, a unique archive of royal fashion from the 18th century to the present day and includes Diana, Fashion and Style.

The John Madejski Garden. Photo: Morley von Sternberg

Victoria & Albert Museum

V&A South Kensington is the world's greatest museum of art and design, with collections unrivalled in their scope and diversity.

Discover 3000 years' worth of amazing artefacts from many of the world's richest cultures including ceramics, furniture, fashion, glass, jewellery, metalwork, photographs, sculpture, textiles and paintings.

Complementing the Museum's permanent collection, the V&A's programme of changing exhibitions and displays, cover a broad range of subjects from design and fashion to photography and architecture.

Major exhibitions feature multiple rooms of objects and installations while smaller displays are sometimes located in just a single case.

British Gallery. Norfolk House Music room, 1756
© Victoria and Albert Museum

Access

The V&A offers a range of facilities to make your visit more enjoyable.

If you have any enquiries regarding facilities and services for disabled people, please contact the Disability and Access Officer by telephone on **+44 (0)20 7942 2766**, by textphone on **+44 (0)20 7942 2002**, or by email **disability@vam.ac.uk**. Further details can be found on our web site at **www.vam.ac.uk/disability**

Entry to the museum is free and people with access needs are entitled to free admission to V&A exhibitions with up to two friends. All V&A events are accessible to disabled people, including BSL interpretation and other support as required. A friend/carer can accompany disabled visitors free of charge. All assistance dogs are welcome.

The V&A is spread over seven levels and a number of interconnecting buildings. The Museum map shows which routes are non-accessible for wheelchairs (or pushchair) due to steps but please ask a member of staff if you need help at any time.

V&A Café © V&A Images

Jewellery Gallery © Edina van der Wyck

Parking

Blue Badge parking is available on Exhibition Road, directly outside the Exhibition Road entrance.

Shopping

The V&A Gift Shop has a full range of gifts, toys, jewellery and cards. The V&A Bookshop is devoted to books and, in addition, reflects our current major exhibition.

Eating

The V&A Café offers hot dishes, salads, sandwiches, pastries and cakes, as well as hot and cold drinks, wine and beer. All food is prepared and cooked on the premises using fresh food, bought daily.

The Café is located in the V&A's original refreshment rooms, the Morris, Gamble and Poynter Rooms. These three rooms formed the first museum restaurant in the world and were intended as a showpiece of modern design, craftsmanship and manufacturing.

Opening Hours

10.00 to 17.45 daily

10.00 to 22.00 Fridays (selected galleries remain open after 18.00.).

Closing commences 10 mins before time stated. Closed 24, 25 & 26 December. The tunnel entrance (not wheelchair accessible) to the V&A is open from 10.00 - 17.30 daily (10.00- 20.00 on Friday), but may be closed on occasion, on the advice of London Underground.

**V&A South Kensington, Cromwell Road, London SW7 2RL
t: +44 (0)20 7942 2000 web: www.vam.ac.uk**

V&A Exterior © V&A Images

Dali Universe

SE1 South Bank | Waterloo

Bankside Gallery

Gallery

P& & 🦮 abc ⠢

48 Hopton Street SE1 9JH
t: 020 7928 7521 **f:** 020 7928 2820
e: info@banksidegallery.com
www.banksidegallery.com
Open: During exhibitions daily: 11.00-18.00. Due to display preparation time, gallery will close in between - check online or by phone. **Admission:** Free. **Access:** 2 parking bays on street. Ramp at main entrance. Ramps to allow wheelchair access to most areas of the gallery. **Description:** Bankside Gallery is the gallery of the Royal Watercolour Society and the Royal Society of Painter-Printmakers. The gallery runs a changing programme of exhibitions of contemporary watercolours and original prints by members of the two societies.

Dali Universe

Museum

&wc 🦮

County Hall, South Bank SE1 7PB
t: 0870 7447485 **f:** 020 7620 3120
e: info@thedaliuniverse.com
www.thedaliuniverse.com
Open: Daily: 9.30-18.00. Last entry 17.00.

Admission: Adult £14.00. Child (15-17) £9.00. Child (7-14) £7.00. Under 7 £5.00. Concessions £12.00. Family (2xA. 2xC) £38.00. **Access:** Wheelchair and ramp access to County Hall is restricted, but access to the gallery is available via the South Bank near the County Hall Gallery. Contact in advance for update and advice. **Description:** The surreal Dali Universe at County Hall Gallery contains over 500 Dali artworks, including the Lobster Telephone, Mae West Lips Sofa and the original canvas in the Hitchcock film, 'Spellbound'. Relocating July 2010 – check website for details.

Design Museum

Museum

P& & &wc 🦮 abc ⠢

28 Shad Thames SE1 2YD
t: 0207 940 8790 **f:** 020 7378 6540
e: info@designmuseum.org
www.designmuseum.org/
Open: Daily: 10.00-17.45. Last admission 17.15. Closed 25, 26 Dec. **Admission:** Adult £8.50. Child (under 12) free. Concessions £6.50. Students £5. Free for Design Museum members. **Access:** All areas accessible by level access or by lift. **Description:** The Design Museum is the world's leading museum devoted to contemporary design in every form from furniture to graphics, and architecture to industrial design. Exhibitions demonstrate both the richness of the creativity to be found in all forms of design, and its importance.

Florence Nightingale Museum

Museum

P& & &wc 🦮 abc ⠢

St Thomas Hospital, 2 Lambeth Palace Road SE1 7EW
t: 020 7620 0374 **f:** 020 7928 1760
e: info@florence-nightingale.co.uk
www.florence-nightingale.co.uk
Open: Daily: 10.00-17.00. Closed Good Friday and Easter Sunday. **Admission:** Adult £5.80. Child £4.80. Concession £4.80. Family £16.00 (2xA,4xC). **Access:** The museum is all on ground level, with a slight ramp down to the entrance. **Description:** Discover Florence Nightingale's personal artefacts, a life-size reconstruction of a Crimean ward scene and an audio-visual presentation, which reveals her life from a serious and solitary child to an internationally recognised figure. New museum to open in 2010.

Hayward Gallery

Gallery

P & | WC & | abc ••

Southbank Centre, Belvedere Road SE1 8XX
t: 020 7921 0887 **f:** 020 7928 0063
e: visual-arts@hayward.org.uk
www.southbankcentre.co.uk/find/visual-arts
Open: Check for each exhibition. Closed 25 Dec.
Admission: Prices vary by exhibition. **Access:** Unstepped access to the Hayward Gallery is the lift located in Southbank Centre Car park - the Hayward Gallery. Access to both levels by ramp or lift. Contact 0871 663 2587 for further information.
Description: Hayward Gallery is the heart of the visual arts at Southbank Centre, putting on major exhibitions and commissioning new artworks in the gallery.

HMS Belfast

Historic Attraction

WC & | abc ••

Morgans Lane, Tooley Street SE1 2JH
t: 0207 940 6300 **f:** 0207 403 0719
e: hmsbelfast@iwm.org.uk
hmsbelfast.iwm.org.uk/
Open: 1 Mar-31 Oct: 10.00-18.00 (last admission 17.00).
1 Nov-28 Feb: 10.00-17.00 (last admission 4.00 pm). Closed 24, 25, 26 Dec. **Admission:** Adults £10.70. Children free.

Senior citizens/students £8.40. Disabled/unemployed £6.40. Carers free. **Access:** Access to some of the areas below decks impossible for wheelchair users. A limited tour of the ship including the Quarterdeck, the Boat Deck and the Walrus Café is possible. Access to the ship is via a gangway with a wheelchair lift to lower you on board. **Description:** HMS Belfast is the largest surviving example of Britain's 20th century naval power and is now moored on the Thames between Tower and London Bridge. HMS Belfast provides 9 decks of history from the Captain's Bridge to the sailors' mess deck, operations room and engine rooms.

Imperial War Museum

Museum

& | WC & | abc ••

Lambeth Road SE1 6HZ
t: 020 7416 5000 **f:** 020 7416 5374
e: mail@iwm.org.uk
london.iwm.org.uk
Open: Daily: 10.00-18.00. Closed 24, 25, 26 Dec.
Admission: Free (except for some special exhibitions).
Access: Step-free access is through the Park Entrance. All areas of the museum are accessible to wheelchairs except the upstairs of the 1940s house in The Children's War exhibition. Lifts serve all floors. **Description:** Discover the story of those who have lived, fought and died in conflict from the First World War to the present day. Learn about the conditions endured by First World War troops, explore the role of espionage and find out about children who lived through evacuation.

Imperial War Museum © Britainonview

The Tower of London

The Tower of London

Think of the Tower and what springs to mind? Beefeaters, ravens, executions and keeping people out? You probably don't think 'accessible' but you'd be wrong. We welcome everyone to explore our stories.

Mobility problems?

The Tower is set on a hill with uneven stairs, narrow passageways and cobbles! So wheelchair access is limited, apart from the Jewel House, which is accessible, where you can see the world-famous Crown Jewels. Both our access leaflet and more detailed access guide use a traffic-light rating system to help you get around. The popular Yeoman Warder guided tour offers an alternative route for people unable to climb steps.

Other access needs?

British Sign Language guided tours are available. Yeoman Warders on guided tours carry portable induction loops.

Assisted descriptive tours of the Jewel House and White Tower for blind and partially-sighted visitors use raised 2D image cards. The Welcome Centre has magnifying sheets for enlarging captions and exhibit information.

We also have audio guides (additional fee), including one for blind and partially-sighted visitors.

White Tower information comes in Braille and tactile format. The 'Hands on History' display is on the top floor and there's a 'handling point' in the basement, which has a lift. There are tactiles in the Lower Salt Tower and the Wall Walk.

So buy a ticket (helper entry free) and experience 1000 years of history at your own pace, in your own way.

And don't forget to visit the other Historic Royal Palaces – all working to improve access and willing to help.

Information: 0844 482 7777

Tickets: 0844 482 7799

Type Talk: 18001 0844 482 7777

Visitor Services: 020 3166 6266

Email: VisitorServices.TOL@hrp.org.uk

Web: www.hrp.org.uk/toweroflondon

Making the Modern World Hall

Interactive Rotation Station

The Science Museum

The Science Museum, South Kensington, is renowned for its unique collections, innovative interactive galleries and its family and adult events.

Whether it's launching a rocket, marvelling at the Apollo 10 command module, controlling a magnetic cloud or being inspired by the works of renowned artists, the Science Museum brings science to life and life to science. With around 15,000 original objects on display, 800 interactive experiences and an IMAX 3D Cinema the size of 4 double-decker buses, the Science Museum has something for everyone.

The Science Museum's trained team of Explainers are always on hand, presenting lively and electrifying demonstrations in regular live science shows. Elsewhere in the Museum, look out for interesting figures from the past as a group of convincing drama characters transport you back in time to meet the scientists who have changed the world. The Museum also offers BSL events on the first Saturday of each month while the audio descriptions of the on line exhibitions aim to engage a wider and more diverse audience.

Younger visitors can throw themselves into the interactive heavens of Pattern Pod and The Garden to explore and enjoy construction areas, water zones and demonstrations which will be sure to engage all the senses.

To be part of the action step inside the spectacular

IMAX 3D Cinema! Dive into an underwater adventure or blast into space for an experience from another dimension. Why not also take a trip on Force Field, our motion effects simulation theatre.

Home to one of the world's most magnificent collections of science, industry, technology and medicine, the Science Museum is a great place to get breathtakingly close to iconic objects. Stephenson's Rocket in our awe-inspiring Making the Modern World gallery and Amy Johnson's Gipsy Moth in the spectacular Flight gallery are just a few of our gallery treasures. There's also the Exploring Space gallery which is packed with real-life rockets, satellites and probes.

Shop till you drop in the marvellous Science Museum Store for unique and interesting science-inspired gifts and gadgets for all ages, or relax in one of our mouth-watering eateries.

Every part of the Museum is accessible by ramp or lift, with the exception of raised walkways in the Flight and Ships galleries and the simulators.

The Science Museum South Kensington SW7 2DD
web: www.sciencemuseum.org.uk **t:** 0870 870 4868

The Merlin Entertainments London Eye

Has become an iconic part of the London skyline

Designed with accessibility in mind some of the main features include:

- Ticket Hall and capsules wheelchair accessible
- Disabled guests pay discounted rate with one carer free of charge
- Proof of disability is not requested
- T-loops available in the London Eye ticket office and on London Eye River Cruise which has full accessibility including disabled lift access to both upper and lower decks
- All guide dogs welcome at London Eye and River Cruise
- Staff undergo in-house, tailor-made disability awareness training
- Fast-track groups of less than four to front of the queue

Disabled guest booking line: 09.00 to 17.00 Monday-Sunday

t: +44 (0)871 222 0188 email: accessiblebooking@londoneye.com web: www.londoneye.com

Lambeth Palace

`Historic Attraction`

Lambeth Palace Road SE1 7JU
t: 020 7898 1200
www.archbishopofcanterbury.org
Open: By pre-booked guided tour only. There is currently a 6-month waiting list for places on tours. **Admission:** Adult £8.00. Child free. **Access:** Most of the routes within the palace are accessible to visitors unable to climb stairs. There is a series of lifts and ramps to help visitors. **Description:** One of the few medieval buildings left in London. It is the London residence of the Archbishop of Canterbury with extensive ecclesiastical library. Visitors are taken on a guided tour of the Crypt, Guard Room, Chapel and the Library.

London Dungeon

`Attraction`

28-34 Tooley Street SE1 2SZ
t: 020 7403 7221 **f:** 020 7378 1529

e: londondungeon@merlinentertainments.biz
Open: Daily. Opening times vary so check before you go. Closed Dec 25. **Admission:** Adult £21.95. Child: £15.95. Concessions (student/60+) £19.95. Prices for guidance only. Carer free. **Access:** The dungeon has wheelchair access, however certain rides are not suitable for disabled customers. Boat Ride is inaccessible to wheelchair users. **Description:** The darkest moments in the capital's history are brought to life at the London Dungeon. Live actors, shows, rides and interactive special effects offer a unique experience. All the exhibitions are based on real historical events, from Jack the Ripper to the Great Fire of London, torture and the plague.

London Eye

`Attraction`

Westminster Bridge Road, County Hall,
Riverside Building SE1 7PB
t: 0870 5000600. Accessibility information: 0870 990 8885
f: 0870 9908882 **e:** accessiblebooking@londoneye.com
www.londoneye.com
Open: May-June, Sept: 10.00-21.00. July- Aug: 10.00-21.30. Oct-Apr: 10.00-20.00. Closed 25 Dec, shorter hours 24

Dec, 1 Jan. **Admission:** Adult £17.50. Child (4-15) £8.75. Under-4 free. Concessions (disabled/60s+) £14.00. **Access:** Fully accessible. Fast-track service for disabled guests. Assistance with boarding available. Wheelchairs available (fully refundable £350 deposit required). **Description:** The Merlin Entertainments London Eye is the place for unrivalled views of the capital. This newest of London's great landmarks was constructed on the South Bank to mark the millennium and has quickly become one of London's must-see visitor attractions.

Movieum of London

Attraction/Museum

Riverside Building, 1st Floor SE1 7PB
t: 020 7202 7040 **e:** mike@themovieum.com
www.themovieum.com
Open: Mon-Fri: 10.00-17.00 (last admission: 16.00). Sat, Sun and Bank Hols: 10.00-18.00 (last admission: 17.00). **Admission:** Adults £17.00 (£12.00 online). Children £8.00. Concessions/students £10.00. **Access:** All main areas wheelchair accessible. **Description:** The Movieum of London is a unique interactive museum attraction right next to the London Eye, giving the visitor a unique look behind the scenes of some of the greatest films ever made.

Museum of Garden History

Museum

Lambeth Palace Road SE1 7LB
t: 020 7401 8865 **f:** 020 7401 8869
www.museumgardenhistory.org/
Open: Daily: 10.30-17.00. Closed the first Mon of every month. **Admission:** Adult £6.00. Child (under 16) free. Senior citizens £5.00. Art Fund Members £3.00 .Students/carers free. **Access:** The museum is fully accessible for wheelchairs and entrance for carers of people with disabilities is free. **Description:** The Garden Museum explores and celebrates British gardens and gardening through its collection, temporary exhibitions, events and garden.

Sea Life London Aquarium

Attraction

Westminister Bridge Road, The County Hall SE1 7PB
t: 020 7967 8002 **f:** 020 7967 8029
e: info@londonaquarium.co.uk
www.sealife.co.uk/london

Open: Daily: 10.00-19.00 (last admission 18.00). Closed 25 Dec. **Admission:** Adult £16.00. Child (3-14) £11.75. Under-3 free. Concessions (disabled/senior citizens/students) £14.00. Registered Disabled Child £9.75. Family (2xA, 2xC) £50.00. Carers free. **Access:** Full disabled access with lifts to all levels. **Description:** The new SEA LIFE London Aquarium is home to one of Europe's largest collections of global marine life and includes the Ocean Tunnel, with its graceful Green turtles, a dramatic shipwreck and the nail-biting Shark Walk.

Shakespeare's Globe Theatre

Attraction/Theatre

The Shakespeare Globe Trust, 21 New Globe Walk SE1 9DT
t: 020 7902 1400. 020 7902 1409 for accessible information.
f: 020 7902 1460 **e:** access@shakespearesglobe.com
www.shakespeares-globe.org/
Open: Exhibition and Globe Theatre Tour (check 2010 dates): 2 Mar-22 Apr: Daily: 09.00-17.00. 23 Apr-10 Oct: Mon-Sat 09.00-12.30. Exhibition and Rose Theatre Tour: 13.00-17.00 (Sun: 09.00-11.30 and 12.00-17.00). **Admission:** Exhibition and Globe (Rose) Adult £10.50 (£7.50). Children (5-15) £6.50 (£4.50). Children Under-5 free. Concessions (60+/students) £8.50 (£6.50). Family (2xA, 3xC) £28.00 (£20.00).
Access: Entrance accessible by ramp. Shakespeare's Globe Exhibition is fully wheelchair accessible. Check for details of theatre visits. **Description:** Shakespeare's Globe is a faithful reconstruction of the open-air playhouse designed in 1599 where many of Shakespeare's plays were performed. Shakespeare's Globe Exhibition and theatre tour offer a fascinating introduction to the world-famous Globe Theatre and life in Shakespeare's London.

Southwark Cathedral

Place of Worship

London Bridge SE1 9DA
t: 020 7367 6700 **f:** 020 7367 6730
e: cathedral@southwark.anglican.org
cathedral.southwark.anglican.org/
Open: Daily: 08.00-18.00. **Admission:** Free. **Access:** Access to all levels via lifts or ramps. **Description:** Oldest Gothic church in London (c1220) with interesting memorials connected with the Elizabethan theatres of Bankside. Window and memorial to William Shakespeare, burial place of his brother Edmond.

Tower Bridge © Britainonview

Tate Modern

Gallery

Bankside SE1 9TG
t: 020 7887 8888. Minicom 020 7887 8687
e: visiting.modern@tate.org.uk
www.tate.org.uk/modern/
Open: Sun-Thurs: 10.00-18.00. Fri-Sat: 10.00-22.00. Last admission into exhibitions 17.15 (Fri, Sat 21.15). Closed 24, 25, 26 Dec. **Admission:** Free except for major exhibitions (Carers free). **Access:** Parking (book in advance). Wheelchairs and electric scooters available on request. Accessible entrance (River entrance) and access to all floors by lift. Assistance Dogs. Accessible toilets. Induction loop. **Description:** Britain's national museum of modern and contemporary art from around the world is housed in the former Bankside Power Station. The awe-inspiring Turbine Hall displays works by artists such as Cézanne, Bonnard, Matisse, Picasso, Rothko, Dalí, Pollock, Warhol and Bourgeois.

Tower Bridge Exhibition

Historic Attraction

Tower Bridge Road SE1 2UP
t: 020 7403 3761 **f:** 020 7357 7935
e: enquiries@towerbridge.org.uk
www.towerbridge.org.uk
Open: Apr-Sept: 10.00-18.30 (last admission 17.30). Oct-Mar: 09.30-18.00 (last admission 17.00). Closed 24, 25, 26 Dec. **Admission:** Adult £7.00. Child (5-15) £3.00. Under-5 free. Concessions £5.00. **Access:** Accessible at all levels by

lifts. Videos with commentary. Interactive units viewable from wheelchairs. **Description:** Inside the Tower Bridge Exhibition you will learn about how the world's most famous bridge works and the history behind its creation.

Winston Churchill's Britain at War Experience

Attraction

64-66 Tooley Street SE1 2TF
t: 020 7403 3171 **f:** 020 7403 5104
e: info@britainatwar.org.uk
www.britainatwar.co.uk
Open: Nov-Mar, Daily: 10.00-16.30. Apr- Oct, Daily: 10.00-17.00. Closed 25, 26 Dec. **Admission:** Adults £11.45. Child (5-15) £5.50. Under-5 free. Concessions (students/ 60+) £5.50. Family Tickets (2xA, 2xC) £29.00. Discount voucher online. **Access:** Level access at entry. The museum has disabled access to most Areas. Contact the museum should you have any special requirements. **Description:** Journey back through a realistic and educational adventure to the home front of World War Two Britain. See the London Underground air-raid shelter where thousands spent sleepless nights. Learn about Winston Churchill, rationing, the British women in munitions factories, the evacuation of school children, the blackout and lots more.

EC1 Clerkenwell | Finsbury

Museum of St Bart's Hospital

Museum

St Bartholomew's Hospital, West Smithfield EC1A 7BE
t: 020 7601 8152/8150
www.bartsandthelondon.nhs.uk/aboutus/st_bartholomews_hospital.asp
Open: Tues-Friday: 10.00-16.00 (closed over Christmas and New Year, Easter and public holidays). **Admission:** Free. **Access:** Wheelchair access by arrangement. Induction loop. **Description:** Set in the historic North Wing of St Bartholomew's Hospital, the Museum tells the story of this renowned institution, celebrates its achievements and explains its place in history. Objects from the hospital's unique historical collections are exhibited, including works of art, and surgical and medical equipment used in the hospital.

EC2 Barbican | City

Bank of England Museum
Museum

Threadneedle Street EC2R 8AH
t: 020 7601 5491
For accessibility information 020 7601 5545
f: 020 7601 5808 **e:** museum@bankofengland.co.uk
www.bankofengland.co.uk/education/museum
Open: Mon-Fri: 10.00-17.00. Christmas Eve: 10.00-13.00.
Closed Sat, Sun and Bank Hols. **Admission:** Free.
Access: Portable ramps (phone in advance to use) give
access to all areas. Coaches and cars can stop briefly to
set down. **Description:** The museum is housed within the
Bank of England which traces the history of the Bank from its
foundation. There are gold bars dating from ancient times to the
modern market bar, coins and a unique collection of banknotes.

Barbican
Theatre/Concert Hall

Barbican Centre, Silk Street EC2Y 8DS
t: 020 7638 4141(Switchboard). 020 7638 8891 (Box Office)
e: info@barbican.org.uk
www.barbican.org.uk
Open: Mon-Sat: 09.00-23.00. Sun and Public Hols: 12.00-
23.00. **Admission:** Check prices for individual events.
Access: The main entrance at Silk Street is ramped and lifts
give access to all levels. All venues have seating for wheelchair
users – please inform of any access requirements on booking.
Description: The Barbican is Europe's largest arts centre
all under one roof. It comprises a concert hall, 2 theatres, 3
cinemas, 2 art galleries, library, 2 trade exhibition halls, 5
conference rooms, foyers, shops and conservatory.

Guildhall
Historic Attraction

Gresham Street EC2P 2EJ
t: 020 7606 3030 **f:** 020 7332 1996
e: guildhall.events@cityoflondon.gov.uk
www.guildhall.cityoflondon.gov.uk
Open: Phone to check – only open when not being used for
private events. **Admission:** Free. **Access:** Level access at
entrance. Access to most floors by lift or stair lift.
Description: The City of London's home at Guildhall has
witnessed traitors' trials, heroes' welcomes, freedom
ceremonies and glittering state occasions. Home to the
municipal government since the 12th century, it is a rare
example of Medieval civic architecture, and is a Grade I
listed building.

Museum of London
Museum

150 London Wall EC2Y 5HN
t: 020 7001 9844. 020 7814 5660 for accessible information.
f: 0870 4443851 **e:** info@museumoflondon.org.uk
www.museumoflondon.org.uk/English/
Open: Daily: 10.00-18.00 (last admission:17.30). Closed:
24, 25, 26 Dec. **Admission:** Free. **Access:** Fully accessible.
Lifts to entrance from car park and street. Lifts to all floors.
Description: The Museum of London an unforgettable journey
through London's past. Discover London, see how the city
changed as Romans gave way to Saxons, and wonder at
the splendour of medieval London. The new galleries telling
London's story from 1666 to the present day will open in 2010.

Tate Modern © Tate Photography

Tate Modern

Access at Tate Modern

Tate Modern has become such a firmly established must-see on the London tourist route that it's hard to remember a time before it existed. Tate Modern opened in May 2000 at the same time as a small flurry of other visitor attractions, such as the London Eye and the Millennium Bridge.

Tate Modern occupies the site of the old Bankside Power Station, which was the younger and smaller sister of Battersea Power Station. Tate acquired the site in 1995 and spent five years transforming it into a world-class national gallery of international modern art.

One significant issue is that Tate Modern receives around five million visitors per year, so even though the architects created an accessible building it was always intended for around two million visitors a year and, at times, it can feel quite busy. This is being addressed

by a major building project, Transforming Tate Modern, which will increase space by 60%. As you would expect, Tate Modern is busiest at the weekend and during school holidays and half terms. It is useful to know that the galleries are somewhat quieter on late night openings, Friday and Saturday, until 22.00.

When visiting Tate Modern, we hope you find the building accessible and enjoy participating in some of the events for disabled visitors. The building has flat level access throughout with the exception of the Turbine Hall ramp

Café on Level 7

Turbine Hall

which can easily be avoided by entering the gallery at one of the three ground level entrances rather than using the lower-ground main entrance. Throughout, doors are either automatic or held open with magnets (except toilet doors). Tate Modern is one of the only visitor attractions in London to have a Changing Places facility, which provides additional access to meet the needs of visitors with more profound disabilities.

For blind visitors, we can offer touch tours of the collection. We have found that most blind visitors book in advance but if you unexpectedly pop in to visit, do ask at the Information Desk as it is often possible to provide a touch tour guide at very short notice. For deaf visitors, we provide monthly BSL talks. These are always on the first Friday of the month at 19.00. There is no need to book, just turn up, follow the signage, and join the crowd, always at least 70 deaf visitors, who have made First Fridays at Tate Modern an unofficial Deaf Club.

Accessible car parking is still available at Tate Modern, but now that work has started on the new building project the car park has moved to the staff entrance end of the building. During the major building project, when parking at Tate Modern, you will be escorted through some of the behind-the-scenes spaces in order to get to the galleries; we hope you will enjoy this glimpse of some parts of the building that the public rarely get to see. Some of the roads in the vicinity will see quite a bit of building work going on but we commit to keeping good access on the Tate Modern site.

Tate Modern, Holland Street, Bankside, London SE1 9TG
t: 020 7887 888   **web:** www.tate.org.uk

Yeoman guard at the Tower of London © Britainonview

EC3 AldgateTower Hill

Tower of London

Historic Attraction

P& & &ʷᶜ 🦮 abc •: 🤟

Tower of London EC3N 4AB
t: 0844 4827777 **f:** 020 7488 4153
e: visitorservices_tol@hrp.org.uk
www.hrp.org.uk/TowerOfLondon
Open: 1 Mar-31 Oct: Tues-Sat 09.00-17.30. Sun-Mon:
10.00-17.30. Last admission 17.00. 1 Nov-28 Feb: Tues-Sat
09.00-16.30. Sun-Mon 10.00-16.30. Last admission 16.00.
Closed 24, 25, 26 Dec, 1 Jan. **Admission:** Adult £17.00.
Child (5-15) £9.50. Under-5 free. Concessions (disabled/
students/60+) £14.40. Carers free. **Access:** The Jewel House
and the Crown Jewels are fully accessible to all visitors. The
Tower is a historic building with difficult stairs and passageways
and wheelchair access is limited - downloadable pdf on website
recommended for details. **Description:** The Tower of London,
founded by William the Conqueror in 1066, is one of the most
famous castles in the world and home to the Crown Jewels and
the Beefeaters. Despite a grim reputation as a place of torture
and death, this powerful and enduring fortress has been a royal
palace, an armoury and even a zoo.

EC4 City | St Paul's

Central Criminal Court (Old Bailey)

Historic Attraction

 &ʷᶜ

Old Bailey EC4M 7EH
t: 020 7248 3277 **f:** 020 7248 5735
e: ccc.enquiries@cityoflondon.gov.uk
www.cityoflondon.gov.uk/Corporation/LGNL_Services/Advice_
and_benefits/Legal_advice/central_criminal_court.htm
Open: Mon-Fri: 10.00-1300, 14.00-17.00 approx. Closed
Bank Hol Mons and the day immediately after.
Admission: Free. Visitors must be over-14. **Access:** Disabled
access via main or side door. **Description:** Universally known
as the Old Bailey, this is the probably the most famous criminal
court in the world, and has been London's principal criminal
court for centuries. There is no public access to the precincts of
the Central Criminal Court but the public galleries are open each
day for viewing of trials in session.

St Paul's Cathedral

Place of Worship

P& & &ʷᶜ 🦮 abc •:

The Chapter House, St Paul's Churchyard EC4M 8AD
t: 020 7246 8346. Accessibility information: 020 7246 8350
(Mon-Fri, 09.00-17.00). **f:** 020 7248 3104
e: visits@stpaulscathedral.org.uk
www.stpauls.co.uk/
Open: Mon- Sat: 08.30-16.30 (last admission). 1.5-hour
guided tours (in English only) of the Cathedral and Crypt are
available at 10.45, 11.15, 13.30 and 14.00.
Admission: Adult £11.00. Child £3.50. Seniors £10.00.
Students £8.50. Family (2xA, 2xC) £25.50. Tours: Adult £3.00.
Child (under 16) £1.00. Concessions £2.50. **Access:** Access
for wheelchair users is via the South Churchyard. Permanent
ramps for wheelchair users in the Crypt allow access to the
whole area. On the Cathedral Floor, the only inaccessible area is
the American Chapel behind the High Altar.
Description: Sir Christopher Wren designed St Paul's, one
of London's most historic landmarks. Inside, you can enjoy
the cathedral's awe-inspiring interior filled with monuments to
famous Britons and beautiful mosaics and carvings, as well as
experiencing the Whispering Gallery.

LONDON OUTER – **NORTH**

N1 Islington

London Canal Museum
Museum

12-13 New Wharf Road N1 9RT
t: 020 7713 0836 **f:** 020 7689 6679
e: info@canalmuseum.org.uk
www.canalmuseum.org.uk/
Open: Tues-Sun, and Bank Hol Mon's: 10.00-16.30. Closed on other Mons. Open late until 19.30 on the first Thurs of each month. Closed on 24, 25, 26, 31 Dec. **Admission:** Adult £3.00. Child (5-15) £1.50. Under-5 free. Concessions (senior/student/unwaged) £2.00. **Access:** Access is level and there are lift alternatives to all staircases. No access to the cabin of the narrow boat Coronis, but virtual tour available.
Description: The museum tells the colourful story of London's canals, their people, cargoes, boats and trade, and the horses that pulled the boats and carts on the streets. See the recreated stable and Horse Power exhibition.

N3 Finchley

Jewish Museum
Museum

4 Shakespeare Road N3 1XE
t: 020 8371 7373 **f:** 020 8371 7374
e: admin@jewishmuseum.org.uk
www.jewishmuseum.org.uk

Freud Museum

Open: The museum is closed for refurbishment and will reopen in spring 2010. Check for all details.
Description: The Jewish Museum is a leader in celebrating Jewish life and cultural diversity. The exhibitions, education programmes and activities encourage a sense of discovery and creativity and are designed to build interfaith understanding.

LONDON OUTER – **NORTH WEST**

NW3 Hampstead

Camden Arts Centre
Gallery

Arkwright Road Hampstead NW3 6DG
t: 020 7472 5500 **f:** 020 7472 5501
e: info@camdenartscentre.org
www.camdenartscentre.org
Open: Tues-Sun 10.00-18.00. Wed 10.00-21.00. Closed Mon and Bank Hols. **Admission:** Free. **Access:** Level access through alternative entrance. Lifts to all floors. **Description:** The beautiful and sensitively designed building combines the original Victorian gothic features with a contemporary urban design to enhance space and light. The new galleries attract artists of the highest calibre, able to display a broad range of work.

Freud Museum
Museum

20 Maresfield Gardens NW3 5SX
t: 020 7435 2002 **f:** 020 7431 5452 **e:** info@freud.org.uk
www.freud.org.uk
Open: Wed-Sun: 12.00-17.00. **Admission:** Adults £6.00. Child (12-16) £3.00. Under-12 free. Senior citizens £4.50. Concessions £3.00 (students/disabled/unemployed).
Access: There is no lift inside the museum. The step-free front entrance gives access to ground floor rooms: Hall, Freud's Study, Dining Room, Museum Shop and Toilet.
Description: London home of Sigmund Freud and his family who came to England in 1938 as refugees from Nazi-occupied Vienna. Freud was able to bring with him his library papers, collection of antiquities and furniture, including his desk and famous couch.

Kenwood House

Historic Attraction

Hampstead Lane NW3 7JR
t: 020 8348 1286.
www.english-heritage.org.uk
Open: Daily: 11.30-16.00. Closed 24, 25, 26 Dec and 1 Jan.
See site notices for opening hours of grounds.
Admission: Free. **Access:** Mobility vehicle for those
with difficulty walking from the Car Park to the House and
Restaurant. Level access at entrance. Access to ground floor
but not upstairs. **Description:** Kenwood House, in fashionable
Hampstead, has a world-famous art collection. The house, set
in a tranquil leafy parkland with sweeping views over London,
has splendid interiors with art masterpieces by Vermeer,
Rembrandt, Turner, Reynolds and Gainsborough.

NW8 St Johns Wood

Lords MCC Museum

Attraction

Lord's Ground NW8 8QN
t: 020 7616 8595 **f:** 020 7266 3825 **e:** tours@mcc.org.uk
www.lords.org/history/tours-of-lords/
Open: Tours: Mon-Fri: 10.00, 12.00 and 14.00. Sat-Sun:
10.00, 12.00 and 14.00. No tours 25, 26 Dec, 1 Jan and
major match days (check). **Admission:** Adults £14.00. Child
£8.00. Concessions: (seniors/students) £8.00. Family ticket
(2xA, 2xC) £37. **Access:** Most areas accessible except the
upper floor of the museum. **Description:** Guided tour of Lord's
Cricket ground, the headquarters of cricket, including the Long
Room, MCC Museum, Real Tennis Court, Mound/Grand Stand,
Investec Media Centre and Indoor School.

NW9 Colindale

Royal Air Force Museum

Museum

Grahame Park Way NW9 5LL
t: 020 8205 2266. 020 8358 4818 for accessible information
f: 020 8200 1751 **e:** london@rafmuseum.org
www.rafmuseum.org.uk/

Open: Daily: 10.00-18.00 (except Grahame White factory:
10.00-12.00). Last admission 17.30. Closed 24, 25, 26 Dec,
1 Jan and 11-15 Jan (check 2010 dates). **Admission:** Free.
Access: Access to all areas (lifts to 1st floor).
Description: This world-class collection of over 100 aircraft,
aviation and wartime memorabilia offers a fascinating day out.
It includes the 3D cinema in Milestones of Flight and an awe-
inspiring sound and light show that recreates the
Battle of Britain.

HA9 Wembley

Wembley Stadium

Attraction

Wembley Stadium, Empire Way HA9 0WS
t: 0844 8002755 **e:** info@thestadiumtour.com
www.thestadiumtour.com
Open: Daily: 10.00-16.30. Closed 25, 26 Dec, 1 Jan and
before and after major events (check). Pre-booking advised.
Admission: Adult £15.00. Child (5-15) £8.00. Concessions
(disabled/60+/students) £8.00. Family (2xA, 2xC) £38.00.
Access: All areas accessible by lift. **Description:** Take the
unforgettable Wembley Stadium Tour. Go behind the scenes
into England's changing rooms. Follow in the footsteps of
legends, through the players' tunnel towards the hallowed turf.

LONDON OUTER – EAST

E1 Whitechapel

The Old Truman Brewery

Attraction

91 Brick Lane E1 6QL
t: 020 7247 3959
e: events@trumanbrewery.com
www.trumanbrewery.com
Open: Check opening times and timing of events online
or by phone. Box Office Hours 09.30-19.00.
Admission: Check event prices by phone or online.
Access: The venue is accessible for wheelchair users.
Accessible by lift. On-site parking is available.
Description: Old Truman Brewery is a site featuring a variety
of spaces for markets and exhibitions. It hosues 200 small,
creative businesses featuring fashion designers, artists
and D.J's.

Whitechapel Art Gallery

80-82 Whitechapel High Street E1 7QX
t: 020 7522 7888 **f:** 020 7377 1685
e: info@whitechapelgallery.org
www.whitechapelgallery.org/
Open: Tues-Wed, Fri-Sun: 11.00-18.00. Thurs: 11.00-21.00.
Closed Mon. **Admission:** Free. **Access:** Entrance is at street
level and all the galleries are wheelchair accessible. There is a
lift servicing all levels. **Description:** The Whitechapel Gallery
is internationally renowned for its exhibitions of modern and
contemporary art and its pioneering education and public
events programmes.

E2 Bethnal Green

Geffrye Museum

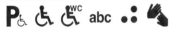

Kingsland Road E2 8EA
t: 020 7739 9893 **e:** info@geffrye-museum.org.uk
www.geffrye-museum.org.uk/
Open: Tues-Sat: 10.00-17.00. Sun and Bank Hol Mons:
12.00-17.00. Closed Mon (except Bank Hols), Good Friday,
24-26 Dec, 1 Jan. **Admission:** Free. Check separate details
for Restored Historic Almshouse: Adult £2.00. Child (under
16) free. **Access:** All main displays are located on the ground
floor. Entrance and gardens are ramped and fully accessible for
wheelchairs. **Description:** The Geffrye presents the history of
the English domestic interior from 1600 to the present day. A
series of period rooms containing fine collections of furniture,
paintings and decorative arts reflect the changing tastes and
styles of the urban middle classes. The grounds have
attractive gardens.

Museum of Childhood (Victoria and Albert)

Cambridge Heath Road E2 9PA
t: 020 8983 5200 **f:** 020 8983 5225 **e:** moc@vam.ac.uk
www.vam.ac.uk/moc
Open: Daily:10.00-17.45 (last admission 17.30). First Thurs of
every month: 18.00-21.00. Closed 24, 25, 26 Dec.
Admission: Free. **Access:** The museum is wheelchair
accessible. Gently sloped approach to the front entrance of
the museum with interior lift and ramp access to all public
areas. Check website for other facilities. **Description:** The
national Museum of Childhood is a branch of the Victoria and
Albert Museum. It houses toy collections, (including dolls,
dolls' houses, games and puppets), of international range and
importance, along with displays of children's costume and
nursery antiques.

Kenwood House

© English Heritage

Eltham Palace – Entrance Hall

Historical Delights

English Heritage offers a range of exciting days out in London

Wellington Arch

Set in the heart of Royal London at Hyde Park Corner, Wellington Arch is a landmark for Londoners and visitors alike. For glorious panoramas over London's Royal Parks and the Houses of Parliament, take the lift to the balconies just below the largest bronze sculpture in Europe, surmounting the arch.

Parking: Disabled visitors may be set down outside the entrance by prior arrangement. **Access:** Level floors throughout. Lift to all floors. Wheelchair access to viewing platform. Numerous chairs available. **Visually impaired visitors:** Hands-on models of the

Kenwood House

All images © English Heritage

Quadriga Sculpture. Easy reading display panels. **Deaf/hard of hearing visitors:** Induction loop available in shop. **Toilets:** Accessible toilet in basement (via lift). Staff assistance required. **Shop:** Level access.

Eltham Palace

Combining Art Deco and ocean liner style, plus 19 acres of gardens, Eltham Palace and Gardens is a stunning masterpiece of twentieth-century design. Textile magnates Stephen and Virginia Courtauld built their glamorous Art Deco showpiece in 1936, next to the remains of a medieval palace, originally Henry VIII's boyhood home.

Parking: Car park 200m from entrance. Disabled visitors may park or be set down near main entrance. Use intercom system at front gate for assistance or call in advance. Access over uneven bridge. **Access to house:** Level access to ground floor (ramp into Great Hall). Stairs to first floor are steep but there is a lift. Two wheelchairs available. **Access to gardens:** Most areas accessible over grass and paths. Some uneven ground. Visually impaired visitors should be aware of many low walls and deep moat. **Visually impaired visitors:** Gardens include fragrant rose garden and triangular garden. **Deaf/hard of hearing visitors:** Audio tour with hearing loop. **Toilets:** Accessible toilet on ground floor. **Shop:** Level access. **Refreshments:** Level access.

ENGLISH HERITAGE

Wellington Arch

Rangers House

Kenwood House

Set in tranquil parkland with panoramic views over London, the property boasts sumptuous interiors and important paintings by many great artists, from Rembrandt to Vermeer. Outside there is beautiful parkland, lakeside walks and meandering woodland paths to explore and enjoy.

Parking: 500m from entrance. Free parking for Blue Badge Holders. Five hatched bays designated for disabled drivers. Manual wheelchair users may need an assistant for car park surface. Disabled visitors may be set down in front of the house, via intercom at the East Lodge. Mobility vehicle available, request via intercom in West Lodge Park. **Access to house:** Wheelchair and shooting sticks available in house. Ground floor all level. Chairs provided. The polished wooden floors may be a little slippery for assistance dogs. **Access to grounds:** Many areas accessible via loose hoggin gravel paths and grass. Manual wheelchair users may choose to

bring an assistant. Seats available. **Visually impaired visitors:** Cornices, fire surrounds, balusters, etc may be touched using cotton gloves provided. Bird song, animal sounds and flower scents in grounds. Garden objects on display to touch and smell in the visitor centre. Visually impaired pack available. **Toilets:** Accessible toilets (near restaurant). **House and Garden shops:** Access via shallow ramp. **Refreshments:** Access via ramp.

Ranger's House

An elegant Georgian villa built in 1723, became the official residence of the 'Ranger of Greenwich Park'. It houses the Wernher Collection - an astounding display of medieval and Renaissance works of art, all purchased by the diamond magnate Sir Julius Wernher (1850-1912)

Parking: Outside house, but limited. Disabled visitors may be set down in side yard near wheelchair lift. Intercom system available to request gate opening. Wheelchairs: One provided. **Access to house:** Steps at front entrance. Alternative side entrance using wheelchair lift. Ground floor all accessible. Easy stairs to upper floor with one handrail. Chairlift available to first-floor exhibitions. Several chairs provided. The Wernher Collection is displayed on both the ground and first floors. **Toilets:** Accessible on ground floor.

Find out more at **www.english-heritage.org.uk**

E14 Poplar

Museum of London Docklands

Museum

P♿ ♿ ♿wc 🦮 abc ⠿

No 1 Warehouse West India Quay E14 4AL
t: 020 7001 9844 **f:** 020 7001 9801
e: info.docklands@museumoflondon.org.uk
www.museumindocklands.org.uk/English/
Open: Daily: 10.00-18.00 (last admission: 17.30). Closed: 24-26 Dec. **Admission:** Adult £5.00. Child (under 16) free. Concessions (60+/unwaged) £3.00. Carers/students (NUS) free. **Access:** Fully-accessible lifts to all public areas throughout the museum. **Description:** The Museum in Docklands explores the story of London's river, port and people from Roman times through to recent regeneration. Twelve galleries provide a showcase for artefacts, paintings, engravings and photographs.

E17 Walthamstow

William Morris Gallery

Gallery

P♿ ♿wc 🦮 abc ⠿

Lloyd Park, Forrest Road E17 4PP
t: 020 8527 3782 **f:** 020 8527 7070
e: wmg.enquiries@walthamforest.gov.uk
www.walthamforest.gov.uk/william-morris
Open: Wed-Sun: 10.00-17.00. **Admission:** Free.
Access: The ground floor of the gallery is accessible to

individuals with wheelchairs. No wheelchair access to 1st floor galleries. **Description:** This mid-18th century house was the boyhood home of William Morris. It now has a permanent exhibition on his life and work, including wallpapers, fabrics, carpets and stained glass. Displays of work by his associates and The Century Guild, paintings by Pre-Raphaelites and Frank Brangwyn.

South London Gallery © BritainonView

LONDON OUTER – SOUTH EAST

SE5 Camberwell

South London Gallery

Gallery

♿wc 🦮 abc ⠿

65 Peckham Road SE5 8UH
t: 020 7703 6120 **f:** 020 7252 4730
e: mail@southlondongallery.org
www.southlondongallery.org

National Maritime Museum © Britainonview

Open: Tues-Sun: 12.00-18.00. Closed Mondays.
Admission: Free. **Access:** Wheelchair ramp, a lift in entrance corridor. Accessibility for electric wheelchair users - Spring 2010. **Description:** One of London's most important contemporary art exhibition spaces, having shown artists such as Gilbert and George, Tracey Emin, Mark Quinn and Julian Schnabel.

SE8 Deptford

Eltham Palace and Gardens
Historic Attraction
 abc

Court Yard, off Court Road SE9 5QE
t: 020 8294 2548 **f:** 020 8294 2621
www.english-heritage.org.uk
Open: 1 Feb-31 Mar, Mon-Wed, Sun: 11.00-16.00. 1 Apr-1 Nov: 10.00-17.00. 2 Nov-30 Dec: 11.00-16.00. Closed 31 Dec-31 Jan. **Admission:** Adult £8.30. Child £4.20. Concessions £7.10. Family £20.80. Free to English heritage

members. Garden only: Adult £5.30. Concession £4.50. Child £2.70. **Access:** Level access to ground floor (ramp into Great Hall). Stairs to the first floor are steep. There is a lift to the first floor. Access to gardens: most areas accessible over grass. Some uneven ground. Visually-impaired visitors should be aware of many low walls and deep moat.
Description: Eltham Palace is a unique Art Deco mansion in a medieval setting. Built for millionaires, it reflects the glamour and allure of 1930s fashionable society with its fine interiors and furnishings, combining designs of ocean-liner style, with French influence Art Deco.

SE10 Greenwich

Fan Museum
Museum

12 Crooms Hill, Greenwich SE10 8ER
t: 020 8305 1441 **e:** admin@fan-museum.org
www.fan-museum.org
Open: Tues-Sat: 11.00-17.00. Sun: 12.00-17.00.
Admission: Adults: £4.00. Child (7-15) £3.00. Under-7 free. Concessions: £3.00. Free entry for OAP and disabled visitors from 14.00. **Access:** Ramp at entrance. All floors accessible by lift. **Description:** This unique museum houses the world's finest collection of fans including exquisite examples from the 18th and 19th centuries. Exhibitions are changed every four months.

National Maritime Museum Greenwich/ Queen's House
Museum
 abc

Greenwich, Romney Road SE10 9NF
t: 020 8312 6565. 020 8312 6608 for accessible information.
f: 020 8312 6632 **e:** bookings@nmm.ac.uk
www.nmm.ac.uk
Open: Daily: 10.00-17.00. Closed 24, 25, 26 Dec. Closes 15.00 31 Dec – 12.00 1 Jan. **Admission:** Free. **Access:** All floors accessible by lifts. **Description:** The National Maritime Museum contains models, displays, paintings and trophies from every continent. The series of themed exhibition galleries offer a voyage through the romance of the great ocean liners, the elegance of Prince Frederick's golden barge, the traditions of maritime London and much more.

Thames Barrier

Peter Harrison Planetarium

Attraction

The Royal Observatory, Greenwich SE10 9NF
t: 020 8312 6565 **e:** bookings@nmm.ac.uk
www.nmm.ac.uk/visit/planetarium-shows
Open: Check online or phone for show times.
Admission: Adult £6.00. Child £4.00. Concessions £4.00.
Family ticket, (2xA, 2xC or 1xA, 3xC) £15.00. **Access:** Fully
accessible by lift. Space for wheelchairs (book in advance).
BSL signed shows - first Saturday of the month, 14.00 and
first Wednesday of the month 14.30. **Description:** The new
state-of-the-art planetarium is the centrepiece of the Royal
Observatory's recent spectacular redevelopment project and is
now the only planetarium in London.

Royal Observatory Greenwich

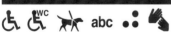

Historic Attraction/Museum

Blackheath Avenue SE10 8XJ
t: 020 8312 6565 **f:** 020 8312 6632
e: bookings@nmm.ac.uk
www.nmm.ac.uk/
Open: Daily, 10.00–17.00. Last planetarium show 16.00.
Closed 24, 25, 26 Dec. Closes at 15.00 on 31 Dec. Open

at 12.00 on 1 Jan. **Admission:** Free. **Access:** Access
by path and ramp to Meridian Garden to reception area.
Astronomy Centre fully accessible by lift. Royal Observatory
has more restricted access. Time Galleries accessible by lift.
Description: The Greenwich Meridian Line, Longitude 0°, is
the centre of world time. You can see the 17th century rooms
occupied by the first Astronomer Royal, the observation room
with its early Tompion clocks and displays on the development
of improved navigation at sea, as well as the Meridian Line.

SE18 Woolwich

Thames Barrier Information and Learning Centre

Attraction

1 Unity Way, Woolwich SE18 5NJ
t: 020 8305 4188 **f:** 020 8855 2146
www.environment-agency.gov.uk/homeandleisure/
floods/38353.aspx
Open: Apr-Sept: 10.30-16.00. Oct-March: 11.00-15.30.
Check before you go. **Admission:** Adult £3.50. Child (5-16)
£2.00. Under-5 free. Concessions £3.00. **Access:** Information
Centre accessible by lift. **Description:** The £500m Thames
Barrier, inaugurated by HM The Queen in 1984, spans 520
metres across the Thames at Woolwich Reach. The 10 steel
gates are raised monthly for testing. There is an exhibition with
a 10-minute video and a working scale model.

SE21 Dulwich

Dulwich Picture Gallery
Gallery

Gallery Road, Dulwich SE21 7AD
t: 020 8693 5254 **f:** 020 8299 8700. 020 8693 5254 for accessibility information
www.dulwichpicturegallery.org.uk
Open: Tues-Fri: 10.00-17.00. Sat-Sun: 11.00-17.00. Closed Mon but open Bank Hol Mons. **Admission:** Adults £5.00. Child (under 18) free. Senior citizens £4.00. Unemployed, disabled, students Art Club members and Friends of Dulwich Picture Gallery, free. Additional charge for exhibitions.
Access: Special parking for disabled visitors next to the main entrance door. Fully accessible to wheelchair users. If you require a wheelchair please ring to book one on 0208 693 5254. **Description:** The Dulwich Picture Gallery has an outstanding collection of 17th and 18th century Old Masters including works by Rembrandt, Van Dyck, Murillo, Poussin, Rubens, Watteau, Gainsborough and Canaletto.

Royal Observatory © Britainonview

SE23 Forest Hill

Horniman Museum and Gardens
Museum

100 London Road SE23 3PQ
t: 020 8699 1872 **f:** 020 8291 5506
e: enquiry@horniman.ac.uk
www.horniman.ac.uk
Open: Daily 10.30-17.30. Closed 24, 25, 26 Dec. Gardens Mon-Sat 07.30-sunset. Sun 08.00-sunset. Closed 25 Dec.
Admission: Free. **Access:** The Museum is wheelchair-friendly with level floors, wide doors, auto-opening entry doors and a lift connecting all gallery areas plus the shop and café.
Description: The Horniman Museum in Forest Hill is a free museum with extensive collections of anthropology, natural history and musical instruments.

LONDON OUTER – SOUTH WEST

SW13 Barnes

London Wetland Centre
Attraction

Queen Elizabeth's Walk SW13 9WT
t: 020 8409 4400 **f:** 020 8409 4401
e: info.london@wwt.org.uk
www.wwt.org.uk/visit-us/london
Open: Daily: 29 Mar-24 Oct (check 2010 dates): 09.30-18.00 (last admission 17.00). 1 Jan-28 Mar and from 25 Oct: 09.30-17.00 (last admission 16.00). Closed 25 Dec.
Admission: Adult £9.50. Child (4-16) £5.25. Under-4 free. Concessions (65+/students/unemployed) £7.10. Family: £26.55 (2xA, 2xC). Carers free. **Access:** The grounds have level access and hard-surfaced paths. Low-level viewing windows and level access to ground-floor bird hides. Lift access to upper floors of visitor centre, observatory and three-storey Peacock Tower hide. No lift in Wildside Hide.
Description: London Wetland Centre is an award-winning wildlife centre close to central London, with 105 acres of beautiful lakes, reed beds and marshes that attract thousands of wild birds each year. Features include a visitor centre.

Wimbledon © AELTC

SW19 Wimbledon

Polka Theatre
Theatre/Concert Hall

   abc

240 The Broadway, Wimbledon SW19 1SB
t: 020 8543 4888 **f:** 020 8545 8326 (Education Department)
e: boxoffice@polkatheatre.com
www.polkatheatre.com
Open: Box Office:Tues-Fri: 9.30-16.30. Sat: 10.00-16.30.
Phone for information on Special events and programme.
Admission: Check prices at Box Office 020 8543 4888.
Access: Polka Theatre has step-free access from street level
through its main entrance at the front of the building. Once in,
there is step-free access to most parts of the building, including
the Adventure Theatre, the café, the playground, the garden,
the workshop, and the adapted toilet. The one exception is the
Main Theatre, where visitors with limited mobility can use the
lift. **Description:** Polka Theatre is one of the few venues in the
UK which is dedicated to producing and presenting work for
young audiences. Since the doors opened in 1979, this unique
venue has been entertaining children with resonant, engaging

and exciting theatre. Polka is committed to making the magic of
theatre available to everyone.

Wimbledon Lawn Tennis Museum
Museum

  abc

All England Lawn Tennis Club, Museum Building SW19 5AE
t: 020 8946 6131 **f:** 020 8947 8752
e: museum@aeltc.com
www.wimbledon.org/en_GB/about/museum/index.html
Open: Tours must be booked in advance. Other than on guided
tours, the museum is only open to tournament ticket-holders
during The Championships. **Admission:** Museum and Tour:
Adult £18.00. Child £13.00. Concession £15.75. Tour only:
Adult £10.00. Child £5.50. Concession £8.75.
Access: Wheelchair access to all public areas. Tour of the
grounds: many sections of the tour are fully accessible, while
others are unsuitable for those in wheelchairs.
Description: The museum provides a remarkable tour of
the traditions, triumphs, sights and sounds that have made
Wimbledon the most coveted title in tennis. Visitors explore the
game's evolution from a garden party pastime to a multi-million
dollar professional sport played worldwide.

KT8 Hampton

Hampton Court Palace
Historic Attraction

Hampton Court Palace KT8 9AU
t: 0844 482 7777. Textphone: 18001 0844 482 7777
(09.00 to 17.00)
e: events@hrp.org.uk
www.hrp.org.uk/HamptonCourtPalace/
Open: Palace and Maze: 29 Mar-24 Oct:10.00-18.00
(last admission: 17.00. 25 Oct-27 Mar: 10.00-16.30 (last
admission: 16.00). Check Gardens and Park times and 2010
dates. **Admission:** Adult £14.00 (£13.00 online). Child (5-16)
£7.00 (£6.50). Under-5 free. Concessions (students/60+)
£11.50 (£10.50). Family (2xA, 3xC) £38.00 (£35.00).
Access: Most of the routes within the palace are accessible to
visitors unable to climb stairs as there is a lift to take visitors to
the State Apartments on the first floor. Accompanying carers
admitted free. **Description:** Henry VIII is most associated with
this majestic palace, extended and developed in grand style
after he acquired it from Cardinal Wolsey. Explore Henry's
majestic palace, the magnificent state apartments and the
vast Tudor Kitchens, the haunted gallery, the baroque
apartments, the formal gardens and the famous
Hampton Court Palace Maze.

KT9 Chessington

Chessington World of Adventures
Attraction

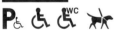

Leatherhead Road, Chessington KT9 2NE
t: 0870 4447777 **f:** 0137 272 5050
www.chessington.com
Open: Check for daily opening times. **Admission:** Adult
£33.00 (£24.00 online). Child (under 12) £22.00 (£17.00).
Under-1m high free. Senior £23.00 (£20.00). Disabled/helpers
(up to two) £20.00 (£18.00). Young disabled £13.00. Family
tickets available. **Access:** Check online or by phone for the
suitability for individual rides for disabled visitors. Guests with
disabilities are required to have at least one helper over the
age of 18 accompany them onto the rides. **Description:** Meet
dragons, brave rollercoasters and have the time of your life at
Chessington World of Adventure. This theme park has rides for
everyone, a children's zoo and shark sea-life centre.

KT16 Chertsey

Thorpe Park
Attraction

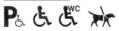

Staines Road, Chertsey KT16 8PN
t: 0870 4444466
www.thorpepark.com
Open: Check for daily opening times. **Admission:** Adult
£35.00 (£28.00 online). Child (under 12) £21.00 (£18.00).
Under-1m high free. Senior £24.00 (£22.00). Disabled/
helpers £20.00 (£18.00). Young disabled £13.00. Family
tickets available. **Access:** Guests registered as disabled are
advised to visit Guest Services on 0870 444 44 66 and to read
the detailed description of the suitability of each ride (www.
thorpepark.com/disabled.php). Wheelchairs £25 deposit.
Assistance dogs not allowed on rides. **Description:** Attention
thrill hunters! For heart-stopping thrills, mind-bending chills
and intense forces with a capital G, Thorpe Park is the ultimate
theme park destination and day out.

LONDON OUTER – WEST

W4 Chiswick

Chiswick House
Historic Attraction

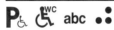

Burlington Lane W42RP
t: 020 8995 0508 **f:** 020 8742 3104
www.chgt.org.uk
Open: House: 1-30 April, Daily: 10.00-17.00. 1 May-1 Nov:
Sun, Mon-Wed, Bank Hols 10.00-17.00, closed Thurs-Sat.
2 Nov-31 Mar closed. Gardens open daily 07.00-dusk.
Admission: Adult £4.40. Child (5-15) £2.20. Concession
£3.70. Under-5 and English Heritage members free. Family
Ticket (2xA, 3xC): £11.00. **Access:** Access via the gravel
courtyard. One step at the entrance and a ramp is available.
All areas of the ground floor can be accessed. First floor can
be reached via a spiral staircase or portico steps. Most of the
garden accessible. **Description:** The Earl of Burlington's home
is an elegant example of British 18th century architecture,
inspired by a love of Italy. Recently installed additions to the
collection of paintings now complement the beautiful painted
and gilded ceilings. The house is also surrounded by Italianate
classical gardens.

Hogarth House

Historic Attraction

Hogarth Lane, Great West Road W4 2QN
t: 020 8994 6757
www.hounslow.info/arts/hogarthshouse/index.htm
Open: Closed for refurbishment at time of going to press.
Normally: 1 Apr-31 Oct: Tues-Fri 13.00-17.00. Sat-Sun:
13.00-18.00. 1 Nov-31 Mar: Tues-Fri: 13.00-16.00. Sat-Sun
13.00-17.00. Closed Mon except Bank Hols, Good Friday,
24-25 Dec and all of Jan. **Admission:** Free.
Access: Check on reopening. **Description:** A collection of
Hogarth's engravings assembled to record the artist's life
and evoke vividly the excesses and miseries of 18th century
England. The engravings, the most extensive on public display,
are interpreted and exhibited to illustrate Hogarth's life
and work.

TW1 Twickenham

Marble Hill House

Historic Attraction

P& &wc ✗ abc ••

Richmond Road, Twickenham TW1 2NL
t: 020 8892 5115 **f:** 020 8607 9976
www.english-heritage.org.uk/server/show/nav.12809
Open: 1 Apr-1 Nov: Sat 10.00-14.00. Sun and Bank Hols
10.00-17.00. 2 Nov-20 Dec, 1 Mar-31 pre-booked groups
only. Closed: 21 Dec-28 Feb. **Admission:** Adult £4.40. Child
£2.20. Concessions £3.70. Family £11.00. **Access:** Disabled
access exterior and ground floor only. First floor limited access
by stairs only. **Description:** An elegant 18th century villa
bordering the Thames, Marble Hill was built for Henrietta
Howard, mistress of George II. Here she entertained courtiers
and literary men, including Pope, Swift and Gay. Intimate
interiors vividly recreate their lifestyle.

Orleans House Gallery

Gallery

P& &wc ✗ abc ••

Riverside, Twickenham TW1 3DJ
t: 020 8831 6000 **f:** 020 8744 0501
e: galleryinfo@richmond.gov.uk
www.richmond.gov.uk/orleans_house_gallery
Open: Apr-Sept, Tues-Sat: 13.00-17.30. Sun, Bank Hols:
14.00-17.30. Oct-Mar, Tues-Sat: 13.00-16.30. Sun, Bank
Hols 14.00-16.30. Gardens open: 09.00 until dusk. Closed
when changing exhibitions. **Admission:** Free.
Access: Wheelchair access to the ground floor of Orleans
House Gallery, Octagon Room, the Coach House, the Stables
Gallery, the Stables Café and the artist in residence studio.
Description: The gallery and adjacent baroque Octagon Room
by James Gibbs, c1720, have a fine permanent collection
of topographical views and a lively programme of temporary
exhibitions, including contemporary crafts.

Thames-side Palladian villa, Marble Hill House © Britainonview

World Rugby Museum and Twickenham Stadium Tours

Museum/Sporting Venue

P♿ ♿ ♿ᵂᶜ 🐕 abc ••

Twickenham Stadium, Rugby Road, Twickenham TW1 1DZ
t: 020 8892 8877 **f:** 020 8892 2817 **e:** museum@rfu.com
www.rfu.com/microsites/museum/
Open: Museum: Tues-Sat, 10.00-17.00. Sun: 11.00-17.00.
Bank Hols 10.00-17.00. Stadium Tours: Tues-Sat: 10.30,
12.00, 13.30, 15.00. Sun: 13.00, 15.00. Closed 24, 25,
26 Dec, 1 Jan and Easter Sunday. No stadium tours on key
match days and the Sundays after. **Admission:** Adult £14.00.
Concessions £8.00. Family ticket (2xA, 3xC) £40.00.
Access: Stadium tour and museum fully accessible.
Description: Twickenham Stadium's World Rugby Museum
where the world's largest collection of rugby memorabilia
helps tell the story of how a schoolboy game became an
internationally renowned professional sport. Paintings, archive
match footage from around the globe.

Rugby Museum, Twickenham © Britainonview

TW7 Isleworth

Osterley Park and House

Historic Attraction

P♿ ♿ ♿ᵂᶜ

Jersey Road, Isleworth TW7 4RB
t: 020 8232 5050 **f:** 020 8232 5080
e: osterley@nationaltrust.org.uk
www.nationaltrust.org.uk/main/w-osterleypark
Open: House: 4 Mar-1 Nov (check 2010 dates): Wed -Sun:
13.00-16.30. 5 Dec-20 Dec: Sat-Sun:12.30-15.30. Check
opening hours park and garden. **Admission:** House and
garden: Adult £8.40 (£7.60 without Giftaid). Child £4.20
(£3.80). Family £21.00 (£18.90). Garden only: Adult £3.70
(£3.35). Child £1.85 (£1.65). **Access:** Parking with transfer
(check availability). Twenty steps (with handrail) to principal
floor, stairclimber available for external steps; unsuitable for
powered or non-standard chairs or if steps are wet. Ground
floor has steps, uneven floors. Stairs to other floors. Grounds
partly accessible. **Description:** The superb 18th century
interiors contain some of the country's best examples of Robert
Adam's work including plasterwork, carpets and furniture. The
house is set in over 350 acres of landscaped park and farmland
complete with ornamental lakes and pleasure grounds.

TW8 Brentford

Syon House and Gardens

Historic Attraction

P♿ ♿ᵂᶜ 🐕 abc ••

Syon Park Brentford TW8 8JF
t: 020 8560 0881. 020-8560-0882 for accessible information
f: 020 8568 0936 **e:** info@syonpark.co.uk
www.syonpark.co.uk/
Open: 18 Mar-31 Oct (check 2010 dates): Wed-Thurs, Sun,
Bank Hol Mons (also Good Friday and Easter Sat):11.00 to
17.00 (last admission 16.00). **Admission:** Adult £9.00. Child
£4.00. Concessions (including disabled) £8.00. Family £20.00.
Gardens and Great Conservatory only: Adults £4.50. Child
£2.50. Concessions £3.50. Family £10.00. **Access:** Entrance
seven steps (stairclimber); 32 steps to 1st floor. For information
on disabled facilities, please contact the Estate Office on 020-
8560-0882. **Description:** Syon House is the London home
of the Duke of Northumberland, remodelled by Robert Adam
and considered to be one of his finest works, with its Great
Conservatory, the private apartments and bedroom used by
the young Queen Victoria. The lush gardens were designed by
Capability Brown.

Red House ©NTPL/Andrew Butler

National Trust

Founded in 1895, the **National Trust** is a charity, membership and voluntary organisation, with over 3.8 million members and over 55,000 volunteers. The Trust has a huge diversity of properties, including historic houses, gardens, industrial monuments, and other built properties. It also cares for countryside areas, including forests, beaches, farmland, moorland, islands, archaeological remains, nature reserves and much more ...

2010 sees the launch of the Trust's Strategy for the next decade. This places emphasis on 'going local', celebrating the distinctive spirit of place and connecting with local communities. This, coupled with an increasing emphasis on properties to improve their visitor experience, offers the opportunity for creativity and innovative ideas which will impact on the enjoyment of a property for everyone, including disabled people.

For many years, Trust properties have endeavoured to become more accessible and welcoming to disabled people. Alongside programmes of access auditing and disability awareness training, property teams are realising the increasing benefits of working with local access groups and disabled people who are willing to be involved in discussions about improving access. These partnerships have led to a spirit of innovation encouraging sites to develop solutions to situations which can often seem complex and challenging. In London, the Trust has developed an exciting partnership with St George's University and English Heritage called 'Heritage 2 Health'. Ham House and Garden, in Richmond-upon-Thames, has now been part of this project for three years, and has hosted events which enable disabled people who have not visited a heritage site before to enjoy a day out and experience health and well-being benefits.

The Trust has an admission policy which entitles the essential companion of a disabled person to have free entry to properties. They also produce an annual publication detailing the access provisions at their properties – the 'Access Guide'. For more information, please contact **01793 817634** or email **enquiries@nationaltrust.org.uk**

To find out more about the National Trust, please visit: **www.nationaltrust.org.uk**

Sutton House, Hackney ©NTPL/Geoffrey Frosh

Ham House ©NTPL/Andreas von Einsiedel

Ham House & Garden

Ham Street, Richmond-upon-Thames, Surrey TW10 7RS
t: 020 8940 1950 **f:** 020 8439 8241
email: hamhouse@nationaltrust.org.uk
web: www.nationaltrust.org.uk/hamhouse

In 1626 William Murray moved to Ham House. A wily Scotsman he earned his living at the court of Charles I where he and the king were close friends and shared a similar taste in art and interior decoration. With the king's patronage William furnished the house fashionably. However, when the Civil War (1642 – 1649) brought a change of power, William was forced to flee to the continent. He left his resourceful wife, Katherine, in charge of the house and estate and their four daughters.

Their eldest daughter Elizabeth was an extraordinary character. Highly intelligent and tenacious, she steered the house ably through Cromwell's rule. Elizabeth inherited a love of fine decoration from her father. The lavish interiors she created at Ham were the height of fashion in the 1670s and today offer an unparalleled example of 17th century courtly taste.

With her second husband, the Duke of Lauderdale, she also created the impressive formal gardens surrounding the house. After Elizabeth's death in 1698, the house was never again comprehensively re-decorated. As you visit today imagine stepping back to an era of luxury!

The intriguing out-buildings include an ice house, a dairy with unusual cast iron "cows' legs", and the earliest known purpose-built still house, the 17th century equivalent of an in-house pharmacy.

Rich in history and atmosphere, Ham was built to impress in its day and it continues to do so today!

Mobility Information: Designated parking, 6 steps to the entrance of the house, ramp available, no handrails. 3 manual wheelchairs available for loan. Ground floor has steps, narrow doorways, small rooms, ramp available. Stairs with handrail to other floors but there is a lift available. There is an accessible WC available in the courtyard opposite the gift shop. Grounds are accessible with some loose gravel paths and cobbled areas. There is a map of an accessible route and also two powered mobility vehicles for loan, but these need to be pre-booked.

Audio/Visual Information: A film provides information about the property on site. It is possible to touch some of the objects and architectural features at Ham, including the panelling, carvings on the Great stairs and the Windsor chairs.

Opening times: Please visit:
www.nationaltrust.org.uk/hamhouse

Osterley Park & House ©NTPL/Andrew Butl

Osterley Park and House

Jersey Road, Isleworth, Middlesex TW7 4RB
t: 020 8232 5050   **f:** 020 8232 5080
email: osterley@nationaltrust.org.uk
web: www.nationaltrust.org.uk/osterley

A true urban oasis, this spectacular mansion surrounded by tranquil gardens, park and farmland is one of the last surviving country estates in London. Once described as the 'palace of all palaces' Osterley was created in the late 18th century by a wealthy banking family to entertain and impress their friends and clients. Today, Osterley offers a fascinating glimpse into the exclusive lifestyle and stories of the Child family and the people 'behind the scenes' that worked to keep the estate running.

Osterley's rare 18th century Garden is currently being restored to its former glory and has attractions throughout the season from spring flowers to autumn colour.

Learn more about life at Osterley in the 18th century with free, user friendly audio visual guides. These informative guides bring the House to life revealing the wealth of stories behind the design, décor and furnishings.

Mobility Information: designated parking; shuttle service from car park to House/Café area; wheelchairs available to borrow; self drive battery vehicles; steps (with handrail) to first floor of House – stair climber available subject to weather/wheelchair compatibility; virtual tour

Visual Information: large print guides and maps; Braille Guides; audio described tour.

Audio Information: Induction loops; signed tour; subtitled introductory film

Please visit the website or contact Osterley for further details.

Opening times/Admission:
Please visit: **www.nationaltrust.org.uk/osterley**

Red House

Red House Lane, Bexleyheath, London DA6 8JF
t: 020 8304 6359
email: redhouse@nationaltrust.org.uk
web: www.nationaltrust.org.uk/redhouse

The 1860 Gothic style house, known as the home of the Arts & Crafts Movement was originally built for the Victorian artist, designer and poet, William Morris by his friend, the renowned architect, Phillip Webb.

Accessibility: The ground floor is reached with ramps. The approach to the shop and cosy tea-room is paved. Small WC not suitable for wheelchairs and has stepped approach. Blue Badge holders are welcome to book one of two parking spaces at front door. Audio guide and touch list available. Booking line: **020 8304 9878**

Sutton House

2&4 Homerton High Street, Hackney, London E9 6JQ
t: 020 896 2264
web: suttonhouse@nationaltrust.org.uk

Built in 1535 by prominent courtier of Henry VIII, Sir Ralph Sadleir, Sutton House retains much of the atmosphere of a Tudor home despite some alterations by later occupants, including a succession of merchants, Huguenot silk weavers, and squatters. Discover oak-panelled rooms, original carved fireplaces and a charming courtyard.

Accessibility: Drop off point and accessible toilet close to level entrance (ramp available) at House. One wheelchair available for loan (book in advance) 020 8986 2264

Mobility Information: There is a drop off point close to the property if you are arriving by car. The House has a level entrance and there is a ramp available. There is one wheelchair available for loan but this needs to be booked in advance. There are stairs to the upper floors. There are also accessible toilet facilities close to the entrance.

For particular queries about accessibility, please contact the property in advance on **020 8986 2264**

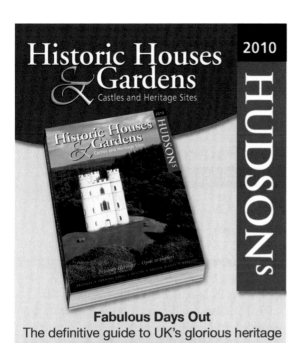

Palm House, Kew Gardens © Britainonview

Kew Bridge Steam Museum
Museum

P& & wc abc ••

Green Dragon Lane, Brentford TW8 0EN
t: 020 8568 4757 **f:** 020 8569 9978 **e:** info@kbsm.org
www.kbsm.org/
Open: Tues-Sun: 11.00-16.00. Closed Mon, except Bank
Hols. **Admission:** Adult £9.50. Accompanied child (under 16)
free. Students/OAPs £8.50. **Access:** Approximately 80% of
the museum is accessible via ramped flooring or a lift. Level
access from the car park to the museum shop and reception
area. Railway carriage has accessible compartment. Access to
the 90" Cornish Beam Engine house is difficult, with two flights
of steps. **Description:** Giant beam engines, the earliest built in
1820, operate under steam and are the largest of their kind in
the world. Housed in a Victorian waterworks visited by Dickens,
these engines pumped London's water for over 100 years.

TW9 | 10 Richmond

Ham House and Garden
Historic Attraction

P& wc abc ••

Richmond TW10 7RS
t: 020 8940 1950 **f:** 020 8439 8241
e: hamhouse@nationaltrust.org.uk
www.nationaltrust.org.uk/main/w-vh/w-visits/w-findaplace/w-
hamhouse
Open: House: 14-25th Feb and 14 Mar-1. Nov: Mon-Wed,
Sat-Sun:12.00-16.00. 28 Feb-8 Mar: Sat-Sun only 12.00-
16.00. Check opening hours for garden only. **Admission:**
Adult £9.00 (£3.00 garden only). Child £5.00 (£2.00). Family
£23.30 (£8.00). **Access:** Six steps to entrance, ramp available,
no handrails. Ground floor has steps, narrow doorways, small

rooms, ramp available. Stairs with handrail to other floors, lift
available (manual wheelchairs only). Grounds fully accessible.
Description: Ham House is Europe's most complete surviving
example of 17th century fashion and power. It was built in 1610
and extended in 1670 when it was at the heart of Restoration
court life. The garden is one of the few formal gardens to
survive the English Landscape movement.

Kew Palace
Historic Attraction

P& & wc

Richmond, Surrey TW9 3AB
t: 0844 4827777. From outside UK: +44 (0)20 3166 6000
e: kewpalace@hrp.org.uk
www.hrp.org.uk/KewPalace/
Open: 10 Apr-27 Sept 2009 (check for 2010 dates): Mon
11.00-17.00. Tues-Sun 10.00 to 17.00. Last admission 16.00.
Admission: Adult £5.00. Child (under 16) free. Concession
(disabled/students/OAPs) £4.00. Carers free. **Access:** Access
to all three floors using the staff-operated lift.
Description: The most intimate of royal palaces, Kew was
used by the royal family between 1729 and 1818. Here George
III, Queen Charlotte and their 15 children enjoyed a relatively
simple domestic routine. They are bought to life through
reminiscences and fascinating personal artefacts.

Royal Botanic Gardens, Kew
Garden

P& & wc abc ••

Richmond, Surrey TW9 3AB
t: 020 8332 5655.
To pre-book mobility scooters: 020 8332 5121
f: 020 8332 5197 **e:** groups@kew.org
www.kew.org/
Open: Daily: 09.30 (except Kew Palace 10.00, Mon 11.00).
Closing varies 17.00-19.30 depending on time of year and
location. Kew Palace open 10 April-27 Sept only. Closed
25-26 Dec. **Admission:** Adult £13.00. Child (under 17) free.
Concessions (disabled/students/OAPs) £11.00. Registered blind
and partially-sighted free. Carers free.
Access: All areas are accessible to wheelchair users, except
no wheelchair access to the Marine display in the Palm
House basement; to the galleries levels in the Palm House
and Temperate House; the upper levels inside the Princess
of Wales Conservatory and Treetop Walkway. Kew Explorer
land train tours gardens - space for one wheelchair and folded
wheelchairs. **Description:** Kew Gardens sits beside the river

Thames between Richmond and Kew in south-west London. Kew Gardens is a World Heritage Site with six magnificent glasshouses, and is home to a remarkable collection of plants from all over the world, including over 14,000 trees.

W12 Shepherds Bush

BBC Television Centre
Attraction

BBC Television Centre, Wood Lane W12 7RJ
t: 0370 9011227. Textphone: 0370 903 0304
f: 028 9032 6453 **e:** bbctours@bbc.co.uk
www.bbc.co.uk/tours
Open: Regular tours Mon-Sat. Pre-booking is essential. Open to anyone aged nine years+ when accompanied by an adult. **Admission:** Adult £9.50. Child (9-15) £7.00. Concession £8.50. Students £7.00. Family ticket (2xA + 2xC or 1xA + 3xC) £27.00. **Access:** Wheelchair access. Lifts available. BBC Television Centre is a large building, so tours cover a fair distance. **Description:** On the award-winning tour of BBC Television Centre you will see what happens inside the most famous TV headquarters in the world. You are likely to see into studios, visit BBC News, take a peek into a dressing-room and have a play in the interactive studio.

W11 Notting Hill

Museum of Brands, Packaging and Advertising
Museum

2 Colville Mews, Lonsdale Road W11 2AR
t: 020 7908 0880 **f:** 020 7908 0950
e: info@museumofbrands.com
www.museumofbrands.com/
Open: Tues-Sat: 10.00-18.00. Sun: 11.00-17.00. Closed Mon except Bank Hols. Closed 25 Dec; 25, 29, 30 Aug 2010. **Admission:** Adults £5.80. Children (7-16) £2.00. Concessions £3.50. Family £14.00. **Access:** Full wheelchair access to all public areas. **Description:** The museum contains 12,000 original items, from motorcars, music, television, holidays and entertainment to branded groceries, sweets and household goods. In the museum's time tunnel you can trace changes in social taste and the evolution of graphic design, marketing and advertising skills.

W14 West Kensington

Leighton House Museum
Museum

12 Holland Park Road W14 8LZ
t: 020 7602 3316 **f:** 020 7371 2467
e: museums@rbkc.gov.uk
www.rbkc.gov.uk/LeightonHouseMuseum/general/
Open: Re-opening 3 April 2010 after refurbishment - check then for all details. **Description:** The former studio-house of the great Victorian artist Frederic, Lord Leighton contains extraordinary period interiors including the Arab Hall. It also houses a permanent exhibition of Victorian paintings, drawings and sculpture.

SL4 Windsor

Windsor Castle
Historic Attraction

Windsor SL4 1NJ (22 miles west of Central London)
t: 0175 386 8286. Accessibility Information: 020 7766 7324
f: 0175 383 2290 **e:** bookinginfo@royalcollection.org.uk
www.royalcollection.org.uk/
Open: Daily, March-Oct: 09.45-17.15 (last admission: 16.00). Nov-Feb: 09.45-16.15 (last admission 15.00). Closed 25, 26 Dec. Check for other days when closed or partially closed. **Admission:** Adult £15.50. Child (under 17) £9.00. Under-5 free. Concessions (60+/student) £14.00. Family £41.00 (2xA, 3xC). Ticket prices reduced when State Apartments closed. **Access:** Access entrance in Engine Court. Most public areas are accessible for wheelchair-users, including the State Apartments. **Description:** Windsor Castle is one of the largest and oldest inhabited castles in the world. A royal home and fortress for over 900 years, the castle remains a working palace today. The magnificent State Apartments are decorated with some of the finest works of art in the Royal Collection.

Windsor Castle © Britainonview

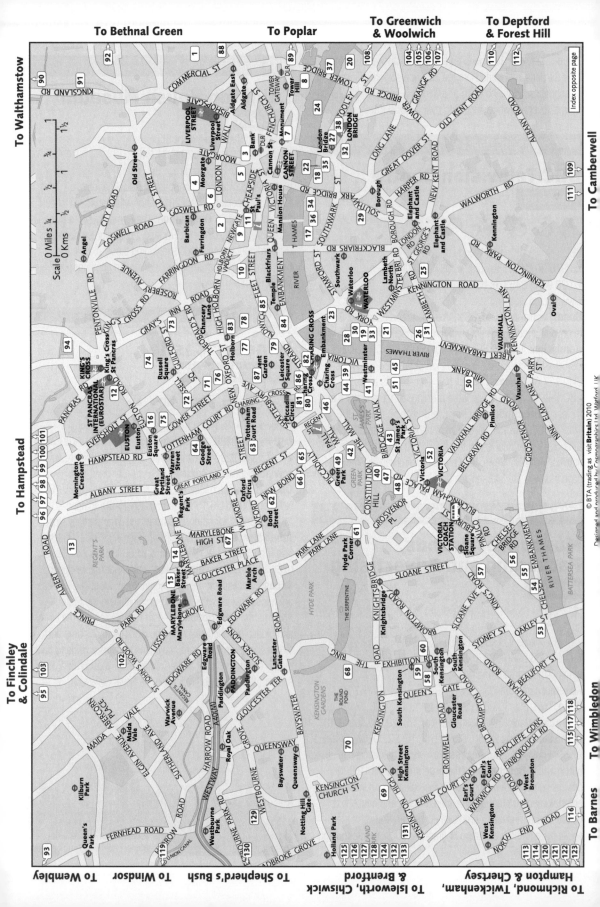

Planning your day

Attractions are grouped by postcode area so that you can work out which ones are close enough to visit on the same day. For a description of the attraction and contact details see pages 80-135

Inner London

1	Old Truman Brewery	E1
2	Museum of St. Bart's Hospital	EC1
3	Bank of England Museum	EC2
4	Barbican	EC2
5	Guildhall	EC2
6	Museum of London	EC2
7	The Monument	EC3
8	Tower of London	EC3
9	Central Criminal Court (Old Bailey)	EC4
10	Dr. Johnson's House	EC4
11	St Paul's Cathedral	EC4
12	British Library	NW1
13	London Zoo	NW1
14	Madame Tussauds	NW1
15	Sherlock Holmes Museum	NW1
16	Wellcome Collection	NW1
17	Bankside Gallery	SE1
18	Clink Prison Museum	SE1
19	Dali Universe	SE1
20	Design Museum	SE1
21	Florence Nightingale Museum	SE1
22	Golden Hinde	SE1
23	Hayward Gallery	SE1
24	HMS Belfast	SE1
25	Imperial War Museum	SE1
26	Lambeth Palace	SE1
27	London Dungeon	SE1
28	London Eye	SE1
29	London Fire Brigade Museum	SE1
30	Moviewm of London changed to the London Film Museum	SE1
31	Garden Museum	SE1
32	Old Operating Theatre, Museum and Herb Garret	SE1
33	Sea Life London Aquarium	SE1
34	Shakespeare's Globe Theatre	SE1
35	Southwark Cathedral	SE1
36	Tate Modern	SE1
37	Tower Bridge	SE1
38	Winston Churchill's Britain at War Experience	SE1
39	Banqueting House	SW1
40	Buckingham Palace (State Rooms)	SW1
41	Churchill Museum and Cabinet war Rooms	SW1
42	Clarence House	SW1
43	Guards Museum	SW1
44	Household Cavalry Museum	SW1
45	Houses of Parliament	SW1
46	Institute of Contemporary Arts	SW1
47	Queen's Gallery	SW1
48	Royal Mews	SW1
49	Spencer House	SW1
50	Tate Britain	SW1
51	Westminster Abbey	SW1
52	Westminster Cathedral	SW1
53	Carlyle's House	SW3
54	Chelsea Physic Garden	SW3
55	National Army Museum	SW3
56	Royal Hospital Chelsea	SW3
57	Saatchi Gallery	SW3
58	Natural History Museum	SW7
59	Science Museum	SW7
60	Victoria and Albert Museum	SW7
61	Apsley House	W1
62	Handel House Museum	W1
63	Photographers' Gallery	W1
64	Pollocks Toy Museum	W1
65	Royal Academy of Arts	W1
66	The Museum at the Royal Institution	W1
67	Wallace Collection	W1
68	Serpentine Gallery	W2
69	Linley Sambourne House	W8
70	Kensington Palace	W8
71	British Museum	WC1
72	Brunei Gallery Soas	WC1
73	Charles Dickens Museum	WC1
74	Foundling Museum	WC1
75	Petrie Museum of Egyptian Archaeology	WC1
76	Political Cartoon Gallery	WC1
77	Freemasons' Hall, Museum and Library	WC2
78	Hunterian Museum (Royal College of Surgeons)	WC2
79	London Transport Museum	WC2
80	National Gallery	WC2
81	National Portrait Gallery	WC2
82	Proud Galleries	WC2
83	Sir John Soane Museum	WC2
84	Somerset House/Courtauld Gallery	WC2
85	St Clements Danes	WC2
86	St Martin in the Fields	WC2
87	Donmar Theatre	WC2

Outer London

88	Whitechapel Arts Gallery	E1
89	Museum of London Docklands	E14
90	William Morris Gallery	E17
91	Geffrye Museum	E2
92	Museum of Childhood (Victoria and Albert)	E2
93	Wembley Stadium	HA9
94	London Canal Museum	N1
95	Jewish Museum	N3
96	2 Willow Road	NW3
97	Camden Arts Centre	NW3
98	Fenton House	NW3
99	Freud Museum	NW3
100	Keats' House	NW3
101	Kenwood House	NW3
102	Lords MCC Museum	NW8
103	Royal Air Force Museum	NW9
104	Fan Museum	SE10
105	National Maritime Museum Greenwich/ Queen's House	SE10
106	Peter Harrison Planetarium	SE10
107	Royal Observatory Greenwich	SE10
108	Thames Barrier Information and Learning Centre	SE18
109	Dulwich Picture Gallery	SE21
110	Horniman Museum and Gardens	SE23
111	South London Gallery	SE5
112	Eltham Palace and Gardens	SE8
113	Thorpe Park	KT16
114	Hampton Court Palace	KT8
115	Chessington World of Adventures	KT9
116	London Wetland Centre	SW13
117	Wimbledon Lawn Tennis Museum	SW19
118	Polka Theatre	SW19
119	Windsor Castle	SL4
120	Marble Hill House	TW1
121	Orleans House Gallery	TW1
122	World Rugby Museum and Twickenham Stadium Tours	TW1
123	Ham House and Garden	TW10
124	Osterley Park and House	TW7
125	Kew Bridge Steam Museum	TW8
126	Syon House and Gardens	TW8
127	Kew Palace	TW9
128	Royal Botanical Gardens, Kew	TW9
129	Museum of Brands, Packaging and Advertising	W11
130	BBC Television Centre	W12
131	Leighton House Museum	W14
132	Chiswick House	W4
133	Hogarth House	W4

A good night guaranteed, across the capital.

Premier Inn has over 40 accessible hotels in greater and central London, and will be the largest provider of budget rooms in London by 2012, making it easier for you to stay away from home.

Our guests tell us they love the value we offer, our clean and comfortable rooms and the warm welcome they receive from our team members. Add to this our unique Good Night Guarantee and you can be assured of a great stay whatever your needs, wherever you need to be.

Book now at **premierinn.com**

Everything's Premier but the Price

Premier Inn

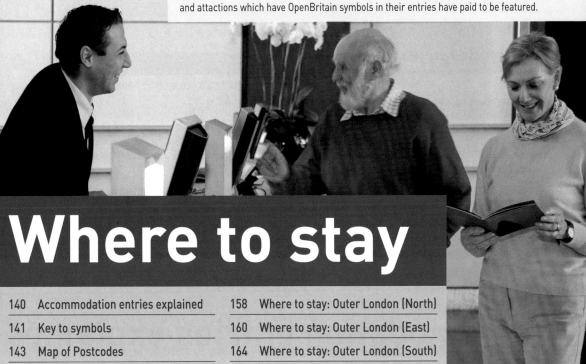

Note: Prices and ratings shown were supplied to us by the proprietors in summer 2009. These may have been changed after this guide has gone to press and we advise that you check at time of booking. Prices are shown in pounds sterling and include VAT where applicable. Properties and attactions which have OpenBritain symbols in their entries have paid to be featured.

Where to stay

Where to Stay aims to provide you with information about accessible accommodation in London. This accommodation has been assessed under either VisitBritain's National Accessible Scheme or has been audited on behalf of the London Development Agency by Direct Enquiries.

Those properties assessed under **VisitBritain's National Accessible Scheme** include standards useful for hearing and visually-impaired guests and standards useful for guests with mobility impairment. Those audited on behalf of the **London Development Agency** must guarantee that they have bedrooms suitable for wheelchair users. For more information go to **directenquiries.com/LDA hotels**.

Within this guide you will find **Hotels**, **Guest Accommodation**, **Bed & Breakfast**, **Guest Houses**, **Camping & Caravan Parks** and **Hostels**.

More detail can be found on:
www.visitlondon.com/accommodation
www.theaa.com/travel
www.enjoyengland.com/stay

Ratings

Star ratings are internationally recognisable and give you a guide to the standard of quality accommodation. Whether rated by **VisitEngland** or the **AA**, these ratings give you information at a glance.

★	No frills, basic facilities
★★	Well maintained with a good level of service
★★★	Friendly, very good quality and well presented
★★★★	Excellent standards, high quality facilities and attentive service
★★★★★	Exceptional service and surroundings. An extra bit of luxury

① ···· SE1 - Southbank | **Novotel London City South** **····⑥**

⑦ ···· AA ★★★★ 53-61 Southwark Bridge Road, Southwark, London SE1 9HH

④ ···· accessible rooms: 12 **t** 020 7089 0400 **e** h3269@accor.com **····②**

Open: All year

Rooms per night:

novotel.com

③ ···· s: £340.00 Central city AA 4 star hotel close to popular

d: £340.00 attractions and London Bridge tube station.

Meals: £10.00

⑤ ···· Access: abc ✏ ✈ 🦮 🛗 ☺ ♿ ♿ ♿ ♿ 🚶 ♿ ♪ General: 🛋 🖥 🅿 ✕ 🍷 🍽 Room: ⛰ Ⓢ ☕

Accommodation entries explained

1 Locations

The establishments are arranged by postcode in Inner London and then alphabetically within each postcode. Each postcode is described by the names of its areas (e.g. WC2 Covent Garden/Holborn/Strand). In Outer London, the establishments are arranged by areas going clockwise (North, East, South and West), and by postcode within these areas.

2 Contact information

Establishment name and booking details including telephone number.

3 Prices

Bed & Breakfast: Per room for B&B and per person for evening meal (d=Double s=Single)

Hotels: Per room for B&B and per person for half board (d=Double s=Single).

Evening Meal: Prices shown are per person per night.

Camping and Caravan Parks: Per pitch per night for touring pitches; per unit per week for caravan holiday homes.

4 Opening

Indicates when the establishment is open.

5 Symbols

An at-a-glance view of services and facilities available. The key to these symbols can be found on page 141

6 Access Statements

'AS' denotes that an Access Statement is available. These can be viewed on openbritain.net

7 Ratings

Quality Rating awarded to the establishment. For more information see pg 139

Key to symbols

Information about many of the accommodation and services and facilities is given in the form of symbols.

Access

Wheelchair user with assistance

Mobility Impaired Walker

Assistance dogs welcome

Designated wheelchair accessible public toilet

Wheelchair accessible restaurant

Wheelchair accessible leisure facilities

Wheelchair accessible bedroom

Fully wheelchair accessible

Facilities for visually impaired

Sign Language used

Hearing facilities

Access trained staff

Accessible lift

Hoist available

Rooms

Text phone/inductive coupler

TV with subtitles

Tea/coffee facilities in all bedrooms

Accessible shower

Seating in shower

Toilet seat raiser

Bedroom(s) on ground floor

General

Children welcome

Designated parking

Ramped or level entrance

Staff available to assist by arrangement

Induction loop system

Licensed bar

Evening meal by arrangement

Special diets by arrangement

Changing Places Facilities

Garden/patio

Overnight holding area

Motor home pitches reserved for day trips off-site

Electrical hook-up points for caravans and tents

Calor Gas/Camping Gaz purchase/exchange service

Chemical toilet disposal point

Motor home waste disposal point

Showers

Laundry facilities

Pitches

Caravans

Motor caravans

Tents

Travelodge.

Over 390 hotels nationwide.
Over 180 hotels in UK city centres.

Rooms from just

£19

Book now
at travelodge.co.uk

Map of Postcodes

This map of London has been divided in postcode areas (using the first part of the postcode). The different regions indicate broad geographic areas – North, East, South East, South West, West and North West. The two central areas – WC (West Central) and EC (East Central) just north of the river form the centre and busiest area of the capital. The areas outside the map are for reference to general location; all are within the Greater London boundaries.

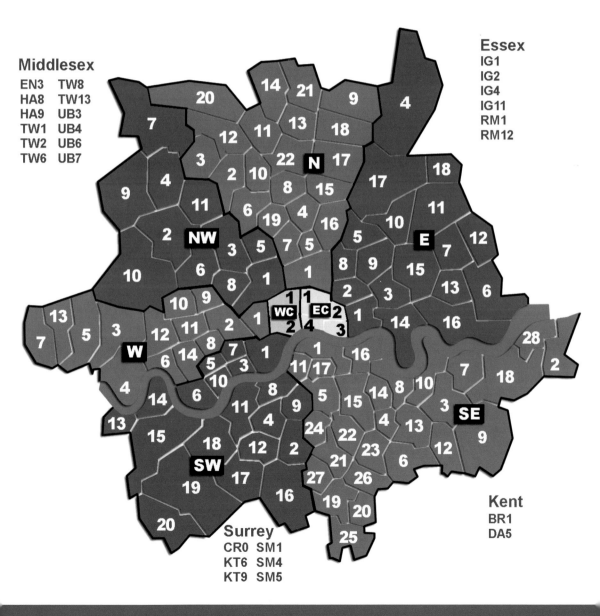

Middlesex

EN3	TW8
HA8	TW13
HA9	UB3
TW1	UB4
TW2	UB6
TW6	UB7

Essex

IG1
IG2
IG4
IG11
RM1
RM12

Surrey

CR0	SM1
KT6	SM4
KT9	SM5

Kent

BR1
DA5

W1 - Marylebone | Hyatt Regency London. The Churchill

AA ★★★★★
accessible rooms: 2

30 Portman Square, Baker Street, London W1H 7BH
t 020 7486 5800
london.churchill.hyatt.com

Access: 🐕 ♿🚶👫♿ General: 🔲 P♿ Room: 🛁

W1 - Marylebone | The Landmark London

AA ★★
accessible rooms: 5

222 Marylebone Road, Marylebone, London NW1 6JQ
t 020 7631 8000 e reservations@thelandmark.co.uk
landmarklondon.co.uk

Access: 📄 🐕 ☺ ♿♿👫♿🚶👫♿ General: 🎠✕🍽🍵 Room: 🛏🔲 WC S

W1 - Marylebone | The Marylebone Hotel

AA ★★★★
accessible rooms: 6

47 Welbeck Street, London W1G 8DN
t 020 7486 6600
doylecollection.com

Access: ♿👫♿ General: 🔲 Room: 🛁

W1 - Marylebone | Park Plaza Sherlock Holmes

AA ★★★★
accessible rooms: 2

108 Baker Street, London W1U 6LJ
t 020 7486 6161 e mwells@pphe.com

parkplaza.com/londonuk_sherlockholmes

Centrally located Park Plaza Sherlock Holmes combines the charm of historic London with modern convenience.

Access: 📄 🐕 ☺ ♿♿👫♿🚶👫♿♿ General: 🎠♿✕🍽🍵 Room: 🛁🛏☕♿

W1 - Marylebone | Travelodge London Marylebone

AA **Budget**
accessible rooms: 2

Harewood Row, Marylebone, London NW1 6SE
t 0871 984 6311
travelodge.co.uk

Access: 📄 🐕 ♿👫♿♿ General: 🔲 Room: 🛁

W1 - Mayfair | Brown's Hotel

AA ★★★★★
accessible rooms: 2

Albemarle Street, Mayfair, London W1S 4BP
t 020 7493 6020 e reservations.browns@roccofortecollection.com
brownshotel.com

Access: 🐕 🛗☺♿♿♿👫♿👫♿ General: 🎠🔲♿✕🍽🍵 Room: 🛁🛏 WC S

W1 - Mayfair | The Chesterfield Hotel

AA ★★★★
accessible rooms: 1

35 Charles Street, Mayfair, London W1J 5EB
t 020 7491 2622
chesterfieldmayfair.com

Access: 🐕 👫♿♿

W1 - Mayfair | **Hilton London Green Park**

Enjoy England   ★★★★   Half Moon Street, Mayfair, London W1J 7BN
accessible rooms: 2   t 020 7629 7522
                     hilton.co.uk/greenpark

Access: 🐕 🛏 ♿ 👤👥

W1 - Mayfair | **Holiday Inn London Mayfair**

AA   ★★★★   3 Berkeley Street, Oxford Street, London W1X 6NE
accessible rooms: 4   t 0800 405 060
                     holiday-inn.co.uk

Access: 🔲 🐕 🛏 ♿ 👤👥 👂 👁   General: 🔲 P♿

W1 - Mayfair | **The Intercontinental Hotel**

AA   ★★★★★   1 Hamilton Place, Park Lane, London W1J 7QY
accessible rooms: 8   t 0800 40 50 60
                     intercontinental.co.uk

Access: 🔲 🐕 🛏 ♿ 👤👥 👁   General: 🔲 P♿

W1 - Mayfair | **London Hilton On Park Lane**

Enjoy England   ★★★★   22 Park Lane, London W1K 1BE
accessible rooms: 5   t 020 7493 8000
                     hilton.co.uk/londonparklane

Access: 🔲 🐕 🛏 ♿ 👤👥 👁   General: 🔲   Room: 🛁

W1 - Mayfair | **London Marriott Hotel Grosvenor Square**

AA   ★★★★   10-13 Grosvenor Square, Mayfair, London W1K 6JP
accessible rooms: 5   t 020 7493 1232
                     marriott.co.uk

Access: 🐕 ♿ 👤👥 👁   General: 🔲 P♿

W1 - Mayfair | **London Marriott Hotel Park Lane**

AA   ★★★★★   140 Park Lane, Park Lane, London W1K 7AA
accessible rooms: 9   t 020 7493 7000
                     marriott.co.uk/hotels/travel/lonpl-london-marriott-hotel-park-lane/

Access: 🔲 🐕 ♿ 👤👥 👂   General: 🔲   Room: 🛁

W1 - Mayfair | **Metropolitan Hotel London**

                     19 Old Park Lane, London W1K 1LB
                     t 020 7447 1000
                     metropolitan.london.como.bz

Access: 🐕 🛏 ♿ 👤👥

W1 - Mayfair | **Millennium Hotel London Mayfair**

AA   ★★★★   39-44 Grosvenor Square, Mayfair, London W1K 2HP
accessible rooms: 2   t 020 7629 9400
                     millenniumhotels.co.uk/millenniummayfair

Access: 🔲 🐕 ♿ 👤👥 👂 👁   General: 🔲 P♿

W1 - Mayfair | Radisson Edwardian Mayfair

AA ★★★★★ Stratton Street, Mayfair, London W1J 8LT
Enjoy England ★★★★★ t 020 7629 7777
accessible rooms: 6 themayfairhotel.co.uk

Access: ⬚ ⤨ 🐕 ♿ ↑ 🧍 ❖ General: 🛗 Room: ⬛

W1 - Piccadilly | Athenaeum Hotel & Apartments

AA ★★★★★ 116 Piccadilly, Piccadilly, London W1J 7BJ
accessible rooms: 2 t 020 7499 3464
athenaeumhotel.com

Access: ⤨ 🐕 🏛 ♿ 🧍 Room: ⬛

W1 - Piccadilly | Radisson Edwardian Hampshire Hotel

AA ★★★★★ 31-36 Leicester Square, London WC2H 7LH
Enjoy England ★★★★★ t 020 7839 9399
accessible rooms: 1 radissonedwardian.com/londonuk_hampshire

Access: ⤨ 🐕 ♿ ↑ 🧍 ❖ General: 🛗 Room: ⬛

W1 - Piccadilly | Radisson Edwardian Leicester Square Hotel

AA ★★★ St. Martins Street, Leicester Square, London WC2H 7HL
Enjoy England ★★★★ t 020 7930 8641
radissonedwardian.com/leicestersquare

Access: ⤨ 🐕 🏛 ↑

W1 - Piccadilly | Thistle Piccadilly

Coventry Street, London W1D 6BZ
t 0871 376 9031
thistle.com

Access: ⬚ ⤨ 🐕 ↑ 🤟 ❖ General: 🛗 P♿

W1 - West End | Best Western Mostyn Hotel

AA ★★★ 4 Bryanston Street, London W1H 7BY
accessible rooms: 1 t 020 7935 2361
mostynhotel.co.uk

Access: ⤨ 🐕 ♿ ❖ Room: ⬛

W1 - West End | The Cumberland

AA ★★★★ Great Cumberland Place, Whitehall, London W1H 7DL
accessible rooms: 10 t 0871 376 9014
guoman.com

Access: ⬚ ⤨ 🐕 ♿ ↑ 🧍 🤟 ❖ General: 🛗 Room: ⬛

W1 - West End | Holiday Inn London Regent's Park

AA ★★★★ Carburton Street, Regent's Park, London W1W 5EE
accessible rooms: 6 t 0800 40 50 60
holiday-inn.co.uk

Access: ⬚ ⤨ 🐕 🏛 ♿ ↑ 🧍 🤟 ❖ General: 🛗

Welcome to Accor hotels

Where friendly staff are on hand in over 36 accessible hotels across London – whatever your needs, whatever your budget.

Three elegant 5 star French Art de Vivre hotels situated in St James, Gatwick and Heathrow T5.

Nine contemporary 4 star hotels across London.

Three individual 3 and 4 star mid-market, London hotels.

14 economy hotels situated throughout London.

New international budget hotels with distinctive personalities: one in central London

Three low-cost London hotels offering the smart traveller a no frills experience at very competitive rates.

For more information and bookings visit or call 0871 663 0624 /accorhotels.com

W1 - West End | The Langham

AA ★★★★★
accessible rooms: 4

1 Portland Place, London W1B 1JA
t 020 7636 1000
london.langhamhotels.co.uk

Access: ♿ 🅰 📱 🦮 ♿🚻 👤👥 🔔 General: 🔼♿ Room: ♨

W1 - West End | London Marriott Hotel Marble Arch

AA ★★★★
accessible rooms: 2

134 George Street, Oxford Street, London W1H 5DN
t 020 7723 1277
londonmarriottmarblearch.co.uk

Access: 📱 🦮 ♿🚻 👤👥 🔔 ⬤ General: 🔼P♿ Room: ♨

W1 - West End | Radisson Edwardian Berkshire Hotel

AA ★★★★
Enjoy England ★★★★
accessible rooms: 2

350 Oxford Street, London W1C 1BY
t 020 7629 7474
radissonedwardian.com

Access: 📱 🦮 ♿🚻 🔔 ⬤ Room: ♨

W1 - West End | Radisson Edwardian Grafton Hotel

AA ★★★★
Enjoy England ★★★★
accessible rooms: 2

130 Tottenham Court Road, Bloomsbury, London W1T 5AY
t 020 7388 4131
radissonedwardian.com/londonuk_Grafton

Access: 📱 🦮 🏨 ♿🚻 👤👥 🔔 ⬤ General: ♿ Room: ♨

W1 - West End | Radisson Edwardian Sussex Hotel

AA ★★★
Enjoy England ★★★

Granville Place, London W1H 6PA
t 020 7408 0130
radissonedwardian.com/londonuk_sussex

Access: 📱 🦮 ♿🚻 👥 ⬤

W1 - West End | Thistle Hotel Marble Arch

AA ★★★★
accessible rooms: 10

Bryanston Street, Marble Arch W1H 7EH
t 0871 376 9027
thistle.com

Access: 📱 🦮 🏨 ♿🚻 👤👥 🔔 General: 🔼 Room: ♨

W1 - West End | YHA London Central

Enjoy England ★★★★

104-108 Bolsover Street, London W1W 6AB
e yha.org.uk

Access: 🦮 👤

WC1 - Bloomsbury | The Bloomsbury Hotel

AA ★★★★
accessible rooms: 5

16-22 Great Russell Street, Bloomsbury, London WC1B 3NN
t 020 7347 1000
doylecollection.com

Access: 🦮 ♿🚻 👥 ⬤ Room: ♨

WC1 - Bloomsbury | Holiday Inn King's Cross

AA ★★★★
accessible rooms: 4

1 King's Cross Road, King's Cross, London WC1X 9HX
t 020 7833 3900
ichotelsgroup.com

Access: 🐕🏛️♿🚶🧍‍ General: ⊡

WC1 - Bloomsbury | Holiday Inn London Bloomsbury

AA ★★★★
accessible rooms: 8

Coram Street, Bloomsbury, London WC1N 1HT
t 0870 400 9222
holiday-inn.co.uk

Access: 🅰️📷🐕🏛️♿🚶🧍‍ 👂◆ General: ⊡P♿

WC1 - Bloomsbury | Imperial Hotel

accessible rooms: 3

61-66 Russell Square, Bloomsbury, London WC1B 5BB
t 020 7837 3655
imperialhotels.co.uk

Access: 🐕🏛️♿🚶🧍‍ General: ⊡P♿ Room: ⛲

WC1 - Bloomsbury | Park Inn Russell Square

AA ★★★★
Enjoy England ★★★★
accessible rooms: 2

92 Southampton Row, Bloomsbury, London WC1B 4BH
t 020 7242 2828
london.russell-square.parkinn.co.uk/

Access: 🐕♿🚶🧍‍ Room: ⛲

WC1 - Bloomsbury | Premier Inn - London Euston

Enjoy England   Budget
accessible rooms: 12

1 Dukes Road, Euston, London WC1H 9PJ
t 0870 238 3301
premierinn.com

Access: 📷🐕🏛️♿🚶🧍‍👂◆ General: ⊡P♿ Room: ⛲

WC1 - Bloomsbury | President Hotel

accessible rooms: 3

Russell Square, Bloomsbury, London WC1N 1DB
t 020 7837 8844
imperialhotels.co.uk

Access: 🐕🏛️♿🚶🧍‍ General: ⊡P♿ Room: ⛲

WC1 - Bloomsbury | Radisson Edwardian Bloomsbury Street Hotel

AA ★★★★
Enjoy England ★★★★
accessible rooms: 2

9-13 Bloomsbury Street, London WC1B 3QD
t 020 7636 5601
RadissonEdwardian.com/Bloomsbury

Access: 📷🐕♿🚶🧍‍👂◆ General: ⊡ Room: ⛲

WC1 - Bloomsbury | Radisson Edwardian Kenilworth Hotel

AA ★★★★
Enjoy England ★★★★
accessible rooms: 2

94-97 Great Russell Street, Bloomsbury, London WC1B 3LB
t 020 7637 3477
radissonedwardian.com/londonuk_kenilworth

Access: 🏛️♿🧍‍ Room: ⛲

WC1 - Bloomsbury | Royal National Hotel

accessible rooms: 10

Bedford Way, Bloomsbury, London WC1H 0DG
t 020 7637 2488
imperialhotels.co.uk

Access: ☑ 🐾 🏛 ♿ 🚶 👫 ? General: 🔛 P♿

WC1 - Bloomsbury | Tavistock Hotel

accessible rooms: 7

Tavistock Square, Bloomsbury, London WC1H 9EU
t 020 7636 8383
imperialhotels.co.uk

Access: 🐾 🏛 ♿ 🚶 👫 General: 🔛 ♿

WC1 - Bloomsbury | Thistle Bloomsbury

AA   ★★★
accessible rooms: 7

Bloomsbury Way, Bloomsbury, London WC1A 2SD
t 0871 376 9006
thistlehotels.com

Access: ☑ 🐾 ♿ ? ♿ Room: 🛁

WC1 - Bloomsbury | Travelodge Farringdon

10-42 Kings Cross Road, Farringdon, London WC1X 9QN
t 0871 984 6274
travelodge.co.uk

Access: ☑ 🐾 👫 ? ♿ General: 🔛

WC1 - Bloomsbury | Travelodge London Kings Cross

AA   Budget
accessible rooms: 7

Gray's Inn Road, Kings Cross, London WC1X 8BH
t 0871 984 6256
travelodge.co.uk

Access: ☑ 🐾 🏛 ♿ 🚶 👫 ? General: 🔛

WC2 - Covent Garden | Radisson Edwardian Mountbatten Hotel

AA   ★★★★
Enjoy England   ★★★★

Seven Dials, Covent Garden, London WC2H 9HD
t 020 7836 4300
radissonedwardian.com/londonuk_mountbatten

Access: ☑ 🐾 ♿ 🚶 👫 ? ♿ General: ♿

WC2 - Covent Garden | Travelodge London Covent Garden

AA   Budget
accessible rooms: 10

10 Drury Lane, Covent Garden, London WC2B 5RE
t 0871 984 6245
travelodge.co.uk

Access: ☑ 🐾 🏛 🚶 👫 ? Room: 🛁

WC2 - Holborn | Grange Holborn Hotel

Enjoy England   ★★★★
accessible rooms: 4

50-60 Southampton Road, Holborn, London WC1X 9QN
t 020 7242 1800
grangehotels.com

Access: ☑ 🐾 🏛 ♿ 👫 ? ♿

WC2 - Strand | **Charing Cross**

AA
accessible rooms: 6   ★★★★   The Strand, St James, London WC2N 5HX
t 0871 376 9012
guoman.com/en/hotels/united_kingdom/london/charing_cross/index.html

Access: ☑ ✖ ⛸ⁿᶜ 🦽 ♪ ✧   General: 🔁   Room: ♨

WC2 - Strand | **The Waldorf Hilton**

Enjoy England   ★★★★   Aldwych, London WC2B 4DD
accessible rooms: 15   **t** 020 7836 2400
hilton.co.uk

Access: ☑ ✖ 🏛 ⛸ⁿᶜ 🚶♪   General: 🔁   Room: ♨

NW1 - Camden | **Holiday Inn Camden Lock**

AA
accessible rooms: 4   ★★★★   28 Jamestown Road, Camden Town, London NW1 7BY
t 0800 405 060
holiday-inn.co.uk

Access: ☑ ✖ 🏛 ⛸ⁿᶜ 🦽🚶♪   General: 🔁   Room: ♨

NW1 - King's Cross | **Ibis London Euston St Pancras**

AA   **Budget**   3 Cardington Street, Euston, Camden, London NW1 2LW
accessible rooms: 8   **t** 020 7388 7777
ibishotel.com

Access: ☑ ✖ ⛸ⁿᶜ 🚶♪ ✧   General: 🔁 **P**♿

NW1 - King's Cross | **Novotel London St Pancras**

AA
accessible rooms: 11   ★★★★   100-110 Euston Road, Euston, London NW1 2AJ
t 020 7666 9000
novotel.com

Access: ☑ ✖ 🏛 ⛸ⁿᶜ 🚶♪   General: 🔁 **P**♿   Room: ♨

NW1 - King's Cross | **Thistle Euston Hotel**

AA
    ★★★★   43 Cardington Street, Euston, London NW1 2LP
t 0870 333 9107
thistle.com

Access: ☑ ✖ 🏛 ⛸ⁿᶜ 🚶♪ ✧   General: 🔁

NW1 - King's Cross | **YHA St Pancras**

79-81 Euston Road, London NW1 2QE
t 020 7388 9998
yha.org.uk

Access: ☑ ✖ 🏛 ⛸ⁿᶜ 🚶♪   General: 🔁

W2 - Bayswater | **Ramada London Hyde Park**

AA
accessible rooms: 6   ★★★★   150 Bayswater Road, Bayswater, London W2 4RT
t 0844 815 9048
ramadajarvis.co.uk

Access: ☑ ✖ 🏛 ⛸ⁿᶜ 🚶♪   General: 🔁 **P**♿   Room: ♨

W2 - Bayswater | Thistle Hyde Park Hotel

AA   ★★★★   90-92 Lancaster Gate, London W2 3NR
t 0871 376 9022
thistlehotels.com

Access: 🖉 🦮 ♪ ♿

W2 - Bayswater | Thistle Kensington Gardens

accessible rooms: 2   104 Bayswater Road, Lancaster Gate, London W2 3HL
t 0871 376 9024
thistle.com

Access: 🖉 🦮 🧍 👫♿ General: P♿ Room: 🛗

W2 - Hyde Park | Hilton London Hyde Park

Enjoy England   ★★★★   129 Bayswater Road, Lancaster Gate, London W2 4RJ
accessible rooms: 2   t 020 7221 2217
hilton.co.uk

Access: 🦮 🏛 ♿ 👫 Room: 🛗

W2 - Paddington | Hilton London Metropole

Enjoy England   ★★★★   225 Edgware Road, Church Street, London W2 1JU
accessible rooms: 20   t 020 7402 4141
hilton.co.uk/londonmet

Access: 🖉 🦮 🏛 ♿ 🧍 👫 ♿ ♪ General: 🔼 P♿ Room: 🛗

W2 - Paddington | Hilton London Paddington

Enjoy England   ★★★★   146 Praed Street, Paddington, London W2 1EE
accessible rooms: 18   t 020 7850 0500
hilton.co.uk/paddington

Access: 🖉 🦮 ♿ 🧍 👫 ♪ ♿ General: 🔼 P♿ Room: 🛗

SW1 - Knightsbridge | Millennium Hotel London Knightsbridge

17 Sloane Street, Knightsbridge, London SW1X 9NU
t 020 7235 4377
millenniumhotels.co.uk

Access: 🦮 🏛 👫 ♪

SW1 - Knightsbridge | Sheraton Park Tower

AA   ★★★★★   101 Knightsbridge, Knightsbridge, London SW1X 7RN
accessible rooms: 4   t 020 7235 8050
sheratonparktower.com

Access: ♿ 🧍 👫 General: 🔼 Room: 🛗

SW1 - St James's | 41 Apartments

accessible rooms: 1   25-27 Catherine Place, London SW1E 6DU
t 020 7958 7760
rubenshotel.com/apartments

Access: 🦮 ♿ 🧍 👫 Room: 🛗

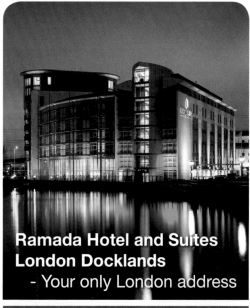

SW1 - St James's | Crowne Plaza London St James

AA   ★★★★   45-51 Buckingham Gate, St James, London SW1E 6AF
Enjoy England   ★★★★   t 0800 405 060
accessible rooms: 3   crowneplaza.co.uk

Access: ⬚ 🐕 🏛 ♿ 🚻 🧍 👫 ⟲ ✦   General: 🛗 ♿

SW1 - St James's | The Royal Horseguards

AA   ★★★★   2 Whitehall Court, St James, London SW1A 2EJ
accessible rooms: 3   t 0871 376 9033
    guoman.com

Access: ⬚ 🐕 ♿ 👫 ⟲   General: 🛗 ♿   Room: 🛏

SW1 - St James's | The Royal Trafalgar

AA   ★★★   Whitcomb Street, St James, London WC2H 7HG
accessible rooms: 4   t 0871 376 9037
    thistle.com

Access: ⬚ 🐕 ♿ 🧍 👫   Room: 🛏

SW1 - St James's | The Rubens At The Palace

AA   ★★★★   39-41 Buckingham Palace Road, St James, London SW1W 0PS
accessible rooms: 1   t 020 7834 6600
    rubenshotel.com

Access: 🐕 ♿ 🧍 👫   Room: 🛏

SW1 - St James's | The Stafford Hotel

accessible rooms: 6   St. James's Place, London SW1A 1NJ
    t 020 7493 0111
    thestaffordhotel.co.uk

Access: 🐕 ♿ 👫 ✦   General: 🛗 ♿   Room: 🛏

SW1 - St James's | Thistle The Grosvenor, London

101 Buckingham Palace Road, London SW1W 0SJ
t 0871 376 9038
thistle.com

Access: 🐕 ♿ 🧍   General: 🛗

SW1 - St James's | The Trafalgar Hilton

accessible rooms: 5   2 Spring Gardens, Trafalgar Square, London SW1A 2TS
    t 020 7870 2900
    hilton.co.uk/trafalgar

Access: ⬚ 🐕 🏛 ♿ 🧍 👫   General: 🛗   Room: 🛏

SW1 - Victoria | Park Plaza Victoria

AA   ★★★★   239 Vauxhall Bridge Road, Victoria, London SW1V 1EQ
accessible rooms: 17   t 020 7769 9999
    victoriaparkplaza.com

Access: ⬚ 🐕 🏛 ♿ 🧍 👫 ⟲   General: 🛗   Room: 🛏

SW1 - Westminster | City Inn Westminster

AA   ★★★★   30 John Islip Street, Belgravia, London SW1P 4DD
accessible rooms: 22   t 020 7630 1000
           cityinn.com/london/

Access: ◻ ⚐ ♿ ♨ ⛟ ⚰ ♊ ?   General: ⬍ P♿   Room: ⚱

SW1 - Westminster | Thistle Westminster Hotel London

AA   ★★★★   Buckingham Palace Road, London SW1W 0QT
           t 0871 376 9039
           thistle.com

Access: ◻ ♿ ⛟ ⚰ ? ⚙   General: ⬍

SW7 - South Kensington | Holiday Inn - Kensington Forum

accessible rooms: 8   Holiday Inn London - Kensington Forum, 97 Cromwell Road, London SW7 4DN
           t 0800 405 060
           holiday-inn.co.uk

Access: ⚠ ◻ ♿ ♨ ⛟ ⚰ ♊ ? ⚙   General: ⬍ P♿ ♿

SW7 - South Kensington | Meininger City Hostel & Hotel London

Enjoy England   ★★★★   65-67 Queen's Gate, London SW7 5JS
           t 020 3051 8173 e welcome@meininger-hostels.com
           meininger-hostels.com

Access: ♿ ⚰

SW7 - South Kensington | Millennium Bailey's London Kensington

           140 Gloucester Road, London SW7 4QH
           t 020 7373 6000
           millenniumhotels.co.uk/millenniumkensington

Access: ◻ ⛟ ? ⚙

SW7 - South Kensington | Millennium Gloucester Hotel London Kensington

AA   ★★★★   4-18 Harrington Gardens, South Kensington, London SW7 4LH
accessible rooms: 6   t 020 7373 6030
           millenniumhotels.co.uk/millenniumgloucester

Access: ◻ ♿ ♨ ⛟ ⚰ ? ⚙   Room: ⚱

SW7 - South Kensington | Radisson Edwardian Vanderbilt

AA   ★★★★   68-86 Cromwell Road, London SW7 5BT
Enjoy England   ★★★★   t 020 7761 9000
accessible rooms: 1   radisson.com/londonuk_vanderbilt

Access: ◻ ♿ ⛟ ⚰   Room: ⚱

W8 - Kensington | Copthorne Tara Hotel London Kensington   AS

AA   ★★★★   Scarsdale Place, Wrights Lane, Kensington, London W8 5SR
accessible rooms: 10   t 020 7937 7211 e reservations.tara@millenniumhotels.co.uk
           millenniumhotels.co.uk/copthornetarakensington

Access: ⚠ ◻ ♿ ♨ ☺ ⛟ ⚰ ♊ ?   General: ⚲ P♿ ✕ ⚑ ☕   Room: ⚱ ⚙ ▣ ⚙

W8 - Kensington | The Milestone Hotel

accessible rooms: 1

1 Kensington Court, London W8 5DL
t 020 7917 1000
milestonehotel.com

Access: ☑ ✕ ♿ ⬆ ♿ ⬗ General: ⬆ ♿

W8 - Kensington | Royal Garden Hotel

accessible rooms: 4

2-24 Kensington High Street, Kensington, London W8 4PT
t 020 7937 8000
royalgardenhotel.co.uk

Access: ☑ ✕ ♿ ⬆ ♿ ? ⬗ General: ⬆ Room: ⬚

SE1 - Southbank | Express By Holiday Inn Southwark

AA **Budget**
accessible rooms: 5

103 Southwark St, Southwark, London SE1 0JQ
t 0800 405 060
hiexpress.co.uk

Access: ☑ ✕ ⬛ ♿ ⬆ ♿ ? General: P♿ Room: ⬚

SE1 - Southbank | Hilton London Tower Bridge

Enjoy England ★★★★
accessible rooms: 13

5 More London, Tooley Street, Southwark, London SE1 2BY
t 020 3002 4300
hilton.co.uk/towerbridge

Access: ☑ ✕ ⬛ ♿ ♿ General: ⬆ Room: ⬚

SE1 - Southbank | London Bridge Hotel

AA ★★★★
accessible rooms: 6

8-18 London Bridge Street, London Bridge, Southwark, London SE1 9SG
t 020 7855 2200
londonbridgehotel.com

Access: ☑ ✕ ⬛ ♿ ⬆ ♿ ? General: ⬆

SE1 - Southbank | Mercure London City Bankside Hotel

AA ★★★★
accessible rooms: 2

77 Southwark Street, Southwark, London SE1 0JA
t 020 7902 0800
accorhotels.com

Access: ☑ ✕ ⬛ ♿ ⬆ ♿ ? General: ⬆ P♿

SE1 - Southbank | Novotel London City South

AA ★★★★
accessible rooms: 12
Open: All year
Rooms per night:

s:	£340.00
d:	£340.00
Meals:	£10.00

53-61 Southwark Bridge Road, Southwark, London SE1 9HH
t 020 7089 0400 e h3269@accor.com

novotel.com

Central city AA 4 star hotel close to popular attractions and London Bridge tube station.

Access: abc ☑ ✕ ⬛ ☺ ♿ ♿ ♿ ♿ ⬆ ♿ ? General: ⬖ ⬆ P♿ ✕ ♟ ⬚ Room: ⬚ ⬒ ⬗

SE1 - Southbank | **Premier Inn - London County Hall**

Enjoy England	**Budget**	Belvedere Road, Lambeth, London SE1 7PB
accessible rooms: 16		t 0870 238 3300
		premierinn.com

Access: ⬚ ⚲ 🏛 ♿ ⚲⚲ ❧ ? General: ⊡

SE1 - Southbank | **Premier Inn - London Southwark**

Enjoy England	**Budget**	Anchor, 34 Park Street, Southwark, London SE1 9EF
accessible rooms: 3		t 0870 990 6402
		premierinn.com

Access: ⬚ ⚲ 🏛 ♿ ⚲⚲ ? General: ⊡ P♿

SE1 - Southbank | **Premier Inn - London Tower Bridge**

Enjoy England	**Budget**	159 Tower Bridge Road, Bermondsey, London SE1 3LP
accessible rooms: 10		t 0870 238 3303
		premierinn.com

Access: ⬚ ⚲ 🏛 ♿ ⚲⚲ ? General: ⊡ P♿

SE1 - Waterloo | **Days Hotel Waterloo**

AA	**Budget**	54 Kennington Rd, Waterloo, Lambeth, London SE1 7BJ
accessible rooms: 2		t 020 7922 1331
		hotelwaterloo.com

Access: ⬚ ⚲ 🏛 ♿ ⚲⚲ ? General: ⊡ P♿ Room: 🛗

SE1 - Waterloo | **Novotel London Waterloo**

AA	★★★★	113 Lambeth Road, Waterloo, Lambeth, London SE1 7LS
accessible rooms: 10		t 020 7793 1010
		novotel.com

Access: ⬚ ⚲ ♿ ⚲⚲ ? General: ⊡ P♿ Room: 🛗

EC1 - Clerkenwell | **Thistle City Barbican**

AA	★★★	120 Central Street, Clerkenwell, London EC1V 8DS
accessible rooms: 1		t 0871 376 9004
		thistle.com

Access: ⬚ ⚲ 🏛 ♿ ⚲⚲ ⚲⚲ ? General: ⊡ P♿

EC1 - Clerkenwell | **Travelodge London City Road**

AA	**Budget**	1-23 City Road, London EC1Y 1AE
accessible rooms: 19		t 0871 984 6333
		travelodge.co.uk

Access: ⬚ ⚲ 🏛 ♿ ⚲⚲ ? General: ⊡ Room: 🛗

EC1 - Finsbury | **Express By Holiday Inn London City**

AA	**Budget**	275 Old Street, Hackney, London EC1V 9LN
accessible rooms: 6		t 0800 405 060
		hiexpress.co.uk

Access: ⚲ 🏛 ♿ ⚲⚲ General: ⊡ P♿ Room: 🛗

EC2 - City | Andaz (formerly Great Eastern Hotel)

accessible rooms: 4

40 Liverpool Street, Bishopsgate, London EC2M 7QN
t 020 7961 1234
london.liverpoolstreet.andaz.hyatt.com

Access: General: Room:

EC3 - City | Grange City Hotel

Enjoy England ★★★★★
accessible rooms: 17

8-14 Cooper's Row, London EC3N 2BQ
t 020 7863 3700
grangehotels.com

Access: General:

EC3 - City | Novotel London Tower Bridge

AA ★★★★

10 Pepys Street, London EC3N 2NR
t 020 7265 6000
novotel.com

Access: General: Room:

EC4 - City | Crowne Plaza City

AA ★★★★
accessible rooms: 10

19 New Bridge Street, London EC4V 6DB
t 0800 405 060
crowneplaza.co.uk

Access: General:

N1 - Islington | Hilton London Islington

Enjoy England ★★★★
accessible rooms: 10

53 Upper Street, Islington, London N1 0UY
t 020 7354 7700
hilton.co.uk

Access: General:

N1 - Islington | Jurys Inn Islington

AA ★★★
accessible rooms: 10

60 Pentonville Road, Islington, London N1 9LA
t 020 7282 5500
jurysinn.com

Access: General: Room:

N1 - Islington | Premier Inn - London King's Cross St Pancras

Enjoy England Budget
accessible rooms: 14

26-30 York Way, King's Cross, London N1 9AA
t 0870 990 6414
premierinn.com

Access: General:

N12 - North Finchley | Comfort Hotel Finchley

accessible rooms: 4

3 Leisure Way, Finchley, London N12 0QZ
t 020 8446 6644
comfortinn.com

Access: General: Room:

EN3 - Enfield | **Premier Inn - Enfield**

Enjoy England **Budget** Innova Park, Corner Of Solar Way, Enfield, London EN3 7XY
accessible rooms: 10 t 0870 238 3306
premierinn.com

Access: ⚡ 🦮 🏢 ᵂᶜ♿ 🧍 🧍♿ ✋ 👁 General: ⬆ **P**♿ ♿

NW2 - Neasden | **Crown Moran Hotel**

AA ★★★★ 142-152 Cricklewood Broadway, Cricklewood, London NW2 3ED
accessible rooms: 6 t 020 8452 4175
crownmoranhotel.co.uk

Access: ⚡ 🦮 🏢 ᵂᶜ♿ 🧍 🧍♿ ✋ General: ⬆ **P**♿ Room: 🛁

NW2 - Neasden | **Holiday Inn Brent Cross**

AA ★★★ Tilling Road, Brent Cross, London NW2 1LP
accessible rooms: 4 t 0800 405 060
holiday-inn.co.uk

Access: ⚡ 🦮 🏢 ᵂᶜ♿ 🧍 🧍♿ ✋ General: ⬆ **P**♿

NW3 - Hampstead | **London Marriott Hotel Regents Park**

AA ★★★★ 128 King Henrys Road, Regents Park, London NW3 3ST
accessible rooms: 5 t 020 7722 7711
marriott.co.uk

Access: 🦮 🏢 ᵂᶜ♿ 🧍 🧍♿ 👁 General: ⬆ **P**♿

NW3 - Hampstead | **Premier Inn - London Hampstead**

Enjoy England **Budget** 215 Haverstock Hill, Hampstead, London NW3 4RB
accessible rooms: 3 t 0870 850 6328
premierinn.com

Access: 🦮 🏢 ᵂᶜ♿ 🧍 🧍♿ General: **P**♿ ♿ Room: 🛁

NW6 - Kilburn | **London Marriott Maida Vale**

AA ★★★★ Plaza Parade, Maida Vale, London NW6 5RP
accessible rooms: 7 t 020 7543 6000
marriott.co.uk

Access: ⚡ 🦮 ᵂᶜ♿ 🧍♿ 👁 General: **P**♿

NW7 - Mill Hill | **Days Hotel London North**

AA **Budget** Welcome Break Services, Mill Hill, London NW7 3HU
accessible rooms: 8 t 020 8906 7000
daysinn.com

Access: 🦮 🏢 ᵂᶜ♿ ♿ 🧍 🧍♿ General: ⬆ **P**♿

HA8 - Edgware | **Premier Inn - London Edgware**

Enjoy England **Budget** 435 Burnt Oak Broadway, Edgware, London HA8 5AQ
accessible rooms: 6 t 0870 990 6522
premierinn.com

Access: ⚡ 🦮 🏢 ᵂᶜ♿ 🧍 🧍♿ ✋ General: ⬆ **P**♿

HA9 - Wembley | **Premier Inn - London Wembley**

Enjoy England | **Budget** | 151 Wembley Park Drive, Wembley, London HA9 8HQ
accessible rooms: 3 | | t 0870 990 6484
| | premierinn.com

Access: ☑ ✝ 🏛 ♿ 🚶 🧑‍🦽 ? ◆ General: 🔼 P♿

E1 - Wapping | **The Tower**

AA | ★★★★ | St. Katharines Way, Tower Bridge, London E1W 1LD
accessible rooms: 10 | | t 0871 376 9036
| | guoman.com

Access: ☑ ✝ ♿ 🧑‍🦽 ? ◆ General: 🔼 P♿ Room: 🛁

E1 - Whitechapel | **Crowne Plaza London Shoreditch**

AA | ★★★★ | 100 Shoreditch High Street, Shoreditch, London E1W 1LD
accessible rooms: 8 | | t 0871 423 4876
| | crowneplaza.com

Access: ☑ ✝ ♿ 🚶 🧑‍🦽 ♣ ? ◆ General: 🔼 P♿

E1 - Whitechapel | **Express By Holiday Inn Limehouse**

AA | **Budget** | 469-475 The Highway, Limehouse, London E1W 3HN
accessible rooms: 6 | | t 0800 405 060
| | hiexpress.co.uk

Access: ☑ ✝ ♿ 🚶 🧑‍🦽 ? General: 🔼 P♿ Room: 🛁

E1 - Whitechapel | **Ibis London City**

AA | **Budget** | 5 Commercial St, Whitechapel, London E1 6BF
accessible rooms: 19 | | t 020 7422 8400
| | ibishotel.com

Access: ☑ ✝ 🏛 ♿ 🚶 🧑‍🦽 ? General: 🔼 Room: 🛁

E1 - Whitechapel | **Premier Inn London City Tower Hill (formerly Sleep Inn)**

Enjoy England | **Budget** | 24 Prescot Street, London E1 8BB
accessible rooms: 9 | | t 0870 423 6498
| | premierinn.com

Access: ☑ ✝ ♿ 🧑‍🦽 ? ◆ Room: 🛁

E1 - Whitechapel | **Travelodge London Liverpool Street**

AA | **Budget** | 1 Harrow Place, Whitechapel, London E1 7DB
accessible rooms: 8 | | t 0871 984 6190
| | travellodge.co.uk

Access: ☑ ✝ 🏛 ♿ 🚶 🧑‍🦽 ? General: 🔼

E4 - Chingford | **Express By Holiday Inn Chingford**

AA | **Budget** | 5 Walthamstow Avenue, Chingford, London E4 8ST
accessible rooms: 5 | | t 0800 405 060
| | hiexpress.co.uk

Access: ☑ ✝ 🏛 ♿ 🚶 🧑‍🦽 ? General: 🔼 P♿ Room: 🛁

E14 - Docklands | Four Seasons Canary Wharf

AA ★★★★★ 46 Westferry Circus, Canary Wharf, London E14 8RS
accessible rooms: 8   t 020 7510 1999

fourseasons.com

Access: ⊘ ⊁ 🛗 ₭ ₥   General: ⬆   Room: ♨

E14 - Docklands | Hilton London Canary Wharf

Enjoy England ★★★★ South Quay, Marsh Wall, London E14 9SH
accessible rooms: 18   t 020 3002 2300

hilton.co.uk

Access: ⊘ ⊁ 🛗 ₭ ⚲ ₥ ♪   General: ⬆ P₊

E14 - Docklands | Ibis London Docklands

AA   Budget   1 Baffin Way, Docklands, London E14 9PE
accessible rooms: 5   t 020 7517 1100

ibishotel.com

Access: ⊘ ⊁ ₭ ₥ ♪ ✦   General: P₊   Room: ♨

E14 - Docklands | London Marriott Hotel West India Quay

AA ★★★★★ 24 Hertsmere Road, Canary Wharf, London E14 4ED
accessible rooms: 18   t 020 7093 1000

marriott.co.uk

Access: ⊁ ₭ ₥ ♪ ✦   General: ⬆   Room: ♨

E14 - Docklands | Travelodge London Docklands

AA   Budget   Coriander Avenue, East India Dock Road, London E14 2AA
accessible rooms: 11   t 0871 984 6192

travelodge.co.uk

Access: ⊁ 🛗 ₭ ⚲ ₥   General: ⬆ P₊

E14 - Poplar | Radisson Edwardian Providence Wharf

Enjoy England ★★★★ 5 Fairmont Avenue, Canary Wharf E14 9PG
t 020 7987 2050   e resnpw@radisson.com

radissonedwardian.co.uk

Access: ⊁ ⚲ ₥

E15 - Stratford | Ibis London Stratford

AA   Budget   1a Romford Road, Stratford, London E15 4LJ
accessible rooms: 6   t 020 8536 3700

ibishotel.com

Access: ⊘ ⊁ 🛗 ₭ ⚲ ₥ ♪   General: ⬆   Room: ♨

E15 - West Ham | Express By Holiday Inn London Stratford

AA   Budget   196 High Street, Stratford, Newham, London E15 2NE
accessible rooms: 6   t 0800 405 060

hiexpress.co.uk

Access: ⊘ ⊁ 🛗 ₭ ⚲ ₥ ♣ ♪   General: ⬆ P₊   Room: ♨

E16 - Canning Town | Crowne Plaza London Docklands

AA   ★★★★   Western Gateway, Royal Victoria Dock, London E16 1AL
accessible rooms: 11   t 0800 405 060

crowneplaza.co.uk

Access: ⬚ 🐕 🗼 ♿ 🚶 ? ♒   General: ⬆ P♿   Room: ♨

E16 - Canning Town | Custom House Hotel

accessible rooms: 15   272-283 Victoria Dock Road, Royal Victoria Dock, London E16 3BY
t 020 7474 0011

customhouse-hotel.co.uk

Access: 🐕 🗼 ♿ ♿ 🚶 🚶   General: ⬆ P♿   Room: ♨

E16 - Canning Town | Etap Hotel London City Airport

accessible rooms: 4   North Woolwich Road, Silvertown, London E16 2EE
t 020 7474 9106

etaphotel.com

Access: 🐕 🗼 ♿ 🚶 🚶   General: ⬆ P♿   Room: ♨

E16 - Canning Town | Express By Holiday Inn London Royal Docks

AA   Budget   1 Silvertown Way, Silvertown, London E16 1EA
accessible rooms: 16   t 0800 405 060

hiexpress.co.uk

Access: ⬚ 🐕 🗼 ♿ ♿ 🚶 🚶 ?   General: ⬆ P♿   Room: ♨

E16 - Canning Town | Ibis London Excel

AA   Budget   9 Western Gateway, Royal Victoria Dock, London E16 1AB
accessible rooms: 18   t 020 7055 2300

ibishotel.com

Access: ⬚ 🐕 🗼 ♿ 🚶 🚶 ?   General: ⬆ P♿   Room: ♨

E16 - Canning Town | Novotel London Excel

AA   ★★★★   7 Western Gateway, Royal Victoria Docks, London E16 1AA
accessible rooms: 13   t 020 7540 9700

novotel.com

Access: ⬚ 🐕 ♿ 🚶 ? ♒   General: ⬆ P♿   Room: ♨

E16 - Canning Town | Premier Inn - London Docklands

Enjoy England   Budget   Royal Victoria Dock, London E16 1SL
accessible rooms: 12   t 0870 238 3322

premierinn.com

Access: 🐕 🗼 ♿ 🚶 🚶   General: ⬆ P♿

E16 - Canning Town | Ramada Hotel & Suites London Docklands [ExCeL]

AA   ★★★★   2 Festoon Way, Royal Victoria Dock, London E16 1RH
t 020 7540 4820   e reservations@ramadadocklands.co.uk

ramadadocklands.co.uk

Access: ☺ ♿ ♿ ♿ 🚶 🚶 ♒   General: 🪑 ⬆ P♿ 🍷 🍽   Room: ♨ 🛏 📺 ♨

E16 - Canning Town | **Travelodge London City Airport**

AA   **Budget**   Hartman Road, Silvertown, London E16 2BZ
accessible rooms: 7   t 0871 984 6290

travelodge.co.uk

Access: ⬚ ⚡ 🏢 ♿ 🚶 👫 ✋   General: **P**♿   Room: ⛲

IG1 - Ilford | **Travelodge London Ilford**

AA   **Budget**   Clements Road, Ilford, London IG1 1BA
accessible rooms: 6   t 0871 984 6194

travellodge.co.uk

Access: ⚡ 🏢 ♿ 🚶 👫   General: ⬚ **P**♿

IG2 - Newbury Park | **Express By Holiday Inn Newbury Park**

AA   **Budget**   713 Eastern Avenue, Newbury Park, London IG2 7RH
accessible rooms: 7   t 020 8709 2200

hiexpress.co.uk

Access: ⬚ ⚡ ♿ 🚶 👫 ✋ ◈   General: ⬚ **P**♿   Room: ⛲

IG4 - Redbridge | **Travelodge London Ilford Gants Hill**

AA   **Budget**   Beehive Lane, Gants Hill, London IG4 5DR
accessible rooms: 1   t 0871 984 6193

travelodge.co.uk

Access: ⬚ ⚡ 🚶 👫 ✋ ◈   General: **P**♿

IG7 - Chigwell | **Vitalise Jubilee Lodge**   AS

Grange Farm, High Road, Chigwell, Essex IG7 6DP
t 0845 345 1970   e bookings@vitalise.org.uk

vitalise.org.uk

Access: ♿ ⬚ 🏢 ☺ ♿ ♿ ♿   General: ✿ **P**♿ ♿ ✕ 🍷 🍴   Room: 🛏 ⛲ ♿ ⬚ 🅢 ☕

IG11 - Barking | **Etap East Barking**

accessible rooms: 4   Highbridge Road, Barking, London IG11 7BA
t 020 8401 7410

etaphotel.com

Access: ⚡ 🏢 ♿ 🚶 👫   General: ⬚ **P**♿   Room: ⛲

IG11 - Barking | **Formule 1 East Barking**

accessible rooms: 4   Highbridge Road, Barking, London IG11 7BA
t 020 850 7078

accorhotels.com

Access: ⚡ 🏢 ♿ 🚶 👫   General: **P**♿

IG11 - Barking | **Ibis London East Barking**

AA   **Budget**   Highbridge Road, Barking, London IG11 7BA
accessible rooms: 4   t 020 8477 4100

ibishotel.com

Access: ⚡ ♿ 👫 ◈   General: **P**♿   Room: ⛲

IG11 - Barking | Premier Inn - Barking

Enjoy England	Budget	Highbridge Road, Barking, London IG11 7BA
accessible rooms: 5		t 0870 990 6318
		premierinn.com

Access: ⬛ 🐕 🏛 ♿ 🚹 🕴 ♪ General: 🔲 P♿

RM1 - Romford | Premier Inn - Romford Central

Enjoy England	Budget	Mercury Gardens, Romford, London RM1 3EN
accessible rooms: 4		t 0870 197 7220
		premierinn.com

Access: ⬛ 🐕 🏛 ♿ 🚹 🕴 ♪ ⬗ General: 🔲 P♿

RM1 - Romford | Premier Inn - Romford West

Enjoy England	Budget	Whalebone Lane North, Chadwell Heath, London RM6 6QU
accessible rooms: 2		t 0870 990 6450
		premierinn.com

Access: ⬛ 🐕 🏛 ♿ 🚹 🕴 ♪ ⬗ General: P♿

RM1 - Romford | Travelodge Romford Central Hotel

AA	Budget	Market Link, Romford, London RM1 1XJ
accessible rooms: 8		t 0871 984 6255
		travelodge.co.uk

Access: ⬛ 🐕 🏛 ♿ 🚹 🕴 ♪ General: 🔲 Room: 🧹

RM12 - Rainham | Premier Inn - Rainham

Enjoy England	Budget	New Road, Wennington, London RM13 9ED
accessible rooms: 3		t 0870 197 7217
		premierinn.com

Access: 🐕 🏛 ♿ 🚹 🕴 ♪ General: 🔲 P♿

SE2 - Abbey Wood | Abbey Wood Caravan Club Site THE CARAVAN CLUB

Enjoy England	★★★★★	Federation Road, Abbey Wood, London SE2 0LS
🚐 (210)		t 020 8311 7708
	£14.60–£21.55	**caravanclub.co.uk**
🚎 (210)		
	£14.60–£21.55	Verdant, gently sloping site with mature trees and
⛺ (100)		spacious grounds, ideal base for exploring.
210 touring pitches		
Open: All year		

Access: Ⓗ 🐕 🏛 ☺ ♿ General: 🔌 📶 🚰 🧺 🔧 ⚡ 🚿 🗑 🚌 Pitch: 🚐 🚎 ⛺

SE3 - Blackheath | Clarendon Hotel

Enjoy England	★★★	8-16 Montpelier Row, Blackheath, London SE3 0RW
accessible rooms: 3		t 020 8318 4321
		clarendonhotel.com

Access: ⬛ 🏛 ♿ 🚹 ♪ General: P♿

SE10 - Greenwich | **Express By Holiday Inn Greenwich**

AA	**Budget**	Bugsby Way, North Greenwich, London SE10 0GD
accessible rooms: 10		t 020 8269 5000
		expressgreenwich.co.uk

Access: ▢ ⚏ 🐕 ♿ 👁♿ ◠ ◈ General: ⊡ P♿ Room: ⚒

SE10 - Greenwich | **Ibis London Greenwich**

AA	**Budget**	30 Stockwell Street, Greenwich, London SE10 9JN
accessible rooms: 2		t 020 8305 1177
		ibishotel.com

Access: 🐕 ♿ 👁♿ ◈ General: P♿ Room: ⚒

SE10 - Greenwich | **Mitre Inn**

accessible rooms: 2		291 Greenwich High Rd, Greenwich, London SE10 8NA
		t 020 8293 0037
		mitrehotel.com

Access: 🐕 🛗 ♿ 👁♿

SE10 - Greenwich | **Novotel London Greenwich**

AA	★★★★	173-175 Greenwich High Rd, Greenwich, London SE10 8JA
accessible rooms: 6		t 020 8312 6800
		novotel.com

Access: ▢ 🐕 🛗 ♿ 👁♿ General: ⊡ P♿

SE16 - Rotherhithe | **Hilton London Docklands, Nelson Dock**

Enjoy England	★★★★	265 Rotherhithe Street, Rotherhithe, London SE16 5HW
accessible rooms: 3		t 020 7231 1001
		hilton.co.uk/docklands

Access: ▢ 🐕 ♿ 👁♿ ◠ ◈ General: P♿

SE16 - Rotherhithe | **YHA Thameside & Conference Centre**

Enjoy England	★★	20 Salter Rd, London SE16 5PR
accessible rooms: 6		t 0870 770 6010
		yha.org.uk

Access: ▢ 🐕 🛗 ♿ 👁♿ ◠ General: ⊡ Room: ⚒

©Britainonview / - Britain on View

OPEN LONDON

DECIDED WHERE TO GO? SEE ATTRACTIONS FOR WHAT TO DO
Ideas and information start on page 78

SE19 - Norwood | Crystal Palace Caravan Club Site

THE CARAVAN CLUB

Enjoy England	★★★★★
🚐 (126)	
	£14.60–£21.55
🚌 (126)	
	£14.60–£21.55
Å (30)	

126 touring pitches
Open: All year

Crystal Palace Road, London SE19 1UF
t 020 8778 7155

caravanclub.co.uk

Busy, friendly site on edge of pleasant park. Close to all of London's attractions.

Access: 🅷 ✕ 🏠 ☺ 🚾♿ General: 🔲🐕🕐🔔 WP 🔥🚐🚜 Pitch: 🚐🚌Å

DA5 - Bexley | Holiday Inn Bexley

AA	★★★
accessible rooms: 2	

Black Prince Interchange, Southwold Road, Bexley, London DA5 1ND
t 0800 405 060

holiday-inn.co.uk

Access: ⬚ ✕ 🏠♿🚾👣✕♿ 🤚 🌼 General: 🔼 P♿ ♿

BR1 - Bromley | Best Western Bromley Court Hotel

AA	★★★

Bromley Hill, Bromley, Kent BR1 4JD
t 020 8461 8600 e enquiries@bromleycourthotel.co.uk

bw-bromleycourthotel.co.uk

Access: abc ⬚ ✕ ☺ ♿🚾♿✕ General: 🐕🌸🔼P♿♿✕🍷🍽 Room: 🚾🖥🍵

SW6 - Fulham | Ibis London Earl's Court

AA	★★★
accessible rooms: 12	

47 Lillie Road, West Brompton, London SW6 1UD
t 020 7610 0880

ibishotel.com

Access: ⬚ ✕ 🏠🚾👣✕ 🤚 General: 🔼P♿

SW6 - Fulham | Jurys Inn Chelsea

AA	★★★
Enjoy England	★★★
accessible rooms: 12	

Imperial Road, Imperial Wharf, London SW6 2GA
t 020 7411 2200

JurysInns.com/ChelseaHotels

Access: ✕ 🏠🚾♿👣✕ General: 🔼 Room: 🏛

SW6 - Fulham | Millennium & Copthorne Hotels At Chelsea Football Club

AA	★★★★
Enjoy England	★★★★
accessible rooms: 8	

Stamford Bridge, Fulham Road, London SW6 1HS
t 020 7565 1400

millenniumhotels.co.uk/millenniumcopthornechelseafc

Access: ✕ 🏠🚾👣✕ General: 🔼P♿ Room: 🏛

SW6 - Fulham | Premier Inn - London Putney Bridge

Enjoy England	Budget
accessible rooms: 8	

3 Putney Bridge Approach, Fulham, London SW6 3JD
t 0870 238 3302

premierinn.com

Access: ⬚ ✕ 🏠🚾👣✕ 🤚 General: 🔼P♿

SW8 - South Lambeth | **Comfort Inn Vauxhall**

accessible rooms: 6

87 South Lambeth Road, Vauxhall, London SW8 1RN
t 020 7735 949
comfortinn.com

Access: ⚲ ⛷ 🏢 ⟨wc⟩ ⟨&⟩ ⟨&⟩ ☊ ⟨ General: 🔼 **P**& Room: 🐜

SW10 - West Brompton | **Wyndham Grand London Chelsea Harbour**

AA

★★★★★ Chelsea Harbour, Chelsea, London SW10 0XG
t 020 7823 3000 e thusband@wyndham.com
wyndhamgrandlondon.co.uk

Access: ⚲ ⟨&⟩ ⟨&⟩ ⟨&⟩ General: 🐎 ✤ 🔼 **P**& ⟨ ⟩ 🍷 Room: 🍵

SW11 - Battersea | **Travelodge London Battersea**

AA   **Budget**
accessible rooms: 5

Southampton House, 192-206 York Road, London SW11 3SA
t 0871 984 6189
travelodge.co.uk

Access: ⚲ ⛷ 🏢 ⟨wc⟩ ⟨&⟩ ⟨&⟩ ☊ General: 🔼 **P**&

SW18 - Wandsworth | **Express By Holiday Inn Wandsworth**

AA   **Budget**
accessible rooms: 8

Smuggler's Way, Battersea, Wandsworth, London SW18 1EG
t 0870 720 1298
ichotelsgroup.com

Access: ⚲ ⛷ 🏢 ⟨wc⟩ ⟨&⟩ ⟨&⟩ ☊ General: 🔼 **P**& Room: 🐜

SW19 - Wimbledon | **Express By Holiday Inn Wimbledon South**

AA   **Budget**
accessible rooms: 5

200 High Street, South Wimbledon, Merton, London SW19 2BH
t 020 8545 7300
exhiwimbledon.co.uk

Access: ⚲ ⛷ 🏢 ⟨&⟩ ⟨&⟩ ☊ ✤ General: 🔼 **P**& ⟨ ⟩ Room: 🐜

SW19 - Wimbledon | **Premier Inn - London Wimbledon South**

Enjoy England   **Budget**
accessible rooms: 7

27 Chapter Way, Merton, London SW19 2RF
t 0870 990 6342
premierinn.com

Access: ⚲ ⛷ 🏢 ⟨&⟩ ⟨&⟩ ☊ General: 🔼 **P**&

SW19 - Wimbledon | **Rose And Crown**

accessible rooms: 1

55 High Street, Wimbledon, Merton, London SW19 5BA
t 020 8947 4713
youngs.co.uk

Access: ⛷ 🏢 ⟨wc⟩ ⟨&⟩ ⟨&⟩

CR0 - Croydon | **Jurys Inn Croydon**

AA

★★★ 26 Wellesley Road, Croydon, London CR0 9XY
accessible rooms: 14   t 020 8448 6000
jurysinn.com

Access: ⛷ 🏢 ⟨wc⟩ ⟨&⟩ ⟨&⟩ General: 🔼 **P**& Room: 🐜

CR0 - Croydon | **Premier Inn - Croydon South**

Enjoy England accessible rooms: 2	Budget	104 Coombe Road, Croydon, London CR0 5RB t 0870 197 7069 premierinn.com

Access: ☑ ✕ 🏛 ♿ ⛹ 🅿 General: 🅿

CR0 - Croydon | **Premier Inn - Croydon West**

Enjoy England accessible rooms: 4	Budget	The Colonnades Leisure Park, 619 Purley Way, Croydon, London CR0 4RQ t 0870 990 6554 premierinn.com

Access: ☑ ✕ 🏛 ♿ 🚶 ⛹ General: 🛗 🅿

SM1 - Sutton | **Holiday Inn London Sutton**

AA accessible rooms: 2	★★★	Gibson Road, Sutton, London SM1 2RF t 0800 405 060 holiday-inn.co.uk

Access: ☑ ✕ 🏛 ♿ 🚶 ⛹ ⬧ General: 🛗 🅿 ♿

SM4 - Morden | **Travelodge London Wimbledon (Morden)**

AA accessible rooms: 3	Budget	Epsom Road, Morden, London SM4 5PH t 0871 984 6196 travelodge.co.uk

Access: ✕ 🏛 ♿ 🚶 ⛹ General: 🅿 Room: 🖌

SM5 - Carshalton | **Greyhound Hotel**

accessible rooms: 1		2 High Street, Carshalton, London SM5 3PE t 020 8647 1511 greyhoundhotel.net

Access: ✕ 🏛 ♿ 🚶 ⛹ General: 🛗

KT6 - Surbiton | **Travelodge Chessington Tolworth**

AA accessible rooms: 5	Budget	Tolworth Tower, Ewell Road, London KT6 7EL t 0871 984 6210 travelodge.co.uk

Access: ☑ ✕ 🏛 ♿ 🚶 ⛹ General: 🛗 🅿 Room: 🖌

KT9 - Chessington | **Holiday Inn London Chessington**

AA accessible rooms: 7	★★★★	Leatherhead Road, Kingston, London KT9 2NE t 0870 890 567 holidayinnchessington.co.uk

Access: ✕ 🏛 ♿ ♿ 🚶 ⛹ General: 🛗 🅿

KT9 - Chessington | **Premier Inn - Chessington**

Enjoy England accessible rooms: 3	Budget	Leatherhead Road, Chessington, Kingston, London KT9 2NE t 0870 197 7057 premierinn.com

Access: ☑ ✕ 🏛 ♿ 🚶 ⛹ General: 🅿 Room: 🖌

TW1 - Twickenham | **Popes Grotto (Young's)**

accessible rooms: 2	Cross Deep, Twickenham, Richmond upon Thames, London TW1 4RB
	t 0889 230 50
	popesgrotto.co.uk

Access: 🐕🏛️♿🚶♿ General: **P**♿

TW2 - Twickenham | **Premier Inn - Twickenham**

Enjoy England Budget	Chertsey Road, Whitton, Richmond upon Thames, London TW2 6LS
accessible rooms: 2	t 0870 990 6416
	premierinn.com

Access: 🖊️🐕🏛️♿🚶♿👂 General: **P**♿

TW6 - Hounslow | **Hilton London Heathrow Airport**

Enjoy England ★★★★	Terminal Four, Heathrow, Hillingdon, London TW6 3AF
accessible rooms: 4	t 020 8759 7755
	hilton.co.uk

Access: 🖊️🐕🏛️♿🚶♿👂 General: 🔲**P**♿ Room: 🧹

TW8 - Brentford | **Holiday Inn London Brentford Lock**

AA ★★★★	High Street, Brentford, Hounslow, London TW8 8JZ
accessible rooms: 5	t 0800 405 060
	holiday-inn.co.uk

Access: 🖊️🐕🏛️♿♿🚶♿👂 General: 🔲**P**♿ Room: 🧹

TW8 - Brentford | **Premier Inn - London Kew**

Enjoy England Budget	52 High Street, Brentford, Hounslow, London TW8 0BB
accessible rooms: 8	t 0870 990 6304
	premierinn.com

Access: 🖊️🐕🏛️♿🚶♿👂 General: 🔲**P**♿

TW13 - Feltham | **Travelodge Feltham**

accessible rooms: 5	Res Centre, Feltham TW13 4EX
	t 0871 984 6319
	travelodge.co.uk

Access: 🐕🏛️♿🚶♿ General: 🔲**P**♿

W3 - Acton | **Express By Holiday Inn London Park Royal**

AA Budget	Victoria Road, North Acton, Ealing, London W3 6UP
accessible rooms: 6	t 020 8896 4460
	exhiparkroyal.co.uk

Access: 🖊️🐕🏛️♿🚶♿👂✦ General: 🔲**P**♿ Room: 🧹

W6 - Hammersmith | **Express By Holiday Inn Hammersmith**

AA Budget	124 King Street, Hammersmith, London W6 0QU
accessible rooms: 7	t 0800 405 060
	hiexpresshammersmith.co.uk

Access: 🖊️🐕🏛️♿🚶♿👂 General: 🔲**P**♿ Room: 🧹

W6 - Hammersmith | Novotel London West

AA	★★★★	Hammersmith International Centre, 1 Shortlands, Hammersmith, London W6 8DR
accessible rooms: 8		t 020 8741 1555
		novotel.com

Access: ☐ ⚹ 🏛 💧⚹🦽 ⟳ General: ⬍ P♿ Room: 🛁

W6 - Hammersmith | Premier Inn - London Hammersmith

Enjoy England	Budget	255 King Street, Hammersmith, London W6 9LU
accessible rooms: 3		t 0870 850 6310
		premierinn.com

Access: ☐ ⚹ 🏛 💧⚹🦽 ⟳ General: ⬍ P♿

W14 - West Kensington | Express By Holiday Inn Earls Court

AA	Budget	North End Road, West Kensington, London W14 9NS
accessible rooms: 5		t 0800 40 50 60
		hiexpress.co.uk

Access: ☐ ⚹ 🏛 💧⚹🦽 ⟳ ⊕ General: ⬍ P♿ Room: 🛁

W14 - West Kensington | K West Hotel & Spa

AA	★★★★	Kensington House, Richmond Way, London W14 0AX
accessible rooms: 6		t 020 8008 6600
		k-west.co.uk

Access: ⚹ 💧⚹🦽 ⊕ General: P♿

UB3 - Hayes | Holiday Inn London Heathrow Ariel

AA	★★★	118 Bath Road, Hayes, London UB3 5AJ
accessible rooms: 4		t 0800 405 060
		holiday-inn.co.uk

Access: ☐ ⚹ 🏛 💧⚹🦽 ⟳ ⊕ General: ⬍ P♿ ♿

UB3 - Hayes | Ibis London Heathrow Airport

AA	Budget	112-114 Bath Road, Hayes, London UB3 5AL
accessible rooms: 7		t 020 8759 4888
		ibishotel.com

Access: ☐ ⚹ 🏛 💧⚹🦽 ⟳ General: ⬍ Room: 🛁

UB3 - Hayes | Premier Inn - Heathrow (M4)

Enjoy England	Budget	Shepiston Lane, Heathrow, London UB3 1RW
accessible rooms: 6		t 0870 990 6612
		premierinn.com

Access: ☐ ⚹ 🏛 💧⚹🦽 ⟳ General: ⬍ P♿

UB3 - Hayes | Radisson Edwardian Heathrow Hotel

AA	★★★★	140 Bath Rd, Hayes, London UB3 5AW
Enjoy England	★★★★	t 020 8759 6311
accessible rooms: 3		radissonedwardian.com/heathrow

Access: ☐ ⚹ 🏛 💧⚹🦽 General: P♿ Room: 🛁

UB4 - Hayes | **Premier Inn - Hayes Heathrow**

Enjoy England   **Budget**   362 Uxbridge Road, Hayes, London UB4 0HF
accessible rooms: 5   t 0870 197 7132
premierinn.com

Access: ⌂ ✈ 🦽 ♿ 👤 🧍 ♈   General: P♿

UB6 - Greenford | **Premier Inn - London Greenford**

Enjoy England   **Budget**   Western Avenue, Greenford, London UB6 8TE
accessible rooms: 2   t 0870 197 7119
premierinn.com

Access: ⌂ ✈ 🦽 ♿ 👤 🧍 ♈   General: P♿

UB7 - West Drayton | **Crowne Plaza London Heathrow**

AA   ★★★★   Stockley Road, West Drayton, London UB7 9NA
accessible rooms: 8   t 0800 405 060
crowneplaza.co.uk

Access: 🅷 ⌂ ✈ 🦽 ♿ 👤 🧍 ♈   General: 🛗 P♿

UB7 - West Drayton | **Holiday Inn London Heathrow**

AA   ★★★★   Bath Road, Corner of Sipson Way, Hillingdon, London UB7 0DP
accessible rooms: 8   t 0800 405 060
holiday-inn.co.uk

Access: ✈ 🦽 ♿ 👤 🧍 ♈ 👁   General: 🛗 P♿   Room: 🧹

UB7 - West Drayton | **Holiday Inn London Heathrow M4**

accessible rooms: 9   Sipson Way, Bath Road, Hillingdon, London UB7 0JU
t 0800 405 060
holiday-inn.co.uk

Access: ⌂ ✈ 🦽 ♿ ♿ 👤 ♈   General: 🛗 P♿

UB7 - West Drayton | **Novotel London Heathrow**

AA   ★★★   Cherry Lane, West Drayton, Hillingdon, London UB7 9HB
accessible rooms: 5   t 01895 431431
novotel.com

Access: ⌂ ✈ 🦽 ♿ ♿ 👤 🧍 ♈ 👁   General: 🛗 P♿

Fish & Chips © Britainonview

Where to eat

This selection of restaurants, cafes, pubs and bars has been inspected by DisabledGo and assessed in detail for accessibility. You can find more detail on their website **www.disabledgo.com**

Here you can either filter the establishments by your specific requirements or you can click on an access guide which will give you an impressive level of detail and, often, photographs.

The restaurants are arranged by postcode in Inner London and then alphabetically within each postcode. The area names appear alongside the postcode (e.g WC1 Bloomsbury). Restaurants in Outer London are arranged by areas starting with the North then clockwise East, South and West) and by postcode within these areas.

Gourmet food at Fables © Britainonview

Bella Pasta at Leicester Square © Britainonview/Jasmine Teer

© Britainonview/Jason Knott

Key to symbols

The symbols have been designed in consultation with disabled people and represent important information that disabled people have told us would be good to find out at a glance. All the venues visited by our surveyors are given symbols; you can narrow your search by filtering your results using the symbols at the top of the results pages.

Access

  Accessible to wheelchair user

  Wheelchair user with assistance

  Mobility Impaired Walker

  Seat Available

WC WC Standard

@ FAX Contacting the venue

  Home Service

P ★★★ Car Parking at Venue

P ★★ Blue Badge Parking Available

P ★ Public Car Park (200m approx)

  Adapted Accommodation

  Sign Language used

  Disability Awareness Training

abc Large print information

  Braille information

  Assistance dogs welcome

  Designated wheelchair accessible public toilet

  Hearing facilities

  Adapted Changing Rooms

Fine Dining in the Capital

Galvin La Chapelle

London has a marvellous selection of top restaurants – here are a few you might like to try for a special meal. We understand that these restaurants are wheelchair friendly, though they have not been independently audited. Please try to book well in advance, and note your requirements when you book.

Galvin La Chapelle

35 Spital Square, London E1 6DY
t: 020 7299 0400
web: www.galvinrestaurants.com
Smart French bistro cuisine, in the trendy Spitalfields district. Wheelchair entrance via the adjoining Galvin Café de Luxe (also worth a visit!). Level access from there into main restaurant.

High Timber Restaurant

8 High Timber Street, London EC4V 3PA
t: 020 7248 1777
web: www.hightimber.com
Featuring hearty food and Cape wines from South Africa, this is a new restaurant close to St Paul's, with views across the Thames. There is lift access from the Millennium Bridge. Level access into the restaurant.

J Sheekey

28 – 32 St Martin's Court, London WC2N 4AL
t: 020 7240 2565
web: www.j-sheeky.co.uk
A fish restaurant and oyster bar in the heart of London's Theatreland. Offers quiet and cosy rooms. Booking essential.

Lutyens Restaurant

Latium Restaurant

21 Berners Street, London W1 3LP
t: 020 7323 9123
web: www.latiumrestaurant.com
Charming Italian restaurant in Fitzrovia which specialises in exceptional ravioli. Level access throughout.

Lutyens Restaurant

85 Fleet Street, London EC4Y 1AE
t: 020 7583 8385
web: www.lutyens-restaurant.com
Named London's Best New Restaurant in 2009 by www.squaremeal.com. French brasserie classics in the splendidly converted former Reuters Building in Fleet Street. Wheelchair access via side entrance (doorman will direct you)

Maze

10-13 Grosvenor Square London W1K 6JP
t: 020 7107 0000
web: www.gordonramsey.com/maze
Stylish, contemporary West End restaurant with one Michelin star, owned by Gordon Ramsey. Located on ground floor of the Marriott Grosvenor Square hotel, and wheelchair entrance is via the main hotel entrance.

Noura Belgravia

16 Hobart Place, London SW1W 0HH
t: 020 7235 9444
web: www.noura.co.uk
A Lebanese restaurant with superior hot and cold mezze, near Victoria Station. Adventurous vegetarian menu also. Level access from the street.

Plateau Restaurant

4th Floor, Canada Place, Canary Wharf London E14 5ER
t: 020 7715 7100
web: www.danddlondon.com/restaurants/plateau
A futuristic restaurant with dramatic views across the rooftops, Plateau offers bold flavour combinations. Fully accessible with lifts from the Canary Wharf shopping centre, blue badge parking.

Roast

Floral Hall, Stoney Street, London SE1 1TL
t: 0845 034 7300
web: www.roast-restaurant.com
Champions of seasonal, artisan British food. Located above the bustle of Borough Market in Southwark, accessible by lift.

Scott's

20 Mount Street, London W1K 2HE
t: 020 7495 7309
web: www.scotts-restaurant.com
A classic seafood restaurant in Mayfair, with level access from the street. Vegetarians, meat-lovers and special diets also catered for.

Roast

Map of Postcodes

This map of London has been divided in postcode areas (using the first part of the postcode). The different regions indicate broad geographic areas – North, East, South East, South West, West and North West. The two central areas – WC (West Central) and EC (East Central) just north of the river form the centre and busiest area of the capital. The areas outside the map are for reference to general location; all are within the Greater London boundaries.

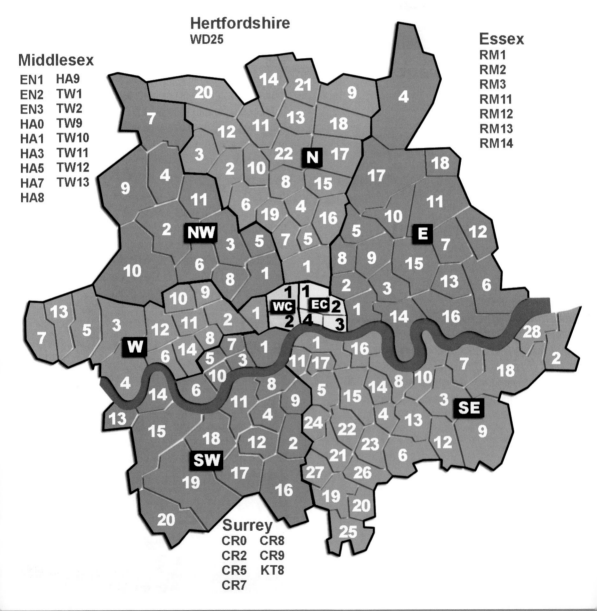

Hertfordshire
WD25

Middlesex

EN1	HA9
EN2	TW1
EN3	TW2
HA0	TW9
HA1	TW10
HA3	TW11
HA5	TW12
HA7	TW13
HA8	

Essex
RM1
RM2
RM3
RM11
RM12
RM13
RM14

Surrey

CR0	CR8
CR2	CR9
CR5	KT8
CR7	

SW1 - Chelsea | Bamford & Sons

31 Sloane Square, London SW1W 8AQ
t 020 7881 8010
bamfordandsons.com

General: 🐕 FÅX 🦽 🏠 🧍 👤 WC ♿ 👥

SW1 - Chelsea | Botanist

7 Sloane Square, London SW1W 8EE
t 020 7730 0077 e reservations@thebotanistonsloanesquare.com
thebotanistonsloanesquare.com

General: 🐕 FÅX 🧍 👤 👥 P

SW1 - Chelsea | Oriel

51 Sloane Square, London SW1W 8AX
t 0871 332 7929
tragus.com

General: 🐕 🦽 🧍 👤 ♿ .: abc

SW1 - Chelsea | Peter Jones

Sloane Square, London SW1W 8EL
t 020 7730 3434 e customer_sevice@peterjones.co.uk
peterjones.co.uk

General: 🐕 FÅX 🦽 🏠 🧍 👤 WC ♿ 👥 .: abc 👂 ♿

SW3 - Chelsea | Ask

300 Kings Road, London SW3 5UH
t 020 7349 9123
askrestaurants.com/

General: 🐕 🦽 🧍 👤 WC 👥

SW3 - Chelsea | Beaufort House

354 Kings Road, London SW3 5UZ
t 020 7352 2828 e joel@bhchelsea.com
chelseavenues.com

General: 🐕 FÅX 🧍 👤 ♿ 👥

SW3 - Chelsea | Big Easy

332-334 Kings Road, Chelsea, London SW3 5UR
t 0207 73524071 e enquiries@bigeasy.uk.com
bigeasy.uk.com

General: 🐕 FÅX 🧍 👤 ♿

SW3 - Chelsea | Bluebird Restaurant & Dining Rooms

350 Kings Road, Chelsea, London SW3 5UU
t 020 7559 1000 e enquiries@bluebird-store.co.uk
bluebird-restaurants.com

General: 🐕 🦽 🧍 👤 WC ♿ 👥

SW3 - Chelsea | Chelsea Potter

119 Kings Road, London SW3 4PL
t 020 7352 9479

General: ⚐ 🧍 ♿

SW3 - Chelsea | Henry J. Bean's

195-197 Kings Road, London SW3 5ED
t 020 7352 9255
henryjbeans.co.uk

General: ⚐ 🧍 ♿

SW3 - Chelsea | Kings Road Steak House And Grill

386 Kings Road, London SW3 5UZ
t 020 7351 9997 e info@kingsroadsteakhouseandgrill.com
kingsroadsteakhouseandgrill.com

General: ⚐ FAX 🧍 ♿ 🚶♿

SW3 - Chelsea | Lucio

257-259 Fulham Road, London SW3 6HY
t 020 7823 3007
luciorestaurant.com

General: ⚐ FAX 🦻 🧍 ♿ 🚶♿

SW3 - Chelsea | Manicomio

83-85 Duke of York Square, King's Road, London SW3 4LY
t 020 7730 3366
manicomio.co.uk

General: ⚐ FAX 🦻 🧍 ♿ ♿wc 🚶♿

SW3 - Chelsea | My Old Dutch

221 Kings Road, London SW3 5EJ
t 020 7376 5650

General: ⚐ 🧍 ♿ 🚶♿

SW3 - Chelsea | Patisserie Valerie

81 Duke of York Square, London SW3 4LY
t 020 7730 7094

General: ⚐ FAX 🦻 ♿

SW3 - Chelsea | Ranoush Juice

338 Kings Road, London SW3 5UR
t 0207 520044
maroush.com

General: ⚐ 🧍 ♿

SW3 - Chelsea | Toms Kitchen

27 Cale Street, London SW3 3QP
t 020 7349 0202 e info@tomskitchen.co.uk
tomskitchen.co.uk

General:

SW3 - Knightsbridge | Brompton Bar & Grill

243 Brompton Road, London SW3 2EP
t 020 7589 8005 e info@bromptonbarandgrill.com
bromptonbarandgrill.com

General:

SW3 - Knightsbridge | Brompton Quarter Cafe

223-225 Brompton Road, Knightsbridge, London SW3 2EJ
t 020 7225 2107 e info@bqcafe.com

General:

SW3 - Knightsbridge | McDonald's

177 Brompton Road, Knightsbridge, London SW3 1NF
t 020 7584 5096
mcdonalds.co.uk

General:

SW3 - Knightsbridge | Richoux

86 Brompton Road, Knightsbridge, London SW3 1ER
t 020 7584 8300 e knightsbridge@richoux.co.uk

General:

SW5 - Earl's Court | Blackbird

209 Earls Court Road, London SW5 9AN
t 020 7835 1855

General:

SW5 - Earl's Court | Burger King

250 Earls Court Road, London SW5 9AD
t 020 7370 2086
burgerking.co.uk

General:

SW5 - Earl's Court | Dragon Palace

207 Earls Court Road, London SW5 9AN
t 020 7370 1461
thedragonpalace.com

General:

SW5 - Earl's Court | **McDonald's**

208 Earls Court Road, London SW5 9QB
t 020 7373 2355

mcdonalds.co.uk

General: 🐕 🦮 🚶 ♿ WC ♿ .: abc

SW5 - Earl's Court | **Nando's**

204 Earls Court Road, London SW5 0AA
t 020 7259 2544 e enquiries@nandos.co.uk

nandos.co.uk

General: 🐕 FAX 🦮 🚶 ♿ ♿

SW7 - South Kensington | **Abbaye**

102 Old Brompton Road, London SW7 3RD
t 020 7373 2403

tragusholdings.com

General: 🐕 🦮 🚶 ♿ WC ♿

SW7 - South Kensington | **Ask**

23-24 Gloucester Arcade, Gloucester Road, London SW7 4SF
t 020 7835 0840

askrestaurants.com

General: 🐕 🦮 🚶 ♿ WC ♿

SW7 - South Kensington | **Beirut Express**

65 Old Brompton Street, London SW7 3JS
t 020 7591 0123

maroush.com

General: 🐕 🚶 ♿ ♿

SW7 - South Kensington | **Black And Blue**

105 Gloucester Road, London SW7 4SS
t 020 7244 7666

blackandbluerestaurant.com

General: 🐕 ♿

SW7 - South Kensington | **Burger King**

85 Gloucester Road, Kensington, London SW7 4SS
t 020 7370 2447

burgerking.co.uk

General: 🐕 FAX 🦮 🚶 ♿ WC ♿ ♿ .: abc

SW7 - South Kensington | **Garfunkel's**

Unit 25-26 Gloucester Arcade, Gloucester Road, London SW7 4SF
t 020 7835 1064

garfunkels.co.uk

General: 🐕 🦮 🚶 ♿ WC ♿ .: abc

SW7 - South Kensington | **Gloucester Arms**

34 Gloucester Road, London SW7 4RB
t 020 7584 0020

General: 🐕‍🦺 🦮 🧍 ♿

SW7 - South Kensington | **Green Door Steakhouse**

152 Gloucester Road, London SW7 4QH
t 020 7373 2010
greendoorsteakhouse.co.uk

General: 🐕‍🦺 🧍 ♿ wc ♿

SW7 - South Kensington | **Hereford Arms**

127 Gloucester Road, London SW7 4TE
t 020 7370 4988

General: 🐕‍🦺 🧍 ♿ wc ♿

SW7 - South Kensington | **Keiko Sushi**

7a Harrington Road, London SW7 3ES
t 020 7591 0606

General: 🐕‍🦺 @FAX 🏠 🧍 ♿ ♿

SW7 - South Kensington | **Le Pain Quotidien**

15-17 Exhibition Road, London SW7 2HE
t 7931568521 e exhibitionroad@lpquk.biz
lepainquotidien.co.uk

General: 🐕‍🦺 @FAX 🦮 🧍 ♿ ♿wc

SW7 - South Kensington | **Little India**

32 Gloucester Road, London SW7 4RB
t 020 7584 3476 e littleindia@btconnect.com

General: 🐕‍🦺 @FAX ♿

SW7 - South Kensington | **Med Kitchen**

25-35 Gloucester Road, London SW7 4PL
t 020 7589 1383 e general@medkitchen.co.uk
medkitchen.co.uk

General: 🐕‍🦺 @FAX 🦮 🧍 ♿ wc

SW7 - South Kensington | **Oddono's Gelati Italiani**

14 Bute Street, London SW7 3EX
t 020 7052 0732

General: 🐕‍🦺 @FAX 🏠 🧍 ♿ ♿

SW7 - South Kensington | **Pasha Lounge And Restaurant**

1 Gloucester Road, London SW7 4PP
t 020 7589 7969
pasha-restaurant.co.uk

General: 🐕 🛵 ♿

SW7 - South Kensington | **Perfect Pizza**

12 Bute Street, London SW7 3EX
t 020 7823 9292
perfectpizza.co.uk

General: 🐕 FAX 🏠 ♿ ♿ ♿

SW7 - South Kensington | **Rocca**

73 Old Brompton Road, London SW7 3JS
t 020 7225 3413 e rocca@roccarestaurants.com
roccarestaurants.com

General: 🐕 FAX ♿ ♿ ♿

W8 - Kensington | **Arcadia Restaurant**

33 Kensington High Street, Kensington Court, London W8 5EB
t 020 7937 4294

General: 🐕 FAX ♿ ♿ ♿

W8 - Kensington | **Archangel**

11-13 Kensington High Street, Kensington, London W8 5NP
t 020 7938 4137 e mark@baronbars.com
archangelw8.com

General: 🐕 FAX ♿ ♿

W8 - Kensington | **Ask**

222 Kensington High Street, London W8 7RG
t 020 7937 5540
askrestaurants.com

General: 🐕 🛵 ♿

W8 - Kensington | **Balans**

187 Kensington High Street, Kensington, London W8 6SH
t 020 7376 0115 e pradybalan@balans.co.uk
balans.co.uk

General: 🐕 FAX ♿ ♿ ♿ abc

W8 - Kensington | **Black & Blue**

215-217 Kensington Church Street, London W8 7LX
t 020 7727 0004
blackandbluerestaurants.com

General: 🐕 ♿ ♿ WC ♿ ♿

W8 - Kensington | **Cafe Rouge**

2 Lancer Square, Kensington, London W8 4EH
t 020 7938 4200
caferouge.co.uk

General: 🐕 🦮 👤 ♿ wc ♿ ♿

W8 - Kensington | **Caffe Uno**

9 Kensington High Street, Kensington, London W8 5NP
t 020 7937 8961   e roger.lord@caffeuno.co.uk
caffeuno.co.uk

General: 🐕 FAX ♿

W8 - Kensington | **Fouberts**

17 Kensington High Street, Kensington, London W8 5NP
t 020 7937 2762

General: 🐕 👤 ♿ ♿

W8 - Kensington | **Giraffe**

7 Kensington High Street, Kensington, London W8 5NP
t 020 7938 1221   e smiles@giraffe.net
giraffe.net

General: 🐕 FAX 🦮 👤 ♿ wc ♿

W8 - Kensington | **Il Portico**

277 Kensington High Street, Kensington, London W8 6NA
t 020 7602 6262

General: 👤 ♿ ♿

W8 - Kensington | **Kensington Place**

201-209 Kensington Church Street, London W8 7LX
t 020 7727 3184   e kpr_res_adm@danddlondon.com
kensingtonplace-restaurant.co.uk

General: 🐕 FAX 🦮 👤 ♿ wc ♿

W8 - Kensington | **Kensington Wine Rooms**

127-129 Kensington Church Street, London W8 7LP
t 020 7727 8142   e richard@greatwinesbytheglass.com
greatwinesbytheglass.com

General: 🐕 FAX 👤 ♿ wc ♿ ♿

W8 - Kensington | **Pizza Hut**

2 Kensington Church Street, London W8 4EP
t 020 7376 1800
pizzahut.co.uk

General: 🐕 🦮 👤 ♿ wc ♿ .: abc

W8 - Kensington | **Prezzo**

35a Kensington High Street, Kensington, London W8 5BA
t 020 7937 2800
prezzoplc.co.uk

General: 🐕 ♿ ⚕ ⚕ ⚕

W8 - Kensington | **Ranoush Juice**

86 Kensington High Street, Kensington, London W8 4SG
t 020 7938 2234 e mail@maroush.com
maroush.com

General: FAX ⚕ ⚕

W8 - Kensington | **Wagamama**

26 Kensington High Street, Kensington, London W8 4PF
t 020 7376 1717
wagamama.com

General: 🐕 ⚕ ⚕ WC ♿ ⚕ ?

W8 - Kensington | **Zaika**

1 Kensington High Street, Kensington, London W8 5NP
t 020 7795 6533 e info@zaika-restaurant.co.uk
zaika-restaurant.co.uk

General: 🐕 FAX ⚕ ⚕ ⚕

EC1 - Clerkenwell | **McDonald's**

6-7 High Holborn, Holborn Circus, London EC1N 2LL
t 020 7831 4202
mcdonalds.co.uk

General: 🐕 FAX ⚕ ⚕ WC ♿ ⚕ .:

EC1 - Clerkenwell | **Sedap**

102 Old Street, London EC1V 9AY
t 020 7490 0200 e info@sedap.co.uk
sedap.co.uk

General: 🐕 FAX ⚕ ⚕ ⚕

EC1 - Islington | **Akiiki**

364 Goswell Road, Islington, London EC1V 7JL
e balaus@overlinebroadband.com

General: 🐕 FAX ⚕ P★★

EC1 - Islington | **Banana Tree Canteen**

412-416 St John Street, London EC1V 4NJ
t 020 7278 7565 e islington@banana-tree.co.uk

General: 🐕 FAX ⚕ ⚕ WC ♿ ⚕

EC2 - City | All Bar One

127 Finsbury Pavement, London EC2A 1NS
t 020 7256 7577
allbarone.co.uk

General: 🐕 🚶 ♿ WC ♿ ⚲

EC2 - City | Barbican Centre

Silk Street, London EC2Y 8DS
t 020 7638 4141 e info@barbican.org.uk
barbican.org.uk

General: 🐕 FAX ♿ 🚶 ♿ WC ♿ ♿ ⚬ ⚲

EC2 - City | Browns Bar And Brasserie

8 Old Jewry, London EC2R 8DN
t 020 7606 6677
browns-restaurants.com

General: 🐕 FAX ♿ 🚶 ♿ WC ♿ ♿

EC2 - City | Burger King

City Food Court, Liverpool Street Station, London EC2M 7PD
t 020 7920 9664
burgerking.co.uk

General: 🐕 ♿ 🚶 ♿ ♿ ♿

EC2 - City | Corney And Barrow

1 Ropemaker Street, London EC2Y 9HT
t 020 7382 0606 e citypoint@winebar-corbar.co.uk
corney-barrow.co.uk

General: 🐕 FAX ♿ 🚶 ♿ WC ♿ ♿ abc

EC2 - City | Cuban

City Point, 1 Ropemaker Street, London EC2Y 9AW
t 020 7256 2202
thecuban.co.uk

General: 🐕 🚶 ♿ WC ♿ ♿

EC2 - City | Ekachai

9-10 The Arcade, Liverpool Street, London EC2M 7PN
t 020 7626 1155 e city@ekachai.net
ekachai.net

General: 🐕 FAX ♿

EC2 - City | Gaucho

5 Finsbury Avenue, London EC2M 1PG
t 020 7256 6877 e broadgate@gaucho-grill.com
gauchorestaurants.co.uk

General: 🐕 FAX ♿ 🚶 ♿ WC ♿ ♿

EC2 - City | Globe

83 Moorgate, London EC2M 6SA
t 020 7374 2915

General: 🐕 ♿

EC2 - City | Gow's Restaurant And Oyster Bar

81-82 Old Broad Street, London EC2M 1PR
t 020 7920 9645 e gows@ballsbrothers.co.uk
ballbrothers.co.uk

General: 🐕 FAX 📶 👤 ♿ WC ♿ 👥 abc

EC2 - City | Green Man (JD Wetherspoon)

1 Poultry, Bank Station, London EC2R 8EJ
t 020 7248 3529
jdwetherspoon.co.uk

General: 🐕 📶 👤 ♿ WC ♿ 👥

EC2 - City | La Tasca

15-17 Eldon Street, Broadgate, London EC2M 7LA
t 020 7256 2381 e broadgate@latasca.co.uk
latasca.co.uk

General: 🐕 FAX 📶 👤 ♿ WC ♿ 👥 🎧

EC2 - City | McDonald's

25 The Concourse, Liverpool Street Station, London EC2M 7PY
t 020 7377 9562
mcdonalds.co.uk

General: 🐕 📶 👤 ♿ WC ♿ 👥

EC2 - City | Pitcher & Piano

200 Bishopsgate, London EC2M 4NR
t 020 7929 5914 e PandPBishopsgate@pitcherandpiano.com
pitcherandpiano.com

General: 🐕 FAX 👤 ♿ WC ♿ 👥

EC2 - City | Pizza Express

232 Bishopsgate, London EC2M 4QD
t 020 7247 2838
pizzaexpress.com

General: 🐕 FAX 👤 ♿ WC ♿ 👥 .:

EC2 - City | Rack And Tenter

Tenter House, 45 Moorfields, London EC2Y 9AE
t 020 7628 3675

General: 🐕 👤 ♿ WC ♿ 👥

EC2 - City | Wagamama

1 Ropemaker Street, London EC2Y 9AW
t 020 7588 2688
wagamama.com

General: 🐕 FAX 🐕 🧍 👤 wc ♿ 👥 .: abc 🎧

EC3 - Aldgate | Number 49

48-49 Aldgate High Street, London EC3N 1AL
t 020 7265 0975

General: 🐕 👤

EC3 - City | Pitcher & Piano

28 Cornhill, London EC3V 3ND
t 020 7929 3989 e PandPCornhill@pitcherandpiano.com
pitcherandpiano.com

General: 🐕 FAX 🐕 🧍 👤 👥

EC3 - City | Pizza Express

20-22 Leadenhall Market, London EC3V 1LR
t 020 7283 5113
pizzaexpress.com

General: 🐕 FAX 🐕 🧍 👤 wc 👥 .:

EC3 - City | Slug & Lettuce

25 St Mary Axe, London EC3A 8LL
t 020 7929 0245 e SlugandLettuce.StMaryAxe@laurelpubco.com
slugandlettuce.co.uk

General: 🐕 FAX 🐕 🧍 👤 wc 👥

EC4 - City | Cafe Rouge

Ludgate House, Limeburner Lane, London EC4M 7HY
t 020 7329 1234
caferouge.co.uk

General: 🐕 FAX 🐕 🧍 👤 ♿ 👥 .: abc

EC4 - City | Corney And Barrow

10 Paternoster Square, London EC4M 7DX
t 020 7618 9520 e paternoster.square@winebar-corbar.co.uk
corney-barrow.co.uk

General: 🐕 FAX 🐕 🧍 👤 wc ♿ 👥 abc

EC4 - City | Heeltap And Bumper

2-6 Cannon Street, London EC4M 6XX
t 020 7248 3371

General: 🐕 FAX 🧍 👤 wc 👥

EC4 - City | McDonald's

147 Cannon Street, London EC4N 5BP
t 020 7626 0827
mcdonalds.co.uk

General: 🐕 🧍 ♿ wc ♿

EC4 - City | Paternoster Chop House

Warwick Court, Paternoster Square, London EC4M 7DX
t 020 7029 9400
danddlondon.com

General: 🐕 FAX 🦽 🧍 ♿ wc ♿ ♿ abc

EC4 - City | Perc%nto

26 Ludgate Hill, London EC4M 7DR
t 020 7778 0010
etruscarestaurants.com

General: 🐕 FAX 🦽 🧍 ♿ ♿ ♿

EC4 - City | Pizza Express

7-9 St Bride Street, London EC4A 4AS
t 020 7583 5126
pizzaexpress.com

General: 🐕 FAX 🦽 🧍 ♿ wc ♿ .: 🎧

EC4 - City | Press House Wine Bar

1 St Brides Passage, London EC4Y 8EJ
t 020 7353 5059
presshousewinebars.co.uk

General: 🐕 FAX 🧍 ♿ wc ♿ ♿

EC4 - City | Punch Tavern

99 Fleet Street, London EC4Y 1DE
t 020 7353 6658 e john@punchtavern.com
punchtavern.com

General: 🐕 FAX 🧍 ♿ ♿

EC4 - City | Singapura

1-2 Lime Burner Lane, London EC4M 7HY
t 020 7329 1133 e john@singapuras.co.uk
singapuras.co.uk

General: 🐕 FAX 🧍 ♿ ♿ ♿

EC4 - City | Tao Restaurant And Bar

11-11a Bow Lane, London EC4M 9AL
t 020 7248 5833 e comments@etruscarestaurants.com
etruscarestaurants.com

General: 🐕 FAX 🧍 ♿ ♿

EC4 - City | Thai Square

1 Great St Thomas Apostle Street, London EC4V 2BH
t 020 7329 0001
thaisq.com

General: 🐕 FAX 🚶 ♿ WC 👨‍🦼

EC4 - City | Vivat Bacchus

47 Farringdon Street, London EC4A 4LL
t 020 7353 2648 e info@vivatbacchus.co.uk
vivatbachus.co.ok.

General: 🐕 FAX 🚶 ♿ WC 👨‍🦼 👨‍🦼

EC4 - City | Wagamama

4 Great St Thomas Apostle, Off Queen Victoria Street, London EC4V 2HE
t 020 7248 5766
wagamama.com

General: 🐕 🚲 🚶 ♿ WC 👨‍🦼 👨‍🦼 .: abc 🔔

EC4 - City | Ye Old Watling

29 Watling Street, London EC4M 9AL
t 020 7248 8935

General: 🐕 🚶 ♿ WC 👨‍🦼 👨‍🦼

N1 - Islington | Ah-So Japanese Teppanyaki Restaurant And Bar

206 Upper Street, Islington, London N1 1RQ
t 020 7704 1890 e enquiries@ah-soislington.co.uk

General: 🐕 FAX 🚲 🚶 ♿ WC 👨‍🦼

N1 - Islington | Almeida Restaurant

30 Almeida Street, London N1 1AD
t 020 7354 4777
almeida-restaurant.co.uk

General: 🐕 FAX 🚶 ♿ WC 👨‍🦼

N1 - Islington | Angel Mangal

139 Upper Street, London N1 1QP
t 020 7359 7777

General: 🐕 FAX 🚶 ♿ 👨‍🦼

N1 - Islington | Ask

Business Design Centre, 52 Upper Street, London N1 0PN
t 020 7226 8728
askcentral.co.uk

General: 🐕 🚲 🚶 ♿ WC 👨‍🦼 👨‍🦼 ♿

N1 - Islington | Barnsbury

209-211 Liverpool Road, Islington, London N1 1LX
t 020 7607 5519
thebarnsbury.co.uk

General: 🐕 FAX 🚶 👤 ♿

N1 - Islington | Bierodrome

173 Upper Street, London N1 1XS
t 020 7226 5835 e info@bierodrome-islington.co.uk
belgo-restaurants.co.uk

General: 🐕 FAX 👤

N1 - Islington | Browns

7-9 Islington Green, London N1 2XH
t 020 7226 2555
browns-restaurant.co.uk

General: 🐕 🚲 🚶 👤 WC ♿ 👥 .:

N1 - Islington | Carluccio's

305-307 Upper Street, London N1 2TU
t 020 7359 8167 e islington@carluccios.com
carluccios.com

General: 🐕 FAX 🚲 🚶 👤 WC 👥 ?

N1 - Islington | Cruse9

62-63 Haliford Street, Islington, London N1 3HF
t 020 7354 8099 e info@cruse9.com
cruse9.com

General: 🐕 FAX 🚶 👤 WC 👥

N1 - Islington | Cuba Libre

72 Upper Street, Islington, London N1 0NY
t 020 7354 9998 e info@cubalibrelondon.co.uk
cubalibrelondon.co.uk

General: 🐕 FAX 🚶 👤 👥 P

N1 - Islington | Driver

224 Wharfdale Road, London N1 9RY
t 020 7278 8827 e info@thedriverlondon.co.uk
thedriverlondon.co.uk

General: 🐕 FAX 🚲 🚶 👤 ♿

N1 - Islington | Elk In The Woods

39 Camden Passage, Islington, London N1 8EA
t 020 7226 3535 e info@the-elk-in-the-woods.co.uk
the-elk-in-the-woods.co.uk

General: 🐕 FAX 👤 P

N1 - Islington | **Firezza**

276 St. Pauls Road, Islington, London N1 2LH
t 020 7359 7400
firezza.co.uk

General: 🐕 📠 🚶 ♿ ♿

N1 - Islington | **Flaming Nora**

177 Upper Street, London N1 1RG
t 0845 835 6672
flamingnora.com

General: 🐕 📠 🚴 🚶 ♿ wc ♿ ♿

N1 - Islington | **Florence**

50 Florence Street, Islington, London N1 2DU
t 020 7354 5633

General: 🐕 🚶 ♿ ♿ ♿

N1 - Islington | **Frederick's Restaurant**

106 Islington High Street, Islington, London N1 8EG
t 020 7359 2888 e eat@fredericks.co.uk
fredericks.co.uk

General: 🐕 📠 🚶 ♿ ♿ 🅿

N1 - Islington | **Gallipoli Again**

120 Upper Street, London N1 1QP
t 020 7359 1578 e administratorcafegallipoli.com
gallipolicafe.com

General: 🐕 📠 🚴 🚶 ♿ ♿

N1 - Islington | **Giraffe**

29-31 Essex Road, London N1 2SA
t 020 7359 5999 e islington@giraffe.net
giraffe.net

General: 🐕 📠 🚶 ♿ wc ♿ ♿ abc

N1 - Islington | **Glassworks**

N1 Centre, Upper Street, London N1 0PS
t 020 7354 6100 e P4015@jdwetherspoon.co.uk
LloydsNo1.co.uk

General: 🐕 📠 🚶 ♿ wc ♿ ♿ abc

N1 - Islington | **Hamburger Union**

341 Upper Street, Islington, London N1 0PB
t 020 7359 4436 e upperstreet@restaurantdivision.co.uk
hamburgerunion.com

General: 🐕 📠 🚶 ♿ wc ♿ ♿ 🅿

N1 - Islington | **House**

63-69 Canonbury Road, Islington, London N1 2DG
t 020 7704 7410 e info@inthehouse.biz
inthehouse.biz

General:

N1 - Islington | **Jacko's**

202 Essex Road, Islington, London N1 3AP
t 020 7354 3955

General:

N1 - Islington | **La Porchetta**

141 Upper Street, London N1 1QY
t 020 7288 2488

General:

N1 - Islington | **La Tasca**

21 Essex Road, Islington, London N1 2SA
t 020 7226 3272 e islington@latasca.co.uk
latasca.co.uk

General:

N1 - Islington | **Living Room - Islington**

Suncourt House, 18-26 Essex Road, Islington, London N1 8LN
t 020 7288 9090 e islington@thelivingroom.co.uk
thelivingroom.co.uk

General:

N1 - Islington | **Maghreb Moroccan Restaurant**

189 Upper Street, Islington, London N1 1RG
t 020 7226 2305
maghrebrestaurant.co.uk

General:

N1 - Islington | **Masala Zone**

30 Upper Street, London N1 0NU
t 020 7359 3399 e info@realindianfood.com
realindianfood.com

General:

N1 - Islington | **McDonald's**

251-252 Upper Street, Islington, London N1 1RY
t 020 7354 4392 e 01134@uk.mcd.com
mcdonalds.co.uk

General:

N1 - Islington | **Med Kitchen**

334 Upper Street, London N1 0PB
t 020 7226 7916 e upper.n1@medkitchen.co.uk
medkitchen.co.uk

General: 🐕 @FAX 🧍 👤 🧑‍🦽 ⚡

N1 - Islington | **Metro Bar And Grill**

270 Upper Street, London N1 2UQ
t 020 7226 1118 e metrobargrill@gmail.com

General: 🐕 @FAX 🛁 🧍 👤 WC ♿ 🧑‍🦽

N1 - Islington | **Nando's**

323-324 Upper Street, London N1 2XQ
t 020 7288 0254
nandos.co.uk

General: 🐕 @FAX 🧍 👤 WC 🧑‍🦽 .: abc

N1 - Islington | **Pasha**

301 Upper Street, London N1 2TU
t 020 7226 1454 e pasharestaurant@yahoo.co.uk
pasharestaurant.co.uk

General: 🐕 @FAX 🧍 👤 abc

N1 - Islington | **Rajmoni**

279 Upper Street, Islington, London N1 2TZ
t 020 7354 1270
rajmoni-islington.co.uk

General: 👤

N1 - Islington | **Rodizio Rico**

77-78 Upper Street, Islington, London N1 0NU
t 020 7354 1076 e rodizion1@rodiziorico.com
rodiziorico.com

General: 🐕 @FAX 🧍 👤 WC ♿ 🧑‍🦽 ⚡

N1 - Islington | **Say Pasta**

117 Upper Street, Islington, London N1 1RG
t 020 7226 3080 e info@saypasta.co.uk
saypasta.co.uk

General: 🐕 @FAX 🧍 👤 WC 🧑‍🦽

N1 - Islington | **Steam Passage**

44-46 Upper Street, London N1 0PN
t 020 7226 5882
thefourteenfourty.com

General: 🐕 @FAX 🧍 👤 WC 🧑‍🦽

N1 - Islington | **Strada**

105-106 Upper Street, London N1 1QN
t 020 7226 9742

strada.co.uk

General: 🐕 FAX 🚶 ♿

N1 - Islington | **Thai Square**

347 Upper Street, London N1 0PD
t 020 7704 2000 e thaisqangel@btconnect.com

thaisq.com

General: 🐕 FAX 🚶 ♿ WC ♿ abc

N1 - Islington | **Tortilla**

13 Islington High Street, London N1 9LQ
t 020 7833 3103

tortilla.co.uk

General: 🐕 🚶 ♿ WC ♿ ♿

N1 - Islington | **Vineyard**

179 Upper Street, Islington, London N1 1RG
t 020 7226 6276 e vineyard.islington@barracudagroup.com

barracudagroup.com

General: 🐕 FAX 🚶 ♿ WC ♿ ♿ abc

N1 - Islington | **Wagamama**

N1 Centre, Upper Street, London N1 0P
t 020 7226 2664 e islington@wagamama.com

wagamama.com

General: 🐕 FAX 🐾 🚶 ♿ WC ♿ ♿ .: abc ♪

N1 - Islington | **Yo! Sushi**

N1 Centre, 39 Parkfield Place, Islington, London N1 0PS
t 020 7359 3502 e yo.islington@yosushi.co.uk

yosushi.com

General: 🐕 FAX 🚶 ♿ WC ♿ ♿

N4 - Finsbury Park | **Nando's**

106 Stroud Green Road, London N4 3EN
t 020 7263 7447

nandos.co.uk

General: 🐕 🚶 ♿ WC ♿ .: abc

N5 - Highbury | **Junction**

2A Corsica Street, London N5 1JJ
t 020 7226 1026 e junction@bpubsltd.co.uk

orchid.co.uk

General: 🐕 FAX ♿

N5 - Highbury | **La Pasta Italiano**

17-19 Highbury Corner, London N5 1RA
t 020 7609 6792

General: ✂ FAX 👤 ♿ ♿

N7 - Holloway | **Millennium Cafe Restaurant & Bar**

500 Holloway Road, London N7 6JA
t 020 7263 8230

General: ✂ 🐾 ♿ ♿ WC P

N7 - Holloway | **Morgan M**

489 Liverpool Road, Holloway, London N7 8NS
t 020 7609 3560
morganm.com

General: 👤 ♿ ♿

N7 - Holloway | **Woodstore Bar & Grill**

North Road, London N7 9EF
t 020 7700 1858 e info@woodstorebarandgrill.com
woodstorebarandgrill.com

General: ✂ FAX 👤 ♿ WC ♿ ♿

N9 - Lower Edmonton | **Cart Overthrown**

Montagu Road, Lower Edmonton, Middlesex N9 0ER
t 020 8803 7658 e 0242@greeneking.co.uk
hungryhorse.co.uk

General: ✂ FAX 👤 ♿ WC ♿ ♿ P

N9 - Lower Edmonton | **Kimiz Ocakbasi & Barbeque Restaurant**

325 Fore Street, Edmonton, London N9 0PD
t 020 8803 6060

General: ✂ 🐾 🏠 👤 ♿ WC ♿ ♿

N9 - Lower Edmonton | **Stag And Hounds**

371 Bury Street West, Edmonton, London N9 9JW
t 020 8360 7412

General: ✂ 🐾 👤 ♿ WC ♿ ♿ P

N11 - New Southgate | **Harvester**

338 Bowes Road, New Southgate, London N11 1AN
t 020 8368 4456

General: ✂ 🐾 👤 ♿ WC ♿ ♿ .: P

N13 - Palmers Green | **Carucci**

222 Green Lanes, Palmers Green, London N13 5UD
t 020 8882 8833

General: 🐕 🚹 🚻 ♿ 👫

N14 - Southgate | **Cathay Chinese Restaurant**

23 Ashfield Parade, Southgate, London N14 5EH
t 020 8882 8989

General: 🐕 🚹 🚻 ♿ 👫

N14 - Southgate | **Chococcino**

6 Ashfield Parade, Southgate, London N14 5AB
t 020 8886 4070 e info@chococcino.com
chococcino.com

General: 🐕 @FAX 🚹 🚻 ♿ 👫

N14 - Southgate | **IOs**

22 The Broadway, The Bourne, Southgate, London N14 6PH
t 020 8447 8715 e info@iosloungebarandrestaurant.com

General: 🐕 🚲 🚹 🚻 wc 👫

N14 - Southgate | **Ye Olde Cherry Tree**

The Green, Southgate, London N14 6EN
t 020 8886 1808

General: 🐕 🚲 🚹 🚻 wc ♿ 👫 🅿

N18 - Upper Edmonton | **Istanbul**

11 Angel Corner Parade, Fore Street, Edmonton, London N18 2QH
t 020 8345 6270

General: 🏨 🚹 🚻 ♿

N19 - Archway | **Hamlet Cafe**

435-437 Hornsey Road, London N19 4DX
t 020 7281 9488

General: 🐕 🚲 🚹 🚻 wc ♿ 👫 🅿

N19 - Archway | **Mosaic**

24 Junction Road, London N19 5RE
t 020 7272 3509
mosaic-restaurant.co.uk

General: 🐕 🚲 🚹 🚻 👫

N19 - Archway | **Spaghi Pizzeria Ristorante**

6 Archway Close, London N19 3TD
t 020 7687 2066
spaghi.co.uk

General: 🐕 🦮 🚶 👩‍🦽 ♿

EN1 - Enfield | **Bar Ten**

8-10 Silver Street, Enfield, Middlesex EN1 3ED
t 020 8364 5005 e birol123abc@yahoo.co.uk
bar-ten.co.uk

General: 🐕 FAX 🚶 👩‍🦽 wc ♿ ♿

EN1 - Enfield | **Caffe Uno**

15 Silver Street, Enfield, Middlesex EN1 3EF
t 020 8367 0337
caffeuno.co.uk

General: 🐕 🦮 🚶 👩‍🦽 wc ♿

EN1 - Enfield | **Old Orleans**

202 Southbury Road, Enfield, Middlesex EN1 1UY
t 020 8366 2656 e oldorleans.enfield@intertainuk.com
oldorleans.com

General: 🐕 FAX 🦮 🚶 👩‍🦽 wc ♿ ♿ P★★★

EN1 - Enfield | **Outback Steak House**

Southbury Road, Enfield, Middlesex EN1 1YQ
t 020 8367 7881 e ob3@outbackpom.com
outbackpom.com

General: 🐕 FAX 🚶 👩‍🦽 wc ♿ ♿ P★★★

EN1 - Enfield | **T.G.I. Friday's**

Enfield Retail Park, Great Cambridge Road, Enfield, Middlesex EN1 3RZ
t 020 8363 5200

General: 🐕 FAX 🦮 🚶 👩‍🦽 wc ♿ ♿ 🔊 P★★★

EN2 - Enfield | **Burlingtons Fish Restaurant**

53 Windmill Hill, Enfield, Middlesex EN2 7AE
t 020 8366 5656 e burlingtonsfishrestaurant.co.uk
burlingtonsfishrestaurant.co.uk

General: 🍷♿ 🐕 🚶 👩‍🦽 ♿ ♿

EN2 - Enfield | **Nando's**

2 The Town, Enfield, Middlesex EN2 6LE
t 020 8366 2904

General: 🐕 FAX 🚶 👩‍🦽 .: abc

EN2 - Enfield | **Palmers**

45 Church Street, Enfield, Middlesex EN2 6AJ
t 020 8363 1411

General: 🐕 @FAX 🚶 ♿ ♿WC ♿

EN2 - Enfield | **Pearsons**

11-14 The Town, Enfield, Middlesex EN2 6LJ
t 020 8373 4200 e info@pearsons-enfield.co.uk
pearsons-enfield.co.uk

General: 🐕 @FAX 🚲 🏨 🚶 ♿ wc ♿WC ♿ 🕐 ♿

EN2 - Enfield | **Plough**

Cattlegate Road, Crews Hill, Enfield, Middlesex EN2 9DJ
t 020 8363 4386 e info@theploughcrewshill.com
theploughcrewshill.com

General: 🐕 @FAX 🚲 🚶 ♿ ♿WC ♿ P★★★

EN2 - Enfield | **Quixotes**

Windmill Hill, Enfield, Middlesex EN2 7AF
t 020 8367 9779

General: 🚲 🚶 ♿ ♿WC

EN2 - Enfield | **Ridgeway**

76 The Ridgeway, Enfield, Middlesex EN2 8JF
t 020 8363 7537

General: 🐕 🚲 🚶 ♿ wc ♿ P★★★

EN2 - Enfield | **Robin Hood**

240 The Ridgeway, Enfield, Middlesex EN2 8AP
t 0208 36333781

General: 🐕 🚲 🚶 ♿ wc ♿WC ♿ P★★★

EN2 - Enfield | **Rose And Crown**

185 Clay Hill, Enfield, Middlesex EN2 9AJ
t 020 8366 0864

General: 🐕 🚲 🚶 ♿ wc ♿ P★★★

EN2 - Enfield | **Toby Carvery Whitewebbs**

Whitewebbs Road, Crews Hill, Enfield, Middlesex EN2 9HH
t 020 8366 0542

General: 🐕 🚲 🚶 ♿ wc ♿WC ♿ P★★★

EN3 - Enfield | **Inn On The Park**

Innova Park, Corner of Solar Way, Enfield, Middlesex EN3 7XY
t 01992 718481

General: 🐕 🐾 🚶 ♿ wc 🚻 ♿ P

EN3 - Enfield | **Meze Bar & Restaurant**

500-504 Hertford Road, Enfield, Middlesex EN3 5SS
t 020 8804 9055 e sunsetgrill@hotmail.co.uk

General: 🐕 FAX 🚶 ♿ 🚻 ♿

EN4 - New Barnet | **Hunters Of Cockfosters**

12-13 Hedden Court Parade, Cockfosters Road, Barnet, London EN4 0DB
t 020 8449 5125
hunters-restaurant.co.uk

General: 🐕 FAX 🐾 🚶 ♿ 🚻 ♿

NW6 - Kilburn | **Brondes Age Bar Restaurant**

328 Kilburn High Road, Kilburn, London NW6 2QN
t 020 7624 9010 e brondesage@aol.com
brondesage.com

General: 🐕 FAX 🚶 ♿ ♿

NW6 - Kilburn | **Cock Tavern**

125 Kilburn High Road, Kilburn, London NW6 6JH
t 020 7624 1820
cocktavern.com

General: 🐕 ♿

NW6 - Kilburn | **Kilburn**

307-309 Kilburn High Road, Kilburn, London NW6 7JR
t 020 7372 7123 e kevin@roninnltd.com
thekilburn.co.uk

General: 🐕 FAX 🐾 🚶 ♿ 🚻 ♿

NW6 - Kilburn | **North London Tavern**

375 Kilburn High Road, Kilburn, London NW6 7QB
t 020 7625 6634 e northlondontavern@realpubs.co.uk

General: 🐕 FAX 🚶 ♿ wc 🚻 ♿

NW6 - Kilburn | **Small And Beautiful Restaurant**

351 Kilburn High Road, Kilburn, London NW6 7QB
t 020 7328 2637

General: 🐕 🚶 ♿ 🚻 ♿

NW9 - Colindale | **Asda**

Capitol Way, Edgware Road, Colindale, London NW9 0AS
t 020 8200 4833
asda.co.uk

General: 🐕 FAX 🦮 🏠 🚶 ♿ wc ♿ᵂᶜ ♿♿ ⏰ ♿ ⭐⭐⭐ ♿

NW9 - Kingsbury | **Blarney Stone**

Blackbird Hill, Kingsbury, Middlesex NW9 8RR
t 020 8205 9845

General: 🐕 🚶 ♿ wc ♿ᵂᶜ ♿♿ ⭐⭐⭐

NW10 - Harlesden | **One Stop Jerk Centre**

212 High Street, Harlesden, London NW10 4SY
t 020 8965 6556 **e** onestopcaribbien@aol.com
onestoprestaurant.co.uk

General: FAX 🚶 ♿ abc

HA0 - Wembley | **Black Horse**

Harrow Road, Wembley, Middlesex HA0 2QP
t 020 8385 2991
emberinns.co.uk

General: 🐕 🦮 🚶 ♿ wc ♿ᵂᶜ ♿♿ ⭐⭐⭐

HA0 - Wembley | **Bootsy Brogans**

89 East Lane, North Wembley, Middlesex HA0 3NJ
t 020 8904 8199 **e** bbwembley@glendola.co.uk
foundationgroup.co.uk

General: 🐕 FAX 🚶 ♿ ♿ ♿ᵂᶜ ♿♿ ⭐⭐⭐

HA0 - Wembley | **Dadima Vegetarian Restaurant**

228 Ealing Road, Alperton, Midllesex HA0 4QL
t 020 8902 1072

General: 🚶 ♿ ♿ᵂᶜ ♿♿

HA0 - Wembley | **Fusilier**

652 Harrow Road, Wembley, Middlesex HA0 2HA
t 020 8903 7863 **e** beerbarrellltd@hotmail.com

General: 🐕 FAX 🚶 ♿ wc ♿ᵂᶜ ♿♿ .: abc ⭐⭐⭐

HA0 - Wembley | **Heather Park**

Heather Park Drive, Wembley, London HA0 1SN
t 020 8795 5654

General: 🐕 🦮 ♿ ⭐⭐⭐

HA1 - Harrow | **Al Dente**

237 Station Road, Harrow, Middlesex HA1 2TB
t 020 8428 8866
aldenterestaurant.co.uk

General: 🐕 🕭 🚶 👤 WC ♿ 👥 🅿

HA1 - Harrow | **Ask**

Unit 28 St. George's Shopping & Leisure, St. Anns Road, Harrow, Middlesex HA1 1HS
t 020 8427 0982

General: 🐕 FAX 🕭 🚶 👤 WC ♿ 👥 abc ♿

HA1 - Harrow | **BHS**

St. Anns Shopping Centre, St. Anns Road, Harrow, Middlesex HA1 1JU
t 020 8427 9314

General: 🐕 🕭 🚶 👤 WC ♿ 👥

HA1 - Harrow | **Burger King**

321 Station Road, Harrow, Middlesex HA1 2AA
t 020 8861 3425 e harrow@sherrygold.co.uk

General: 🐕 FAX 🕭 🚶 👤 WC ♿ 👥

HA1 - Harrow | **Cumberland Hotel (Best Western)**

St. John's Road, Harrow, Middlesex HA1 2EF
t 020 8863 4111 e reservations@cumberlandhotel.co.uk
cumberlandhotel.co.uk

General: 🐕 FAX 🚶 👤 WC ♿ 👥 🅿★★★

HA1 - Harrow | **Freddy's Restaurant Bar & Grill**

190-194 Station Road, Harrow, Middlesex HA1 2RH
t 020 8424 8300 e contact@freddys.ltd.uk
freddys.ltd.uk

General: 🐕 FAX 🚶 👤 WC ♿ 👥 🅿

HA1 - Harrow | **Gaucho's**

86 High Street, Harrow On The Hill, Middlesex HA1 3LW
t 020 8423 3888

General: 🐕 FAX 🚶 👤 abc

HA1 - Harrow | **Harrow Crown Court**

Hailsham Drive, Harrow HA1 4TU
t 020 8424 2294
hmcourts-service.gov.uk

General: 🐕 FAX 🕭 🚶 👤 WC ♿ 👥 .: abc 🔊 🅿★★★

HA1 - Harrow | **Harrow Hotel**

12-22 Pinner Road, Harrow, Middlesex HA1 4HZ
t 020 8427 3435 e info@harrowhotel.co.uk
harrowhotel.co.uk

General: 🐕 @FAX 🧍 🦽 WC ♿WC ♿ P⋆⋆⋆ 🛏

HA1 - Harrow | **Incanto**

41 The High Street, Harrow on the Hill, Middlesex HA1 3HT
t 020 8426 6767 e mail@Incanto.co.uk
Incanto.co.uk

General: 🐕 @FAX 🚴 🧍 🦽 WC ♿

HA1 - Harrow | **Kebabland**

34-36 College Road, Harrow, Middlesex HA1 1BE
t 020 8424 9651

General: 🐕 @FAX 🧍 🦽 WC ♿WC ♿

HA1 - Harrow | **Kentucky Fried Chicken**

Unit 4-5 St. Anns Shopping Centre, Harrow, Middlesex HA1 1AR
t 020 8427 9045

General: 🐕 🧍 🦽 ♿ ♿

HA1 - Harrow | **Lahore Restaurant**

45 Station Road, Harrow, Middlesex HA1 2UA
t 020 8424 8422
indianrestaurant.com

General: 🏠 🦽 ♿WC

HA1 - Harrow | **Lontosa**

152 Station Road, Harrow, Middlesex HA1 2RH
t 020 8427 8926

General: 🐕 @FAX 🧍 🦽 ♿WC ♿

HA1 - Harrow | **Mario's Cafe**

63 Station Road, Harrow, Middlesex HA1 2TY
t 020 8863 4185

General: 🧍 🦽 ♿

HA1 - Harrow | **Mumbai Junction**

231 Watford Road, Harrow, Middlesex HA1 3TU
t 020 8904 2255
mumbaijunction.co.uk

General: 🐕 🧍 🦽 WC ♿WC ♿ P⋆⋆⋆

HA1 - Harrow | **Rising Sun**

Greenford Road, Sudbury Hill, Harrow, Middlesex HA1 3QP
t 020 8422 2575

General: 🧍 🛉 wc ♿ 🧑‍🦽 🅿★★★

HA1 - Harrow | **Royal Oak**

86 St. Anns Road, Harrow, Middlesex HA1 1JP
t 020 8427 0552

General: 🐕 FAX 🐾 🧍 🛉 wc 🧑‍🦽

HA1 - Harrow | **Sakonis**

5/8 Dominion Parade, Station Road, Harrow, Middlesex HA1 2TR
t 020 8863 3399

General: @FAX 🧍 🛉 wc ♿ 🧑‍🦽

HA1 - Harrow | **Sazio**

381 Station Road, Harrow, Middlesex HA1 2AW
t 020 8427 1555 e info@sazio.co.uk
sazio.co.uk

General: 🐕 @FAX 🧍 🛉 🅿

HA1 - Harrow | **St. Ann's Shopping Centre**

St. Ann's Road, Harrow, Middlesex HA1 1AR
t 020 8861 2242
stannsshopping.com

General: 🐕 🐾 🧍 🛉 wc ♿ 🧑‍🦽 abc 🛗 🅿★★★

HA1 - Harrow | **Veggie Inn**

123 Headstone Road, Harrow, Middlesex HA1 1PG
t 020 8863 6144
veggieinn.com

General: 🐕 🧍 🛉 ♿ 🧑‍🦽 🅿

HA1 - Harrow | **Yates's**

269-274 Station Road, Harrow, Middlesex HA1 2TB
t 020 8863 9470 e yates.harrow@townandcitypub.com
yatesbars.co.uk

General: 🐕 @FAX 🐾 🧍 🛉 wc ♿ 🧑‍🦽 .:

HA2 - Harrow | **Futana**

453 Alexandra Avenue, Rayners Lane, Middlesex HA2 9SE
t 020 8868 9085

General: 🐕 @FAX 🐾 🏠 🧍 🛉 🧑‍🦽

HA2 - Harrow | Golden Kitchen

48-50 Station Road, North Harrow, Middlesex HA2 7SE
t 020 8427 1446

General: 🐕 ⚡ 👤 ♿ ♿ ♿

HA2 - Harrow | Jaflong Restaurant

299 Northolt Road, South Harrow, Middlesex HA2 8JA
t 020 8864 7345 e salim_chowdhury315@hotmail.com

General: 🐕 FAX 🍴 👤 ♿ ♿ ♿

HA2 - Harrow | Matrix

Alexandra Avenue, South Harrow, Middlesex HA2 9DL
t 020 8422 2067

General: 🐕 👤 ♿ ♿ ♿ P★★★

HA2 - Harrow | Mediterranean Touch

248 Northolt Road, South Harrow, Middlesex HA2 8DU
t 020 8423 6101

General: 🏠 👤 ♿ ♿ ♿ abc

HA2 - Harrow | Papaya

15 Village Way East, Rayners Lane, Middlesex HA2 7LX
t 020 8866 5582
papaya-uk.com

General: 🐕 🏠 👤 WC ♿ ♿ abc P★

HA2 - Harrow | Rayners Tandoori

383 Alexandra Avenue, Rayners Lane, Middlesex HA2 9EF
t 020 8868 4317

General: FAX 👤 ♿ ♿ ♿

HA2 - Harrow | Royal Nepal

439 Alexandra Avenue, Rayners Lane, Middlesex HA2 9SE
t 020 8866 5988

General: 🐕 FAX 🏠 👤 ♿ ♿

HA2 - Harrow | Star

211 Northolt Road, South Harrow, Middlesex HA2 0LY
t 020 8422 0505

General: 🐕 🍴 👤 WC ♿ ♿

HA2 - Harrow | **Subway**

288 Northolt Road, South Harrow, Middlesex HA2 8EB
t 020 8423 1133
subway.com

General: 🐕 FAX 🐾 🧍 🦽 🧑‍🦼

HA3 - Harrow | **Chasing Dragon**

28 Headstone Drive, Wealdstone, Middlesex HA3 5QH
t 020 8863 8799

General: 🐕 📱 🧍 🦽 ♿ 🧑‍🦼 ⚲

HA3 - Harrow | **Fiddler's Restaurant**

221-227 High Road, Harrow Weald, Middlesex HA3 5EE
t 020 8863 6066 e info@fiddlers-restaurant.co.uk
fiddlers-restaurant.co.uk

General: 🐕 FAX 🧍 🦽 WC 🧑‍🦼 abc

HA3 - Harrow | **Leef Robinson VC**

Uxbridge Road, Harrow Weald, Middlesex HA3 6DL
t 020 8954 6781
whitbread.com

General: 🐕 FAX 🐾 🧍 🦽 WC ♿ 🧑‍🦼 .: abc) ★★★

HA3 - Harrow | **Meeting Palace**

34 High Street, Wealdstone, Middlesex HA3 7AB
t 020 8861 6363

General: 🐕 FAX 🐾 🧍 🦽 WC ♿ 🧑‍🦼 ⚲

HA3 - Harrow | **Miller & Carter**

Brockhurst Corner, Uxbridge Road, Harrow, Middlesex HA3 6DL
t 020 8954 6781
millerandcarter.co.uk

General: 🐕 🐾 🧍 🦽 WC ♿ 🧑‍🦼 ★★★

HA3 - Harrow | **Seven Balls**

Kenton Lane, Harrow Weald, Middlesex HA3 6AW
t 020 8954 4744

General: 🐕 🧍 🦽 ♿ 🧑‍🦼 ★★★

HA3 - Harrow | **Swadisht**

195 Streatfield Road, Kenton, Middlesex HA3 9DA
t 020 8905 0202

General: 🧍 🦽 WC ♿ 🧑‍🦼

HA3 - Harrow | **Three Wishes**

20 The Broadwalk, North Harrow, Middlesex HA3 6ED
t 020 8424 8336

General: 🐕 FAX 🧍 🦽 🚶♿ abc

HA5 - Pinner | **Ask**

246-248 Uxbridge Road, Hatch End, Middlesex HA5 4HS
t 020 8421 6789
askrestaurants.com/

General: 🐕 🕸 🧍 🦽 WC ♿ 🚶♿ ⚲

HA5 - Pinner | **Bacchus**

302 Uxbridge Road, Hatch End, Middlesex HA5 4HS
t 020 8428 4232

General: 🧍 🦽 ♿ 🚶♿ abc

HA5 - Pinner | **Brasserie Chez Gerrard**

15-17 High Street, Pinner, Middlesex HA5 5PJ
t 020 8429 3239
brasseriechezgerard.co.uk

General: 🐕 🕸 🧍 🦽 WC ♿ 🚶♿

HA5 - Pinner | **BRB The Victory**

6 High Street, Pinner, Middlesex HA5 5PW
t 020 8866 5757

General: 🐕 🧍 🦽 WC ♿ 🚶♿

HA5 - Pinner | **Cafe Cocoa**

207 Marsh Road, Pinner, Middlesex HA5 5NE
t 020 8429 8474

General: FAX 🕸 🏠 🧍 🦽 ♿ 🚶♿

HA5 - Pinner | **Caffe Uno**

15-17 High Street, Pinner, Middlesex HA5 5PJ
t 020 8429 3239
caffeuno.co.uk

General: 🐕 🕸 🧍 🦽 WC ♿ 🚶♿

HA5 - Pinner | **Fellini**

410 Uxbridge Road, Hatch End, Middlesex HA5 4HP
t 020 8421 3000
felliniwines.co.uk

General: 🐕 🦽 WC ♿

 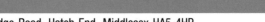

HA5 - Pinner | **Hatch End Tandoori**

282-284 Uxbridge Road, Hatch End, Middlesex HA5 4HS
t 020 8428 9781

General: 🐕 🦮 🏠 🏃 ♿ ⚥ 🅿️

HA5 - Pinner | **JD Wetherspoon - The Village Inn**

402 Rayners Lane, Pinner, Middlesex HA5 5DY
t 020 8868 8551
jdwetherspoon.co.uk

General: 🐕 🏃 ♿ wc ⚥ 🏃 .: 🅿️

HA5 - Pinner | **Moon And Sixpence**

250 Uxbridge Road, Hatch End, Middlesex HA5 4HS
t 020 8420 1074

General: 🐕 🦮 🏃 ♿ ⚥ 🏃 .:

HA5 - Pinner | **Prezzo**

36 High Street, Pinner, Middlesex HA5 5PW
t 020 8966 9916
prezzoplc.co.uk

General: 🐕 🦮 ♿ 🅿️

HA5 - Pinner | **Sakee**

173-175 Marsh Road, Pinner, Middlesex HA5 5PB
t 020 8868 9588

General: 📠 🏃 ♿ wc ⚥ 🏃

HA5 - Pinner | **Sazio**

302 Uxbridge Road, Hatch End, Middlesex HA5 4HR
t 020 8421 4455 e info@sazio.co.uk
sazio.co.uk

General: 🐕 📠 🦮 🏃 ♿ ⚥ 🏃 🅿️

HA5 - Pinner | **Sea Pebbles**

352 Uxbridge Road, Hatch End, Middlesex HA5 4HR
t 020 8428 0203

General: 🐕 🏃 ♿ wc ⚥ 🏃

HA5 - Pinner | **Titash**

52 Bridge Street, Pinner, Middlesex HA5 3JF
t 020 8866 1555

General: 🐕 🦮 🏠 🏃 ♿ ⚥ abc

HA7 - Stanmore | Apollonia

25-27 Church Road, Stanmore, Middlesex HA7 4AR
t 020 8954 5060 e info@apolloniarestaurant.co.uk
apolloniarestaurant.co.uk

General: 🐕 FAX 🧍 ♿ WC ♿ 👨‍🦽 P★★★

HA7 - Stanmore | Crazy Horse

43 Church Road, Stanmore, Middlesex HA7 4AA
t 020 8954 2666 e Info@crazyhorselondon.com

General: 🐕 FAX 🧍 ♿ WC 👨‍🦽 P★★★

HA7 - Stanmore | Jonathans

67 The Broadway, Stanmore, Middlesex HA7 4DJ
t 020 8416 0213
prezzoplc.co.uk

General: 🐕 🧍 ♿ WC ♿ 👨‍🦽

HA7 - Stanmore | Madisons Deli

11 Buckingham Parade, Stanmore, Middlesex HA7 4EB
t 020 8954 9998

General: 🐕 FAX ♿ WC ♿

HA7 - Stanmore | Man In The Moon

1 Buckingham Parade, Stanmore, Middlesex HA7 4EB
t 020 8954 6119
jdwetherspoon.co.uk

General: 🐕 🧍 ♿ WC ♿ 👨‍🦽 .:

HA7 - Stanmore | Memories Of India

12 Buckingham Parade, The Broadway, Stanmore, Middlesex HA7 4EB
t 020 8954 0967

General: 🐕 🏠 🧍 ♿ ♿ 👨‍🦽 P★★

HA7 - Stanmore | Overseas

397 Honeypot Lane, Stanmore, Middlesex HA7 1JJ
t 0208 2045637/ 2040666

General: 🐕 🏠 🧍 ♿ ♿ 👨‍🦽

HA8 - Edgware | Aviv Restaurant

87-89 High Street, Edgware, Middlesex HA8 7DB
t 020 8952 2484
avivrestaurant.com

General: 🐕 FAX ♿ ♿ abc

HA8 - Edgware | **B & K Salt Beef Restaurant**

11 Lanson House, Whitchurch Lane, Edgware, Middlesex HA8 6NL
t 020 8952 8204

General: 🐕 FAX 🛴 🧍 👤 👨‍🦽

HA8 - Edgware | **Malibu Club**

119 High Street, Edgware, Middlesex HA8 7DB
t 020 8905 6890 e malibuclub@aol.com

General: FAX 👤 abc ★★★

HA8 - Edgware | **Satyam Restaurant**

24 Queensbury Station Parade, Edgware, Middlesex HA8 5NR
t 020 8952 3947

General: 🏧 🧍 👤 ♿ 👨‍🦽

HA8 - Edgware | **Zan Zi Bar**

113 High Street, Edgware, Middlesex HA8 7DB
t 020 8952 2986

General: FAX 🛴 🧍 👤 wc 👨‍🦽 abc ★★★

HA9 - Wembley | **Allso Thai**

15 Empire Way, Wembley Park, Wembley, Middlesex HA9 0RQ
t 020 8795 4242

General: 🐕 🛴 🧍 👤 wc ♿ 👨‍🦽

HA9 - Wembley | **Arena Restaurant**

307 Harrow Road, Wembley, Middlesex HA9 6BD
t 020 8902 1849
arenarestaurant.co.uk

General: 🐕 FAX 🧍 👤 ♿ 👨‍🦽

HA9 - Wembley | **Burger King**

413 High Road, Wembley, Middlesex HA9 7AB
t 020 8903 6842
burgerking.co.uk

General: 🐕 🛴 🧍 👤 ♿ 👨‍🦽

HA9 - Wembley | **Ghurka Valley**

305 Harrow Road, Wembley, Middlesex HA9 6BD
t 020 8902 4039

General: 🐕 FAX 🧍 👤

HA9 - Wembley | McDonald's

126 Wembley Park Drive, Wembley Retail Park, Wembley, Middlesex HA9 8TS
t 020 8795 1961 e 0834@uk.mcd.com

mcdonalds.co.uk

General: 🦮 FAX ♿ ⚕ ♿ WC ♿ ♿ .: abc ♪ ♿

HA9 - Wembley | Moore Spice (1966)

Unit 2 Wembley Retail Park, Engineers Way, Wembley HA9 0ER
t 020 8795 1966

moorespice1966.co.uk/

General: FAX ⚕ ♿ WC ♿ ♿ ♿

HA9 - Wembley | Triangle Restaurant

8-9 Neeld Parade, Wembley, Middlesex HA9 6QU
t 020 8902 9720 e mail@thetrianglelondon.com

thetrianglelondon.com

General: 🦮 FAX ⚕ ♿ ♿ ♿

HA9 - Wembley | Wembley Tandoori Restaurant

133 Wembley Park Drive, Wembley, Middlesex HA9 8HQ
t 020 8902 2243

General: 🦮 FAX ⚕ ♿ ♿ ♿

WD24 - Watford | Frankie & Benny's

Woodside Leisure Park, Garston, Watford, Hertfordshire WD25 7JZ
t 01923 662690

frankieandbennys.com

General: 🦮 FAX ♿ ⚕ ♿ WC ♿ ♿ ♿

E1 - Aldgate | Indian Spice

152 Brick Lane, Aldgate East, London E1 6RU
t 020 7247 1012

city-spice.co.uk

General: FAX ♿ ⚕ ♿ ♿

E1 - Aldgate | Lane, The

12-20 Osborne Street, Aldgate East, London E1 6TE
t 020 7456 1067 e info@thelanebarandrestaurant.com

thelanebarandrestaurant.com

General: 🦮 FAX ⚕ WC ♿

E1 - Aldgate | Princess Of Prussia

15 Prescott Street, Tower Hill, London E1 8AZ
t 020 7702 0723 e princess-of-prussia@hotmail.co.uk

princess-of-prussia.com

General: 🦮 FAX ♿ ⚕ ♿ ♿ ♿

E1 - Aldgate | **Sonargaon**

32-38 Osbourne Street, Aldgate East, London E1 6DT
t 020 7377 8005
sonargaon.com

General: 🐾 FAX 👤 👥 WC 🧑‍🦽

E1 - Mile End | **2 Tasty**

226 Mile End Road, London E1 6PU
t 020 7791 2055

General: 🏧 👤 👥 ♿ 🧑‍🦽

E1 - Spitalfields | **Giraffe**

Unit 1 Crispin Place, Spitalfields, London E1 6DW
t 020 3116 2000 e spitalfields@giraffe.net
giraffe.net

General: 🐾 FAX 👤 👥 WC ♿ 🧑‍🦽

E1 - Spitalfields | **Nando's**

114-118 Commercial Street, Spitalfields, London E1 6NF
t 020 7650 7775
nandos.co.uk

General: 🐾 🚴 👤 👥 WC 🧑‍🦽 abc P★

E1 - Spitalfields | **Water Poet**

9-11 Folgate Street, Spitalfields, London E1 6BX
t 020 7426 0495

General: 🐾 👤 👥 🧑‍🦽 abc P★

E1 - Wapping | **Dickens Inn**

St. Katherine's Way, London E1W 1UH
t 020 7488 2208 e dickensinn@btinternet.com
dickensinn.co.uk

General: 🐾 FAX 🚴 👤 👥 WC 🧑‍🦽

E1 - Wapping | **Mala Indian Restaurant**

2 Marble Quay, St. Katherine's Dock, St. Katherines Way, London E1W 1UH
t 020 7480 6356
mala-restaurant.co.uk

General: FAX 👤 👥 WC ♿ 🧑‍🦽

E1 - Wapping | **Prospect Of Whitby**

57 Wapping Wall, Wapping, London E1W 3SH
t 020 7481 1095 e prospect.of.whitby8166@thespiritgroup.com
thespiritgroup.com

General: 🐾 FAX 🚴 👤 👥 WC ♿ 🧑‍🦽 .: abc

E1 - Whitechapel | **Aladin Restaurant**

132 Brick Lane, London E1 6RU
t 020 7247 8210
aladinbricklane.co.uk

General: FAX 🚶 ♿ 🚶♿ 🅿

E1 - Whitechapel | **Alishaan Restaurant**

30 Osborn Street, London E1 6TD
t 020 7392 2100

General: ♿ 🅿

E1 - Whitechapel | **All Star Lanes**

95 Brick Lane, London E1 6QL
t 0202 74229200 e bricklane@allstarlanes.co.uk
allstarlanes.co.uk

General: 🐕 FAX 🚶 ♿ WC ♿ 🚶♿ 🅿

E1 - Whitechapel | **Bar Gramaphone**

60-62 Commercial Street, London E1 6LT
t 020 7377 5332 e info@thegramaphone.co.uk
thegramaphone.co.uk

General: 🐕 FAX ♿ 🅿

E1 - Whitechapel | **Bengal Cusine**

12 Brick Lane, London E1 6RF
t 020 7377 8405

General: 🐕 🚶 ♿ 🚶♿ 🅿

E1 - Whitechapel | **Big Chill Bar**

91-94 Dray Walk, off Brick Lane, London E1 6QL
t 020 7792 9180 e sandra.a@bigchill.net
bigchill.net

General: 🐕 FAX 🛍 🚶 ♿ WC ♿ 🚶♿ abc 🅿

E1 - Whitechapel | **Brown Bear**

139 Leman Street, London E1 8EY
t 020 7481 3792 e thebrownbear@btconnect.com

General: 🐕 FAX 🛍 🚶 ♿ ♿ 🚶♿

E1 - Whitechapel | **Chillies**

76 Brick Lane, London E1 6RL
t 020 7247 7539

General: 🚶 ♿ 🅿

E1 - Whitechapel | **Chutneys**

90 Brick Lane, London E1 6RL
t 020 7247 9686 **e** info@chutneysbricklane.com
chutneysbricklane.com

General: 🐕 FAX 🧍 ♿ WC ♿ ♿ abc ★

E1 - Whitechapel | **Clifton**

1 Whitechapel Road, Whitechapel, London E1 6TY
t 020 7377 5533 **e** theclifton@aol.com
cliftonrestaurant.com

General: 🐕 FAX 🛴 🧍 ♿

E1 - Whitechapel | **Clipper**

104 Brick Lane, London E1 6RL
t 020 7377 0022 **e** turon.miah@hotmale.co.uk
bricklaneclipperrestaurant.co.uk

General: 🐕 FAX 🧍 ♿ ★

E1 - Whitechapel | **Gram Bagla**

68 Brick Lane, London E1 6RL
t 020 7377 6116

General: 🐕 🧍 ♿ ♿ ♿ ★

E1 - Whitechapel | **Herb And Spice Restaurant**

11a Whites Row, London E1 7NF
t 020 7247 4050

General: 🐕 FAX 🧍 ♿ WC ♿ ♿ ★

E1 - Whitechapel | **Hotel Ibis London City**

5 Commercial Street, London E1 6BF
t 020 7422 8400 **e** H5011@accor.com
ibishotel.com

General: 🐕 FAX 🛴 🧍 ♿ WC ♿ ♿ ★ 🍴 ♿ 🛏

E1 - Whitechapel | **Lanes Restaurant & Bar**

East India House, 109-117 Middlesex Street, London E1 7JF
t 020 7247 5050 **e** info@lanesrestaurant.co.uk
lanesrestaurant.co.uk

General: 🐕 FAX 🛴 🧍 ♿ WC ♿ ♿

E1 - Whitechapel | **La Taj**

96 Brick Lane, London E1 6RL
t 020 7247733 **e** info@letaj.co.uk
letaj.co.uk

General: 🐕 FAX 🧍 ♿ WC ♿ ♿ ★

E1 - Whitechapel | **McDonald's**

201-217 Commercial Road, Stepney, London E1 2BT
t 020 7790 8238 e 01127@uk.mcd.com
mcdonalds.co.uk

General: 🐕 FAX 🦮 🚶 👤 WC ♿ 🚻 abc P★★★

E1 - Whitechapel | **Moon Light**

8 Brick Lane, London E1 6RF
t 020 7247 6606 e nurul2@hotmale.co.uk

General: 🐕 FAX 🚶 👤 ♿ 🚻 P★

E1 - Whitechapel | **Pizza Hut**

245-247 Whitechapel Road, Whitechapel, London E1 1DB
t 020 7247 9958
pizzahut.co.uk

General: 🐕 🦮 🚶 👤 WC ♿ 🚻 .: abc

E1 - Whitechapel | **Preem And Prithi Restaurant**

124-126 Brick Lane, London E1 6RL
t 020 7377 5252 e info@preemprithi.co.uk
preemprithi.co.uk

General: 🐕 FAX 🚶 👤 🚻 P★

E1 - Whitechapel | **Sheba Brick Lane**

136 Brick Lane, London E1 6RU
t 020 7247 7824 e shebabricklane@yahoo.co.uk
shebabricklane.com

General: FAX 🚶 👤 🚻 abc P★

E2 - Bethnal Green | **McDonald's**

432-436 Bethnal Green Road, Bethnal Green, London E2 0DJ
t 020 7729 6660 e 00190@uk.mcd.com
mcdonalds.co.uk

General: 🐕 FAX 🦮 🚶 👤 WC ♿ 🚻 .: abc

E2 - Bethnal Green | **Nando's**

366 Bethnal Green Road, Bethnal Green, London E2 0AH
t 020 7729 5783
nandos.co.uk

General: 🐕 🦮 🚶 👤 WC 🚻 .:

E3 - Bow | **Zeera**

554 Mile End Road, Bow, London E3 4PL
t 020 8983 3111 e info@zeeraindiancuisine.com
zeeraindiancuisine.com

General: 🐕 FAX 🚶 👤 WC 🚻

E3 - Mile End | **Morgan Arms**

43 Morgan Street, London E3 5AA
t 020 8980 6389 e themorgan@geronimo-inns.co.uk
geronimo-inns.co.uk

General: 🐕 FAX ⚡ 🚶 ♿ WC 🚻♿

E14 - Docklands | **All Bar One**

42 MacKenzie Walk, South Colonnade, Canary Wharf, London E14 5EH
t 020 7516 0191
mbplc.com

General: 🐕 ⚡ 🚶 ♿ WC 🚻♿ 🚻♿

E14 - Docklands | **Amerigo Vespucci**

25 Cabot Square, Mackenzie Walk, Canary Wharf, London E14 4QA
t 020 7513 0288 e info@amerigovespucci.co.uk
amerigovespucci.co.uk

General: 🐕 FAX ⚡ 🚶 ♿ 🚻♿ 🚻♿

E14 - Docklands | **Brodies Bar/Restaurant**

43 Fisherman's Walk, Cabot Square, Canary Wharf, London E14 5HD
t 020 7719 0202 e brodiescw@kornicis.co.uk
brodiesbars.com

General: 🐕 FAX ⚡ 🚶 ♿ WC 🚻♿

E14 - Docklands | **Browns Restaurant And Bar**

Hertsmere Road, West India Quay, London E14 8JJ
t 020 7987 9777
browns-restaurants.com

General: 🐕 ⚡ 🚶 ♿ WC 🚻♿ 🚻♿

E14 - Docklands | **Burger King**

2nd Floor Cabot Place West, Canary Wharf, London E14 4QT
t 020 7513 2755

General: 🐕 FAX ⚡ 🚶 ♿ WC 🚻♿ 🚻♿ abc ♿

E14 - Docklands | **Chili's**

Cabot Place East, Canary Wharf, London E14 4QS
t 020 7363 5678 e canary@chilis.uk.com
chilis.uk.com

General: 🐕 FAX ⚡ 🏠 🚶 ♿ WC 🚻♿ 🚻♿ ♿

E14 - Docklands | **Davy's**

31-35 Fishermans Walk, Cabot Square, Canary Wharf, London E14 4DH
t 020 7363 6633 e bookings@davy.co.uk
davy.co.uk

General: 🐕 FAX ⚡ 🚶 ♿ WC 🚻♿ 🚻♿

E14 - Docklands | **Emery Hall**

Annabell Close, East India Dock Road, London E14 6DP
t 0202 75151177

General: 🦮 🧍 👤 wc ♿ 👥 ★★★

E14 - Docklands | **Fine Line, The**

29-30 Fishermans Walk, Cabot Square, Canary Wharf, London E14 6DH
t 020 7513 0255 e fineline.canarywharf@fullers.co.uk
thefineline.co.uk

General: 🦮 FAX 🐕 🧍 👤 wc ♿ 👥

E14 - Docklands | **Four Seasons Hotel Canary Wharf**

46 Westferry Circus, Canary Wharf, London E14 8RS
t 020 7510 1999
fourseasons.com

General: 🦮 FAX 🐕 🧍 👤 wc ♿ 👥 .: abc 🦻

E14 - Docklands | **Gourmet Pizza**

18-20 Mackenzie Walk, Canary Wharf, London E14 4QT
t 020 7345 9192
london-eating.co.uk

General: 🦮 FAX 🐕 🏢 🧍 👤 wc ♿ 👥

E14 - Docklands | **Itsu**

Level 2 Cabot Place East, Canary Wharf, London E14 4QT
t 020 7512 5790
itsu.co.uk

General: 🦮 FAX 🏢 🧍 👤 wc ♿ 👥 ♿

E14 - Docklands | **Itsu Japanese & Asian Restaurant**

28A Jubilee Place, 45 Bank Street, Canary Wharf, London E14 5NY
t 020 7512 9650

General: FAX 🧍 👤 👥 ♿

E14 - Docklands | **La Tasca**

Hertsmere Road, West India Quay, Canary Wharf, London E14 4AE
t 020 7531 9990 e canarywharf@latasca.co.uk
latasca.co.uk

General: 🦮 FAX 🐕 🧍 👤 wc 👥 abc

E14 - Docklands | **Ledger Building**

4 Hertsmere Road, Docklands, Tower Hamlets E14 4AL
t 020 7536 7770

General: 🦮 🐕 🧍 👤 wc .: abc

E14 - Docklands | **Museum of London Docklands**

1 Warehouse, Hertsmere Road, West India Quay, London E14 4AL
t 020 7001 9844 e info.docklands@museumoflondon.org.uk
museumoflondon.org.uk

General: 🐕 FAX 🛴 🧍 👤 wc ♿ 🧍♿ 👤★★ abc 🔔

E14 - Docklands | **Nicolas Wine Bar**

Unit 480 1 Canada Square, Canary Wharf, London E14 5AX
t 020 7512 9092

General: 🐕 FAX 🧍 👤 wc ♿ 🧍♿ ♿

E14 - Docklands | **Pizza Express**

200 Calbot Place East, Canary Wharf, London E14 4QT
t 020 7513 0513 e canarywharf.manager@pizzaexpress.com
pizzaexpress.com

General: 🐕 FAX 🏠 🧍 👤 wc ♿ 🧍♿ .:♿

E14 - Docklands | **Plateau**

Canada Place, Canary Wharf, London E14 5ER
t 020 7715 7100
conran.com

General: 🐕 FAX 🛴 🧍 👤 wc ♿ 🧍♿

E14 - Docklands | **Singapore Sam**

2nd Floor Cabot Place West, Canary Wharf, London E14 4QT
t 020 7513 2755

General: 🐕 FAX 🛴 🧍 👤 wc ♿ 🧍♿ abc ♿

E14 - Docklands | **Slug And Lettuce**

30 South Colonnade, Canary Wharf, London E14 4QQ
t 020 7519 1612

General: 🐕 FAX 🧍 👤 wc ♿ 🧍♿

E14 - Docklands | **Smollensky's Bar And Grill**

1 Nash Court, Canary Wharf, London E14 5AG
t 020 7719 0101 e canarywharf@smollenskys.co.uk
smollenskys.co.uk

General: 🐕 FAX 🧍 👤 wc ♿ 🧍♿

E14 - Docklands | **Tiffinbites**

22-23 Jubilee Place, 45 Bank Street, Canary Wharf E14 5NY
t 020 7719 0333 e canarywharf@tiffinbites.com
tiffinbites.com

General: 🐕 FAX 🧍 👤 ♿ 🧍♿ ♿

E14 - Docklands | **Tootsies**

45 Jubilee Place, 45 Bank Street, Canary Wharf, London E14 5NY
t 020 7516 9110 e cw@tootisesrestaurants.co.uk

General: ⚐ FAX ⚐ ⚐ wc ⚐ ⚐

E14 - Docklands | **Via Fossa**

Unit B Port East Buildings, West India Quay, London E14 4AY
t 020 7515 8549

General: ⚐ ⚐ ⚐ ⚐ wc ⚐ ⚐ ⚐

E14 - Docklands | **Wagamamas**

39 Jubilee Place, 45 Bank Street, Canary Wharf, London E14 5NY
t 020 7516 9009
wagamama.com

General: ⚐ ⚐ ⚐ ⚐ wc ⚐ ⚐ ⚐

E14 - Poplar | **1802 Bar Lounge And Dining**

No.1 Warehouse, West India Quay, Hertsmere Road, London E14 4AL
t 0870 444 3886 e calexander@museumindocklands.org.uk
searcys.co.uk

General: ⚐ FAX ⚐ ⚐ wc ⚐ ⚐ abc

E14 - Poplar | **Captain's Table**

16 Market Way, Crisp Street Market, Poplar, London E14 6AH
t 020 7987 0219

General: ⚐ ⚐ ⚐ ⚐

E14 - Poplar | **Eastern Tandoori**

332 Burdett Road, London E14 7DL
t 020 7537 9550
eastern-tandoori.co.uk

General: ⚐ ⚐ ⚐ ⚐ ⚐ ⚐ abc

E14 - Poplar | **McDonald's**

Trafalgar Way, Poplar, London E14 5SP
t 020 7987 0766 e 00557@uk.mcd.com
mcdonalds.co.uk

General: ⚐ FAX ⚐ ⚐ wc ⚐ ⚐ .: P★★★

RM1 - Romford | **Faraglioni**

142 Rushgreen Road, Romford, Essex RM7 0QA
t 01708 748652

General: ⚐ ⚐ ⚐ ⚐ P★★★

RM1 - Romford | **Harefield Manor Hotel**

33 Main Road, Romford, Essex RM1 3DL
t 01708 751901 e enquiries@harefieldmanor.o.uk
harefieldmanor.co.uk

General: 🐕 📠 🕸 🕴 ⅃ wc ♿ 🧑‍🦽 abc ★★★

RM1 - Romford | **La Tasca**

Unit FR5 1st Floor, The Brewery Shopping Centre, Romford, Essex RM1 1AU
t 01708 734662 e romford@latasca.co.uk
latasca.co.uk

General: 🐕 📠 🕸 🕴 ⅃ wc ♿ 🧑‍🦽 ★★★

RM1 - Romford | **Liberty Bell**

Mercury Gardens, Romford, Essex RM1 3EN
t 1708 e romfordcentralpti@whitbread.com

General: 🐕 📠 🕸 🕴 ⅃ wc ♿ 🧑‍🦽 .: abc ★★★

RM1 - Romford | **Outback Steakhouse**

Unit 1D 1st Floor, The Brewery Shopping Centre, Romford, Essex RM1 1AU
t 01708 737955 e ob2@outbackpom.com
outbackpom.com

General: 🐕 📠 🕸 🕴 ⅃ wc ♿ 🧑‍🦽 ★★★

RM1 - Romford | **Shanghai**

44 North Street, Romford, Essex RM1 1BH
t 01708 743162

General: 🕴 ⅃ wc ♿ 🧑‍🦽 ★

RM2 - Gidea Park | **Harvester**

91 Main Road, Gidea Park, Romford, Essex RM2 5EL
t 01708 738811
harvester.co.uk

General: 🐕 🕸 🕴 ⅃ wc ♿ 🧑‍🦽 .: ★★★

RM3 - Romford | **Mayland Golf Club**

Colchester Road, Romford, Essex RM3 0AZ
t 01708 341777 e maylands@maylandgolf.com
maylandsgolf.com

General: 🐕 📠 ⅃ abc ★★★

RM11 - Hornchurch | **Ardleigh And Dragon**

124 Ardleigh Green Road, Hornchurch, Essex RM11 2SH
t 01708 442 550

General: 🐕 🕸 🕴 ⅃ wc ♿ 🧑‍🦽 ★★★

RM11 - Hornchurch | **Harrow**

130 Hornchurch Road, Hornchurch, Essex RM11 1DP
t 01708 462 611

General: ⚬ ⚬ ⚬ ⚬ wc ⚬ ⚬ P✦✦✦ ⚬

RM11 - Hornchurch | **Mandarin Palace**

197-201 High Street, Hornchurch, Essex RM11 3XT
t 01708 438003

General: ⚬ ⚬ ⚬ ⚬ P✦✦✦

RM11 - Hornchurch | **Prezzo**

189 High Street, Hornchurch, Essex RM11 3XT
t 01708 455501
prezzorestaurants.co.uk

General: ⚬ ⚬ ⚬ ⚬ wc ⚬ ⚬ P✦

RM11 - Hornchurch | **Tarantino**

51 High Street, Hornchurch, Essex RM11 1TP
t 01708 504030 e tarantinorestaurant@hotmail.com
tarantinos.co.uk

General: ⚬ FAX ⚬ ⚬ ⚬ P✦

RM11 - Hornchurch | **Umberto's Italian Restaurant**

195 High Street, Hornchurch, Essex RM11 3XT
t 01708 475218
umbertosrestaurant.com

General: ⚬ ⚬ ⚬ ⚬ P✦✦✦

RM12 - Hornchurch | **Ask**

Unit 2, 168 High Street, Hornchurch, Essex RM12 6QU
t 01708 464798 e info@askcentral.co.uk

General: ⚬ FAX ⚬ ⚬ wc ⚬ ⚬ P✦

RM12 - Hornchurch | **Compasses-Harvester**

125 Abbs Cross Lane, Hornchurch, Essex RM12 4XS
t 01708 450 240
harvester.co.uk

General: ⚬ ⚬ ⚬ ⚬ wc ⚬ ⚬ .: P✦✦✦

RM12 - Hornchurch | **Good Intent**

Southend Road, Hornchurch, Essex RM12 5NU
t 01708 554644

General: ⚬ ⚬ ⚬ ⚬ wc P✦✦✦

RM12 - Hornchurch | **La Eroma**

25 The Broadway, Hornchurch, Essex RM12 4RW
t 01708 478525

General: 🐕 🚶 ♿ WC 🚻 P

RM12 - Hornchurch | **Railway**

Station Lane, Hornchurch, Essex RM12 6SB
t 01708 440028

General: 🐕 FAX 🚲 🚶 ♿ WC 🚻 👫 P

RM12 - Hornchurch | **Wildwood**

168 High Street, Hornchurch, Essex RM12 6QU
t 01708 471429

General: 🐕 🚶 ♿ WC 🚻 👫 P

RM12 - Hornchurch | **Zizzi**

41 Station Road, Hornchurch, Essex RM12 6JT
t 01708 444740

General: 🐕 🚶 ♿ WC 🚻 👫 P

RM12 - Rainham | **Albion**

Rainham Road, Rainham, Essex RM13 8SS
t 01798 552445

General: 🐕 🚶 ♿ WC 👫 P

RM12 - Rainham | **Willow Farm Brewers Fayre**

New Road, Rainham, Essex RM13 9ED
t 01708 634 825

General: 🐕 🚲 🚶 ♿ WC 🚻 👫 .: abc P

RM14 - Upminster | **Golden Crane**

117 Avon Road, Cranham, Essex RM14 1RQ
t 01708 224701

General: 🐕 🚲 🚶 ♿ WC 🚻 👫 P

RM14 - Upminster | **Huntsman And Hounds**

Ockenden Road, Corbets Tey, Essex RM14 2DN
t 01708 221672

General: 🐕 🚲 🚶 ♿ WC 👫 P

RM14 - Upminster | Jobbers Rest

St Marys Lane, Cranham, Essex RM14 3LT
t 01708 250480

General: ☂ ♿ ♿ ♿ ♿ ♿ abc ★★★

RM14 - Upminster | Kalijeera

32 Corbets Tey Road, Upminster, Essex RM14 2AD
t 01708 222263/228516

General: ☂ ♿ ♿ wc ♿ ♿ ♿

RM14 - Upminster | Optomist

Hacton Lane, Upminster, Essex RM14 2XY
t 01708 641530

General: ☂ ♿ ♿ ♿ wc ♿ ★★★

SE3 - Blackheath | Pizza Express

64-66 Tranquil Vale, Blackheath, London SE3 0BN
t 020 8318 2595
pizzaexpress.com

General: ☂ FAX ♿ ♿ ♿ ♿ .:

SE3 - Blackheath | Strada

5 Lee Road, Blackheath, London SE3 9RQ
t 020 8318 6644 e blackheath@strada.co.uk
strada.co.uk

General: ☂ FAX ♿ ♿ wc ♿ ♿ .: abc

SE4 - Brockley | Brockley Barge (JD Wetherspoon)

184 Brockley Road, Brockley, London SE4 2RR
t 020 8694 7690
jdwetherspoon.co.uk

General: ☂ FAX ♿ ♿ ♿ wc ♿ ♿

SE6 - Catford | A2 Delecious

77a Rushey Green, Catford, London SE6 4AF
t 020 8695 9822 e a2delicious@hotmail.co.uk

General: ☂ ♿ ♿ ♿ ♿

SE6 - Catford | Sapporo Ichiban

13 Catford Broadway, Catford, London SE6 4SP
t 020 8690 8487

General: ☂ FAX ♿ ♿ wc ♿ ♿ ♿

SE6 - Catford | **Tai Won Mein**

90-92 Rushey Green, Catford, London SE6 4HW
t 020 8690 8238

General: 🧍 ♿ ♿ ♿ ⚡

SE6 - Catford | **Turkuaz**

163 Bromley Road, Catford, London SE6 2NZ
t 020 8697 4545
turkuaz.co.uk

General: 🐕 📢 🧍 ♿ ⚡★★★

SE13 - Lewisham | **Davito's**

17 Montpelier Vale, Blackheath, London SE13 7SW
t 020 8852 9226
davitos.com

General: 🧍 ♿ ♿

SE13 - Lewisham | **Madras Restaurant**

244 Lewisham High Street, Lewisham, London SE13 6JU
t 020 8852 6666 e madrasrestaurant@aol.com
madrasrestaurant.co.uk

General: 🐕 📠 🧍 ♿ ♿ ♿ abc

SE13 - Lewisham | **Maggie's Cafe & Restaurant**

320-322 Lewisham Road, Lewisham, London SE13 7PA
t 020 8244 0339 e info@maggiesrestaurant.co.uk
maggiesrestaurant.co.uk

General: 🐕 📠 📢 🧍 ♿ ⚡

SE13 - Lewisham | **Market Tavern**

139-141 Lewisham High Street, Lewisham, London SE13 6AA
t 020 8297 8645 e markettavern@marstons.co.uk
marstonstaverns.co.uk

General: 🐕 📠 📢 🧍 ♿ WC ♿ abc ⚡

SE13 - Lewisham | **Masons Bar Restaurant**

38 Ladywell Road, Ladywell, London SE13 7UZ
t 020 8314 0314
masonladywell.co.uk

General: 🐕 📠 🧍 ♿ ♿

SE13 - Lewisham | **Mixers**

187 Lewisham High Street, Lewisham, London SE13 6AA
t 020 8318 4686

General: 🐕 🧍 ♿ ♿ abc

SE13 - Lewisham | **Palace Chine**

228 Lewisham High Street, Lewisham, London SE13 6JU
t 020 8297 2800

General: 🐕 FAX 📠 🧍 ᵻ WC ♿ ᛘ P***

SE13 - Lewisham | **Pontil's**

The Riverdale Centre, Lewisham, London SE13 7ER
t 020 8318 4710

General: 🐕 FAX 🧍 ᵻ ᛘ ♿

SE13 - Lewisham | **Something Fishy**

117-119 Lewisham High Street, Lewisham, London SE13 6AQ
t 020 8852 7075

General: 🐕 🧍 ᵻ ᛘ

SE13 - Lewisham | **Taste Of Lewisham**

19 Lee High Road, Lewisham, London SE13 5LD
t 020 8297 6452

General: 🐕 🧍 ᵻ ᛘ P

SE13 - Lewisham | **Welcome Noodle House**

47-49 Lee High Road, Lewisham, London SE13 5NS
t 020 8297 5268

General: 🐕 🧍 ᵻ ♿ abc

SE14 - New Cross | **Walpole Arms**

407 New Cross Road, New Cross, London SE14 6LA
t 020 8692 2080

General: 🐕 🧍 ᵻ ᛘ

SE23 - Forest Hill | **Capitol**

11-21 London Road, Forest Hill, Lewisham, London SE23 3TW
t 020 8291 8920
jdwetherspoon.co.uk

General: 🐕 🧍 ᵻ WC ᛘ .:

SE26 - Sydenham | **Dolphin**

121 Sydenham Road, Sydenham, London SE26 5HB
t 020 8778 8101
thedolphinsydenham.com

General: 🐕 🧍 ᵻ ♿ ᛘ

SE26 - Sydenham | **Puerto Mexico**

118 Sydenham Road, Sydenham, London SE26 5JX
t 020 8778 1222

General: ⚹ 👤 👤 wc 👤 👤

SE26 - Sydenham | **Two Half's**

42 Sydenham Road, Sydenham, London SE26 5QF
t 020 8778 0649

General: ⚹ 👤 👤 wc 👤 👤 abc 👤

BR1 - Bromley | **McDonald's**

Old Bromley Road, Bromley, Kent BR1 4JY
t 020 8460 4160
mcdonalds.co.uk

General: ⚹ 👤 👤 wc 👤 👤

SW10 - West Brompton | **Vignt-quatre**

325 Fulham Road, London SW10 9QL
t 020 7376 7224 e vigntquatre@longshotpic.com

General: ⚹ FAX 👤 👤 👤

SW10 - World's End | **Osteria Dell'Arancio**

383 Kings Road, London SW10 0LP
t 020 7349 8111 e info@osteriadellarancio.co.uk
osteriadellarancio.co.uk

General: ⚹ FAX 👤 👤 wc 👤 👤

SW11 - Battersea | **Asparagus**

1-13 Falcon Road, Battersea, London SW11 2PL
t 020 7801 0046
jdwetherspoon.co.uk

General: ⚹ 👤 👤 wc 👤 👤 .:

SW11 - Clapham | **All Bar One**

32-38 Northcote Road, Clapham, London SW11 1NZ
t 020 7223 9763
allbarone.co.uk

General: ⚹ 👤 👤 wc 👤 👤

SW11 - Clapham | **Bank**

33-37 Northcote Road, Clapham, London SW11 1NJ
t 020 7924 7387 e thebank@fullers.co.uk
fullers.co.uk

General: ⚹ FAX 👤 👤 👤 wc 👤

SW11 - Clapham | **Marzano**

53 Northcote Road, Clapham, London SW11 1NJ
t 020 7228 8860 e manager@marzanorestaurants.co.uk

General: 🐕 FAX 🚿 👤 👥 WC ♿ 👥 👥 ✋ ♪

SW12 - Balham | **Balham Tup**

21 Chestnut Grove, Balham, London SW12 8JB
t 020 8772 0546 e balhamtup@inventiveoperations.com

General: 🐕 👤 👥 ♿ 👥

SW12 - Balham | **Bedford**

77 Bedford Hill, Balham, London SW12 9HD
t 020 8682 8940 e info@thebedford.co.uk
thebedford.co.uk

General: 🐕 FAX 👥

SW12 - Balham | **Blithe Spirit**

157 Balham High Road, Balham, London SW12 9AU
t 020 8772 0082 e blithespirit.london@marstons.co.uk

General: 🐕 🚿 👤 👥 WC 👥

SW12 - Balham | **Clarence**

90-92 Balham High Road, Balham, London SW12 9AG
t 020 8772 1155 e enquiries@clarencebalham.com
clarencebalham.com

General: 🐕 FAX 👤 👥 WC 👥 ✋

SW12 - Balham | **Coffee Max**

104 Bedford Hill, Balham, London SW12 9HR
t 020 8673 3120

General: 🐕 🚿 👤 👥 ♿

SW12 - Balham | **Dish Dash**

11-13 Bedford Hill, Balham, London SW12 9ET
t 020 8673 5555 e eat@dish-dash.com
dish-dash.com

General: 🐕 FAX 👤 👥 WC 👥

SW12 - Balham | **Exhibit Bar & Restaurant**

Balham Station Road, Balham, London SW12 9AU
t 020 8772 6556 e exhibit@exhibitbars.com
theexhibit.co.uk

General: 🐕 FAX 👤 👥 WC ♿ 👥

SW12 - Balham | **Fine Burger Restaurant**

37 Bedford Hill, Balham, London SW12 9EY
t 020 8772 0266 e balham@fineburger.co.uk
fineburger.co.uk

General: ⚥ @FAX ⚦ ♿ ♿ ♿ abc

SW12 - Balham | **Jackdaw And Rook**

100 Balham High Road, Balham, London SW12 9AA
t 020 8772 9021 e jackdaw.rook@fullers.co.uk

General: ⚥ ⚥ ⚦ ♿ wc ♿ ♿

SW12 - Balham | **Moon Under Water (JD Wetherspoon)**

Balham High Road, Balham, London SW12 9BP
t 020 8673 0535
jdwetherspoon.co.uk

General: ⚥ ⚦ ♿ wc ♿ ♿ .:

SW12 - Balham | **Nando's**

116-118 Balham High Road, Balham, London SW12 9AA
t 020 8675 6415
nandos.co.uk

General: ⚥ @FAX ⚦ ♿ wc ♿ ♿

SW12 - Balham | **Pizza Express**

47 Bedford Hill, Balham, London SW12 9EY
t 020 8772 3232 e balham.manager@pizzaexpress.com
pizzaexpress.com

General: ⚥ @FAX ⚥ ⚦ ♿ wc ♿ ♿ .:

SW13 - Barnes | **Ask**

108 Station Road, Barnes SW13 0LJ
t 020 8878 9300
askrestaurants.com

General: ⚥ ⚦ ♿ wc ♿ ♿

SW14 - East Sheen | **Bellinis Pizzeria**

313 Upper Richmond Road, East Sheen, Surrey SW14 8QR
t 020 8287 4114

General: ⚥ ♿

SW14 - East Sheen | **Lal Bagh**

467 Upper Richmond Road, East Sheen SW14 7PU
t 020 8878 0010

General: ⚥ ⊞ ⚦ ♿ ♿

SW14 - East Sheen | Leonardo Wine Bar & Restaurant

459 Upper Richmond Road West, East Sheen SW14 7PR
t 020 8878 3408

General: FAX ⚕ ⚕ ⚕ ⚕

SW14 - East Sheen | Naked Turtle

505 Upper Richmond Road West, East Sheen SW14 7DE
t 020 8878 1995 e info@naked-turtle.com
naked-turtle.com

General: ⚕ FAX ⚕ ⚕ ⚕ ⚕ ⚕

SW14 - East Sheen | Pala Kebab House

238 Upper Richmond Road West, East Sheen, Surrey SW14 8AG
t 020 8876 1514

General: ⚕ ⚕ ⚕ ⚕

SW14 - East Sheen | Sophitia Thai Cuisine

431 Upper Richmond Road, East Sheen SW14 7PG
t 020 8878 3588

General: ⚕ ⚕ ⚕

SW14 - Mortlake | Tapestry

1 Lower Richmond Road, Mortlake, London SW14 7EZ
t 020 8878 7177 e tapestrybar@hotmail.com
tapestrybar.co.uk

General: ⚕ FAX ⚕ ⚕ wc ⚕ ⚕

SW15 - Putney | 40 Degrees Grill

40 Upper Richmond Road, Putney, London SW15 2RX
t 020 8875 1231 e info@40degreesgrill.co.uk
40degreesgrill.co.uk

General: ⚕ FAX ⚕ ⚕ ⚕ ⚕ abc

SW15 - Putney | Arab Boy

289 Upper Richmond Road, Putney, London SW15 6SP
t 020 8788 5154

General: ⚕ ⚕ ⚕ ⚕

SW15 - Putney | Cafe Rouge

200 Putney Bridge Road, Putney, London SW15 2NA
t 020 8788 4257
caferouge.co.uk

General: ⚕ FAX ⚕ ⚕ ⚕ .: abc

SW15 - Putney | **Coat & Badge**

8 Lacy Road, Putney, London SW15 1NL
t 020 8788 4900
geronimo-inn.co.uk

General: 🐕 FAX 🦽 🚶 🧏 WC ♿ 🧑‍🦽 abc

SW15 - Putney | **Friends Oriental Food Hall**

4 Chelverton Road, Putney, London SW15 1RH
t 020 8788 0599

General: 🐕 FAX 🚶 🧏 WC ♿ 🧑‍🦽

SW15 - Putney | **Hare & Tortoise**

296-298 Upper Richmond Road, Putney, London SW15 6TH
t 020 8394 7666 e putney@hareandtortoise-restaurants.co.uk
hareandtortoise-restaurants.co.uk

General: 🐕 FAX 🚶 🧏 WC 🧑‍🦽

SW15 - Putney | **Jim Thompsons**

408 Upper Richmond Road, Putney, London SW15 6JP
t 020 8788 3737 e jim-thompsons@orchidgroup.co.uk
orchidgroup.co.uk

General: 🐕 FAX 🦽 🚶 🧏 WC 🧑‍🦽

SW15 - Putney | **McDonald's**

84 Putney High Street, Putney, London SW15 1RB
t 020 8780 9834
mcdonalds.co.uk

General: 🐕 🦽 🚶 🧏 🧑‍🦽

SW15 - Putney | **Mezza**

56 Lower Richmond Road, Putney, London SW15 1JT
t 020 8780 3883

General: 🦽 🚶 🧏 ♿ 🧑‍🦽

SW15 - Putney | **Moomba**

5 Lacy Road, Putney, London SW15 1NH
t 020 8785 9151 e reservations@moomba.co.uk
moomba.co.uk

General: 🐕 FAX 🚶 🧏 🧑‍🦽

SW15 - Putney | **Nando's**

148 Upper Richmond Road, Putney, London SW15 2SW
t 020 8780 3651
nandos.co.uk

General: 🐕 FAX 🦽 🚶 🧏 🧑‍🦽 .: abc

SW15 - Putney | **Pappa & Ciccia**

90 Lower Richmond Road, Putney, London SW15 1LL
t 020 8789 9040
pappaciccia.com

General: 🦮 FAX 🏠 🧍 ♿ ♿ .: abc

SW15 - Putney | **Pizza Express**

144 Upper Richmond Road, Putney, London SW15 2SW
t 020 8789 1948 e putney.manager@pizzaexpress.com
pizzaexpress.com

General: 🦮 FAX 🧍 ♿ ♿ .:

SW15 - Putney | **Putney Station**

94-98 Upper Richmond Road, Putney, London SW15 2SP
t 020 8780 0242

General: 🦮 🧍 ♿ WC ♿ ♿

SW15 - Putney | **Real Greek Souvlaki And Bar**

31 Putney High Street, Putney, London SW15 1SP
t 020 8788 3270 e putney@therealgreek.com
therealgreek.com

General: 🦮 FAX ♿ 🧍 ♿ WC ♿ abc

SW15 - Putney | **Rocket Riverside**

Brewhouse Lane, Putney, London SW15 2NS
t 020 8789 7875
rocketrestaurant.co.uk

General: 🦮 FAX 🧍 ♿ WC ♿ ♿

SW15 - Putney | **Royal China**

3 Chelverton Road, Putney, London SW15 1RN
t 020 8780 1520

General: FAX 🏠 🧍 ♿ ♿ ♿ .: abc

SW15 - Putney | **Spencer Arms**

237 Lower Richmond Road, Putney, London SW15 1HJ
t 020 8788 0640 e info@spencerarms.co.uk
thespencerarms.co.uk

General: 🦮 ♿ 🧍 ♿ WC ♿ ♿

SW15 - Putney | **Thai Square Putney Bridge**

2-4 Lower Richmond Road, Putney, London SW15 1LB
t 020 8780 1811 e thaisqputney@btconnect.com
thaisquare.net

General: 🦮 FAX 🧍 ♿ WC ♿

SW15 - Putney | **V81**

30 Putney High Street, Putney, London SW15 1SQ
t 020 8780 5252

General: ✗ FAX ▲ ♿ ♿ abc

SW17 - Tooting | **Blue Pumpkin**

16-18 Ritherdon Road, Balham, London SW17 8QD
t 020 8767 2660 e info@bluepumpkin.co.uk
bluepumpkin.co.uk

General: ✗ FAX ▲ ♿ wc ♿ ♿

SW17 - Tooting | **Curry Express**

47 Upper Tooting Road, Tooting, London SW17 7TR
t 020 8672 6433 e heartmanek@yahoo.com

General: ✗ FAX ▲ ♿ ♿ abc

SW17 - Tooting | **Dexters Bar & Grill**

20 Bellevue Road, Wandsworth Common, London SW17 7EB
t 020 8767 1858 e enquiries@tootsiesrestaurants.com
tootsiesrestaurants.com

General: ✗ FAX ▲ ♿ wc ♿ abc

SW17 - Tooting | **Golden Grill**

115 Mitcham Road, Tooting, London SW17 9PE
t 020 8672 0550

General: ✗ ▲ ♿ ♿

SW17 - Tooting | **Gurkas Diner**

1 The Boulevard, Balham High Road, Balham, London SW17 7BW
t 020 8675 1188
gurkasdiner.co.uk

General: ✗ ▲ ♿ wc ♿ ♿

SW17 - Tooting | **Jasmins Fish & Chips Bar**

20 Mitcham Road, Tooting, London SW17 9NA
t 020 8772 7172

General: ✗ ▲ ♿ ♿ ♿ abc

SW17 - Tooting | **McDonald's**

42-44 Mitcham Road, Tooting, London SW17 5NA
t 020 8672 0139
mcdonalds.co.uk

General: ✗ ▲ ♿ wc ♿ ♿ .: abc

SW17 - Tooting | **Mirch Masala**

213 Upper Tooting Road, Tooting, London SW17 7TG
t 020 8672 7500 e tooting@mirchmasalarestaurant.co.uk
mirchmasalarestaurant.co.uk

General: FAX 🏠 👤 👥 👫 abc

SW17 - Tooting | **Mixed Spice**

2b Tooting Bec Road, Tooting, London SW17 8BD
t 020 8767 6269

General: 🐕 🏠 👤 👥 👫

SW17 - Tooting | **Piccolino**

27-29 Bellevue Road, Wandsworth, London SW17 7EF
t 020 8767 1713 e wandsworth.piccolino@ircplc.co.uk
individualrestaurantcompanyplc.co.uk

General: 🐕 FAX 👤 👥 WC 👫 abc

SW17 - Tooting | **Pizza Express**

198 Trinity Road, Tooting, London SW17 7HR
t 020 8672 0200
pizzaexpress.com

General: 🐕 FAX 🚲 🏠 👤 👥 WC 👫 .: abc 🎵

SW17 - Tooting | **Tooting Kebab Fish & Chips**

66 Mitcham Road, Tooting, London SW17 9MN
t 020 8672 0796

General: 🐕 👤 👥 👫 abc

SW18 - Wandsworth | **Alma**

499 Old York Road, Wandsworth, London SW18 1TF
t 020 8870 2537 e alma@youngs.co.uk
thealma.co.uk

General: 🐕 FAX 🚲 👤 👥 WC 👫 P★★★

SW18 - Wandsworth | **Blend**

111-113 Wandsworth High Street, Wandsworth, London SW18 4HY
t 020 8874 7746
blendwandsworth.co.uk

General: 🐕 👤 👥 WC 👫

SW18 - Wandsworth | **Brewers Inn**

147 East Hill, Wandsworth, London SW18 2QB
t 020 8874 4128 e brewersinn@youngs.co.uk
brewersinn.co.uk

General: 🐕 FAX 🚲 👤 👥 WC 👫 P★★★

SW18 - Wandsworth | **Colins Fish And Chicken Bar**

193 Garratt Lane, Wandsworth, London SW18 4DR
t 020 8870 3809

General: 🐕 🧍 ♿ ♿ abc

SW18 - Wandsworth | **Doukan**

350 Old York Road, Wandsworth, London SW18 1SS
t 020 8870 8280 e talktous@doukan.co.uk
doukan.co.uk

General: 🐕 FAX 🧍 ♿

SW18 - Wandsworth | **Earl Spencer**

260-262 Merton Road, Southfields, London SW18 5JL
t 020 8870 9244 e theearlspencer@hotmail.com
theearlspencer.co.uk

General: 🐕 FAX 🧍 ♿ ♿

SW18 - Wandsworth | **Global Bar And Restaurant**

350 Old York Road, Wandsworth, London SW18 1SS
t 020 8870 5491 e parties@gimr.co.uk
globalrestaurant.co.uk

General: 🐕 FAX 🧍 ♿

SW18 - Wandsworth | **Grid Inn**

22 Replingham Road, Southfields, London SW18 5LS
t 020 8874 8460
jdwetherspoon.co.uk

General: 🐕 🧍 WC ♿ .:

SW18 - Wandsworth | **Kens Cafe & Restaurant**

62 West Hill, Wandsworth, London SW18 1RU
t 020 8265 4136

General: 🐕 ♿

SW18 - Wandsworth | **Konnigans**

344-346 Old York Road, Wandsworth, London SW18 1SS
t 020 8871 1496 e caroline@konnigansrestaurant.co.uk
konnigansrestaurant.co.uk

General: 🐕 FAX 🏠 🧍 ♿

SW18 - Wandsworth | **McDonald's**

1 Marl Road, Swandon Way, Wandsworth, London SW18 1JT
t 020 8871 2880 e 00429@mcdonalds.co.uk
mcdonalds.co.uk

General: 🐕 FAX 🧍 WC ♿ abc P★★★

SW18 - Wandsworth | Nilima

175 Replingham Road, Southfields, London SW18 5LY
t 020 8871 2078

General:

SW18 - Wandsworth | Old Garage

20 Replingham Road, Southfields, London SW18 5LS
t 020 8874 9370
greeneking.co.uk

General:

SW18 - Wandsworth | Old Sergeant

104 Garratt Lane, Wandsworth, London SW18 4DJ
t 020 8874 4099 e theoldsergeant@googlemail.com

General:

SW18 - Wandsworth | Pizza Express

539 Old York Road, Wandsworth, London SW18 1TG
t 020 8877 9812
pizzaexpress.com

General:

SW18 - Wandsworth | Queen Adelaide (Youngs)

35 Putney Bridge Road, Wandsworth, London SW18 1NP
t 020 8874 1695 e queenadelaide@youngs.co.uk
thequeenadelaide.co.uk

General:

SW18 - Wandsworth | Riverpoint

94 Point Pleasant, Wandsworth, London SW18 1PP
t 020 8871 9267
riverpointrestaurant.co.uk

General:

SW18 - Wandsworth | San Pietro Italian Restaurant

189 Garratt Lane, Wandsworth, London SW18 4DR
t 020 8871 9464 e info@san-pietro.co.uk
san-pietro.co.uk

General:

SW18 - Wandsworth | Spur Steak And Grill

Southside Shopping Centre, Garratt Lane, Wandsworth, London SW18 4TF
t 020 8874 0831 e mohawkspur@btconnect.com
spurcorp.com

General:

SW18 - Wandsworth | **Thai**

362 Old York Road, Wandsworth, London SW18 1SP
t 020 8877 2724

General: 🐕 @FAX 🏠 🚶 ♿ 🧑‍🦽

CR0 - Croydon | **Auberge Cafe**

Level 3, The Whitgift Centre, Croydon CR0 1LP
t 020 8680 8337
towncentrerestaurants.co.uk

General: 🐕 🚶 ♿ 🧑‍🦽 ♿

CR0 - Croydon | **Bagattis Restaurant**

56-58 Southend, Croydon CR0 1DP
t 020 8686 9649 e croydon@bagattis.com
bagattis.com

General: 🐕 @FAX 🚶 ♿ WC ♿ 🧑‍🦽

CR0 - Croydon | **Banana Leaf**

7 Lower Addiscombe Road, Croydon CR0 6PQ
t 020 8688 9922

General: 🐕 🚶 ♿ ♿ 🧑‍🦽

CR0 - Croydon | **Burger King**

87 Northend, Croydon CR0 1JH
t 020 8688 4012
burgerking.co.uk

General: 🐕 🚶 ♿ 🧑‍🦽

CR0 - Croydon | **Cafe Venezia**

Unit 80, The Whitgift Centre, Croydon CR0 1UR
t 020 8688 9352

General: 🐕 🚶 ♿ 🧑‍🦽

CR0 - Croydon | **Chiquito Restaurant & Bar**

Unit 3 Valley Park Leisure Development, Beddington Farm Road, Croydon CR0 3JB
t 020 8686 8341
chiquito.co.uk

General: 🐕 🚶 ♿ WC ♿ 🧑‍🦽

CR0 - Croydon | **Connors Fish & Chip Restaurant**

65 Church Street, Croydon CR0 1RH
t 020 8688 7026

General: 🐕 🚶 ♿ ♿ 🧑‍🦽

CR0 - Croydon | **Frankie & Benny's**

Unit 3 Valley Park, Croydon CR0 4YA
t 020 8760 5021
frankieandbennys.com

General: 🐕 ⋀ ♿ wc ♿ ⋀♿

CR0 - Croydon | **Galicia Tapas Bar & Restaurant**

269-275 High Street, Croydon CR0 1QH
t 020 8686 0043

General: 🐕 ⋀ ♿ wc ♿ ⋀♿

CR0 - Croydon | **Jardin De Provence**

40-42 Southend, Croydon CR0 1DP
t 020 8255 0045 e info@jardindeprovence.co.uk
jardindeprovence.co.uk

General: 🐕 FAX ⋀ ♿ wc ♿ ⋀♿

CR0 - Croydon | **Malay House**

60 Lower Addiscombe Road, Croydon CR0 6AA
t 020 8666 0266

General: 🐕 ⋀ ♿ ♿ ⋀♿

CR0 - Croydon | **Pizza Express**

3-5 Southend, Croydon CR0 1BE
t 020 8680 0123
pizzaexpress.com

General: 🐕 FAX ⋀ ♿ ⋀♿ .:

CR0 - Croydon | **Pizza Hut**

38 George Street, Croydon CR0 1PB
t 020 8681 5953
pizzahut.co.uk

General: 🐕 🦽 ⋀ ♿ wc ♿ ⋀♿ .: abc

CR2 - South Croydon | **Kelong**

1b Selsdon Road, Croydon CR2 6PU
t 020 8288 1638 e info@kelong.uk.com
kelong.co.uk

General: 🐕 FAX ⋀ ♿ wc ♿ ⋀♿

CR2 - South Croydon | **Sir Julian Huxley (JD Wetherspoon)**

152-154 Addington Road, Selsdon, Surrey CR2 8LB
t 020 8657 9457
jdwetherspoon.co.uk

General: 🐕 🦽 ⋀ ♿ wc ⋀♿ .:

CR2 - South Croydon | **Toby Carvery & Innkeepers Lodge**

415 Brighton Road, Croydon CR2 6EJ
t 020 8680 4559
toby-carvery.co.uk

General: ⚐ 🚹 👤 wc ♿ 👥 abc P★★★ 🛏

CR5 - Coulsdon | **Kabada**

196 Brighton Road, Coulsdon CR5 2NF
t 020 8668 0568
kabada.co.uk

General: ⚐ 🏠 🚹 👤 ♿ 👥

CR7 - Thornton Heath | **Eastern Promise**

12 High Street, Thornton Heath CR7 8LE

General: ⚐ 🚹 👤 ♿ 👥

CR7 - Thornton Heath | **Humming Bird**

23 Brigstock Road, Thornton Heath, Croydon CR7 7JJ
t 020 8683 1664
hummingbirduk.com

General: ⚐ 🚹 👤 ♿ 👥

CR8 - Purley | **Las Fuentes**

36-40 High Street, Purley, Croydon CR8 2AA
t 020 8763 1983

General: ⚐ 🚹 👤 wc ♿ 👥

CR8 - Purley | **Pizza Express**

960 Brighton Road, Purley CR8 2LP
t 020 8668 9547
pizzaexpress.com

General: ⚐ FAX 🚹 👤 wc 👥 .:

CR9 - Croydon | **Croydon Park Hotel**

7 Altyre Road, Croydon CR9 5AA
t 020 8680 9200 e reservations@croydonparkhotel.com
croydonparkhotel.com

General: ⚐ FAX 🚹 👤 ♿ P★★★

KT8 - Hampton Court | **Blubeckers Restaurant**

3 Palace Gate, Hampton Court, Surrey KT8 9BN
t 020 8941 5959
blubeckers.co.uk

General: ⚐ FAX 🚹 👤 👥

KT8 - Hampton Court | Cafe Fiama

Hampton Court Road, Hampton Court, Surrey KT8 9BY
t 020 8943 2050

General: ⚐ ⚐

KT8 - Hampton Court | Dar Latifa

76 Milton Road, Hampton, Middlesex TW12 2LJ
t 020 8941 4056 e latifa@dar-latifa.com
dar-latifa.com

General: ⚐ FAX ⚐ ⚐ ⚐ ⚐

KT8 - Hampton Court | Doolally

Park Cottage, Lion Gate, Hampton Court Road, East Mosely KT8 9BY
t 020 8943 3111

General: ⚐ ⚐ ⚐ ⚐ ⚐

KT8 - Hampton Court | Jolly Coopers

16 High Street, Hampton TW12 2SJ
t 020 8979 3384 e jane@jollycoopers.freeserve.co.uk

General: ⚐ FAX ⚐ ⚐ ⚐ ⚐ ⚐

TW1 - Twickenham | Cafe Du Bonheur

53 Church Street, Twickenham TW1 3NR
t 020 8891 6338

General: ⚐ FAX ⚐ ⚐ WC ⚐ ⚐

TW1 - Twickenham | Jun Ming

34 Heath Road, Twickenham TW1 4BZ
t 020 8892 3105

General: ⚐ ⚐ ⚐ ⚐ ⚐ ⚐

TW1 - Twickenham | Pizza Express

21 York Street, Twickenham TW1 3JZ
t 020 8891 4126
pizzaexpress.co.uk

General: ⚐ FAX ⚐ ⚐ ⚐ WC ⚐ .:

TW1 - Twickenham | Raefil's Restaurant

Church Street, Twickenham TW1 3NR
t 020 8892 6366

General: ⚐ ⚐ ⚐ ⚐

TW2 - Twickenham | Arthur's On The Green

The Green, Twickenham, Surrey TW2 5AB
t 020 8893 3995 e hello@arthursonthegreen.co.uk
arthursonthegreen.co.uk

General: 🐕 FAX 🚶 ♿ WC ♿ 🚶♿

TW2 - Twickenham | Cafe Venice

49 High Street, Whitton, Twickenham TW2 7LB
t 020 8898 4000

General: 🐕 FAX 🚶 ♿ ♿ 🚶♿ abc

TW2 - Twickenham | Fountain (Beefeater)

Corner Sixth Cross & Staines Road, Twickenham TW2 5PE
t 020 8898 2382
beefeater.co.uk

General: 🐕 FAX 🐾 🚶 ♿ WC ♿ 🚶♿ .: abc ⌒ P★★★

TW2 - Twickenham | Loch Fyne

175 Hampton Road, Twickenham, Middlesex TW2 5NG
t 020 8255 6222 e enquiries@lochfyne.net
lochfyne.com

General: 🐕 FAX 🚶 ♿ 🚶♿ P★★★

TW2 - Twickenham | Spice Of India

27 High Street, Whitton, Twickenham TW2 7LB
t 020 8894 1010
spiceofindiauk.com

General: 🐕 FAX 🏠 🚶 ♿ ♿

TW2 - Twickenham | Winning Post

Chertsey Road, Whitton, Middlesex TW2 6LS
t 020 8894 2772

General: 🐕 🐾 🚶 ♿ WC ♿ 🚶♿ P★★★

TW9 - Richmond | All Bar One

9-11 Hill Street, Richmond Upon Thames TW9 1SX
t 020 8332 7141
mbplc.com

General: 🐕 🚶 ♿ WC 🚶♿

TW9 - Richmond | Browns

3-5 Kew Green, Richmond Upon Thames, Surrey TW9 3AA
t 020 8948 4838
browns-restaurants.com

General: 🐕 FAX 🚶 ♿ WC 🚶♿

TW9 - Richmond | **Cafe Mama**

24 Hill Street, Richmond Upon Thames, Surrey TW9 1TW
t 020 8940 1625 e caffemama@hotmail.co.uk

General:

TW9 - Richmond | **Carluccio's**

31-33 Kew Road, Richmond Upon Thames, Surrey TW9 2NQ
t 020 8940 5037 e richmond@carluccios.com
carluccios.com

General:

TW9 - Richmond | **Duke**

2 Duke Street, Richmond, Surrey TW9 1HP
t 020 8940 4067 e duke@foodandfuel.co.uk
thedukerichmond.co.uk

General:

TW9 - Richmond | **Edward's**

1 Kew Road, Richmond Upon Thames, Surrey TW9 2NQ
t 020 8940 5768
mbplc.com

General:

TW9 - Richmond | **Matsuba**

10 Red Lion Street, Richmond TW9 1RW
t 020 8605 3513 e matsuba10@hotmail.com
matsuba.co.uk

General:

TW9 - Richmond | **McDonald's**

30 The Quadrant, Richmond Upon Thames, Surrey TW9 1DN
t 020 8332 2820 e richmond@mcd.co.uk
mcdonalds.co.uk

General:

TW9 - Richmond | **Pizza Express**

10 Station Approach, Kew TW9 3QB
t 020 8404 6000
pizzaexpress.co.uk

General:

TW9 - Richmond | **Pizzeria Rustica**

32 The Quadrant, Richmond Upon Thames, Surrey TW9 1DN
t 020 8332 6262

General:

TW9 - Richmond | **Strada**

26 Hill Street, Richmond Upon Thames, Surrey TW9 1TW
t 020 8940 3141 e richmond@strada.co.uk
strada.co.uk

General: ⚲ FAX ⚲ 🚶 ♿ WC ♿

TW9 - Richmond | **Tootsies**

Hotham House, Richmond Riverside, Richmond, Surrey TW9 1EJ
t 020 8948 3436 e enquiries@tootsiesrestaurants.com
tootsiesrestaurants.com

General: ⚲ FAX 🚶 ♿ WC ♿ ♿

TW9 - Richmond | **White Swan**

25-26 Old Palace Lane, Richmond Upon Thames, Surrey TW9 1PG
t 020 8940 0959 e info@whiteswanrichmond.co.uk
whiteswanrichmond.co.uk

General: ⚲ FAX ⚲ 🚶 ♿ ♿

TW10 - Richmond | **Don Fernando's**

27F The Quadrant, Richmond Upon Thames, Surrey TW10 1DN
t 020 8948 6447 e info@donfernando.co.uk
donfernando.co.uk

General: ⚲ FAX 🚶 ♿ abc

TW10 - Richmond | **Pembroke Lodge**

Richmond Park, Richmond Upon Thames, Surrey TW10 5HX
t 020 8940 8207 e info@pembrokelodge.uk
pembrokelodge.co.uk

General: ⚲ FAX ⚲ 🚶 ♿ WC ♿ ♿ P★★★

TW10 - Richmond | **Roebuck**

130 Richmond Hill, Surrey TW10 6RN
t 020 8948 2329

General: ⚲ ♿

TW10 - Richmond | **Taj Mahal Tandoori**

9 Petersham Road, Richmond TW10 6UH
t 020 8940 4903

General: ⚲ FAX ▥ 🚶 ♿ ♿

TW11 - Teddington | **Brasserie Gerard**

High Street, Teddington, Middlesex TW11 8EW
t 020 8943 5488 e teddington@paramountrestaurant.co.uk
brasseriegerard.co.uk

General: ⚲ FAX ⚲ 🚶 ♿ WC ♿ ♿ ⁘★ P

TW11 - Teddington | **Charin**

3 Church Road, Teddington, Surrey TW11 8PF
t 020 8943 3331

General: 🚶 ♿ ♿

TW11 - Teddington | **Clock House**

69 High Street, Teddington, Middlesex TW11 8HA
t 020 8977 3909
theclockhousepub.com

General: 🐕 🚶 ♿ ♿ ♿ abc ★★★

TW11 - Teddington | **Estilo Restaurant And Bar**

44 Broad Street, Teddington TW11 8QZ
t 020 8977 6002 e info@barestilo.co.uk
barestilo.co.uk

General: 🐕 FAX 🚶 ♿ wc ♿ ♿

TW11 - Teddington | **Park Hotel**

Park Road, Teddington, Middlesex TW11 0AB
t 020 8614 9700 e reservations.park@foliohotels.co.uk
foliohotels.co.uk

General: 🐕 FAX 🛒 🚶 ♿ wc ♿ ♿ abc 🔊 ★★★ 🛏

TW11 - Teddington | **Red Peppers**

53 Broad Street, Teddington, Surrey TW11 8QZ
t 020 8977 5452

General: 🐕 🚶 ♿

TW11 - Teddington | **Scarpetta**

78 High Street, Teddington TW11 8JD
t 020 8977 8177 e info@scarpetta.co.uk
scarpetta.co.uk

General: 🐕 FAX 🚶 ♿ ♿

TW11 - Teddington | **Tide End Cottage**

8 Ferry Road, Teddington TW11 9NN
t 020 8977 7762

General: 🐕 🚶 ♿ wc ♿ ♿ ★★★

TW13 - Feltham | **McDonald's**

Twickenham Road, Feltham TW13 6HB
t 020 8893 8477
mcdonalds.co.uk

General: 🐕 🛒 🚶 ♿ wc ♿ ♿ .: ★★★

W10 - North Kensington | **Garden Bar & Grill**

41 Bramley Road, London W10 6SZ
t 020 7229 1111 e info@priorybars.com
priorybars.com/station

General: 🐕 FAX 🚹 ♿ ♿ ♿

W10 - North Kensington | **Golborne Cafe Restaurant**

78 Golborne Road, London W10 5PS
t 020 8960 7308

General: 🐕 🚹 ♿ ♿ ♿

W10 - North Kensington | **Palki Indian Cuisine**

44 Goldbourne Road, London W10 5PR
t 020 8968 8764
palki.co.uk

General: 🐕 🚹 ♿ ♿

W11 - Notting Hill | **Ask**

145 Notting Hill Gate, London W11 3LB
t 020 7792 9942
askrestaurants.com

General: 🐕 🚹 ♿ ♿

W11 - Notting Hill | **Bertorelli Ristorante**

17 Notting Hill Gate, Kensington, London W11 3JQ
t 020 7727 7604

General: 🐕 ♿

W11 - Notting Hill | **Burger King**

100 Notting Hill Gate, London W11 3QA
t 020 7229 0699
burgerking.co.uk

General: 🐕 🚹 ♿ ♿

W11 - Notting Hill | **Kebab House Cafe**

24 Notting Hill Gate, Kensington, London W11 3JE
t 020 7221 0616

General: FAX 🚹 ♿

W11 - Notting Hill | **Le Pain Quotidien**

81-85 Notting Hill Gate, London W11 3JS
t 020 7486 6154 e nottinghill@lpquk.biz
lepainquotidien.co.uk

General: 🐕 FAX ♿ 🚹 ♿ wc ♿ ♿ 👫

W11 - Notting Hill | **McDonald's**

108 Notting Hill Gate, Notting Hill, London W11 3QA
t 020 7792 4151
mcdonalds.co.uk

General: 🐕 🐾 🧍 ᛒ WC ᚼᚽ .: abc P★

W11 - Notting Hill | **Mexicali**

147-149 Notting Hill Gate, London W11 3LF
t 020 7243 4148
eatmexicali.com

General: 🐕 ᛒ

W11 - Notting Hill | **Mitre**

40 Holland Park Avenue, London W11 3QY
t 020 7727 6332 e mitre@thespiritgroup.com
thespiritgroup.com

General: 🐕 FAX 🧍 ᛒ WC ᚼᚽ

W11 - Notting Hill | **Nando's**

58-60 Notting Hill Gate, London W11 3HT
t 020 7243 1647 e enquiries@nandos.co.uk
nandos.co.uk

General: 🐕 FAX 🐾 🧍 ᛒ .: abc

W11 - Notting Hill | **New Culture Revolution**

157-159 Notting Hill Gate, London W11 3LF
t 020 7313 9688 e info@newculturerevolution.co.uk
newculturerevolution.co.uk

General: 🐕 FAX 🧍 ᛒ ᚼᚽ

W11 - Notting Hill | **Portobello Gold**

95-97 Portobello Road, London W11 2QB
t 020 7460 4910

General: 🐕 🧍 ᛒ ᚽWC

W11 - Notting Hill | **Wine Factory**

294 Westbourne Grove, Notting Hill Gate, London W11 2PS
t 020 7229 1877
brinkleys.com

General: 🧍 ᛒ

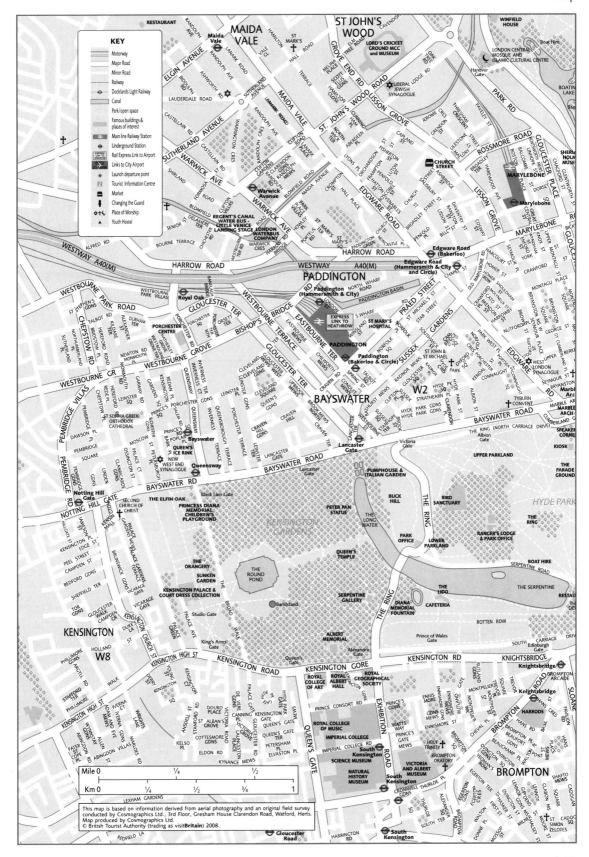

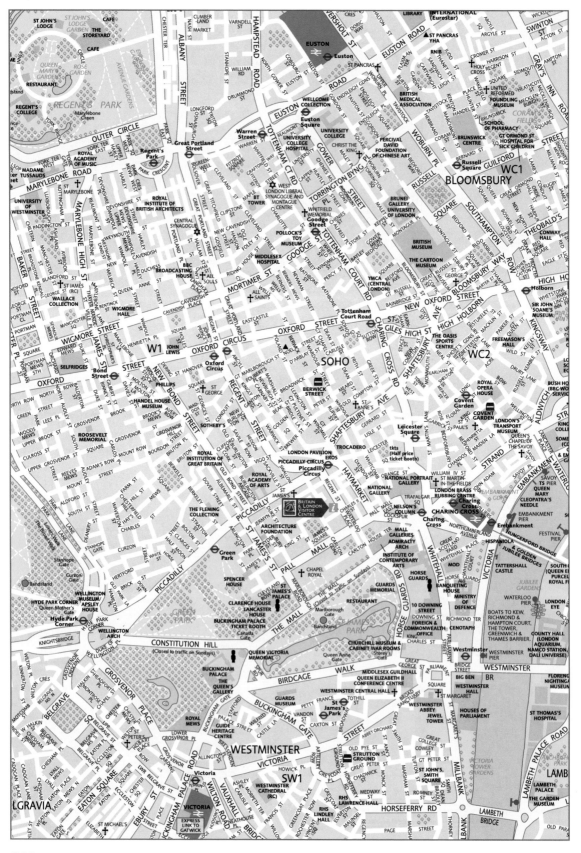

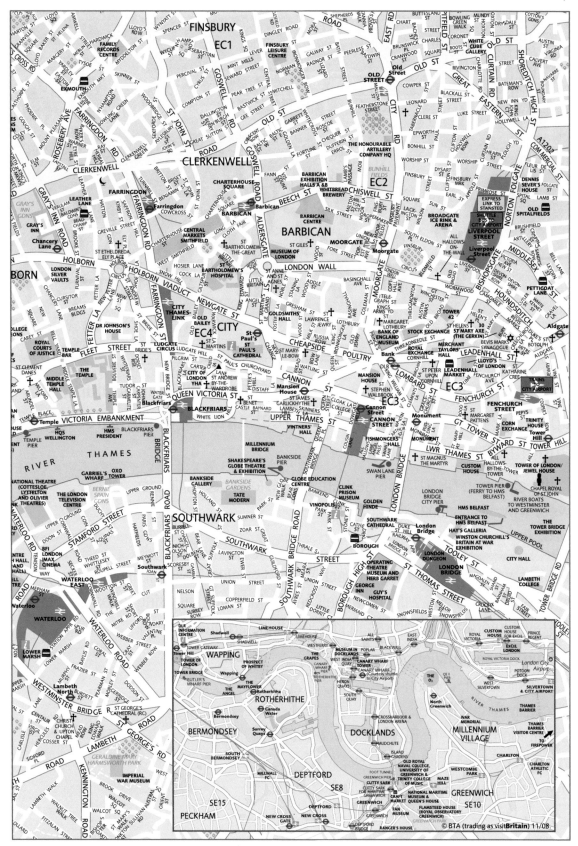

© 2010 photolibrary.

Visitor Information

Visit London can provide online information and booking for special events, theatre tickets, restaurants, accommodation and much more.

Visit London **t:** 08701 566 366 **email:** visitorinfo@visitlondon.com
web: www.visitlondon.com

Tourist & Travel – Information Centres

We know that face-to-face contact is always valued, especially when you are in a new city, so you will find a welcoming face and inspiring ideas at Tourist & Travel Information Centres in key locations around London.

Britain & London Visitor Centre
1 Regent Street, London SW1Y 4XT
Piccadilly Circus Exit 3
Open: Mon 09.30-18.30 (18.00 Oct-Mar)
Tues-Fri 09.00-18.30 (18.00 Oct-Mar)
Sat, Sun & Public Holidays 10.00-16.00
(Sat 09.00-17.00 Jun-Sep)

Tourist Information Centres – Central London

City of London TIC
St Paul's Churchyard, London EC4M 8BX
St. Paul's/Mansion House
Open: Mon-Sat 09.30-17.30
Sun 10.00-16.00

Greenwich TIC
46 Greenwich Church Street,
Greenwich SE10 9BL
Open: Daily 10.00-17.00

Holborn Visitor Information Kiosk
Kingsway, London WC2B 6BG
Holborn
Open: Mon-Fri 08.00-18.00 only

Tourist Information Centres – Outer London

Bexley Hall Place TIC
Bourne Road, Bexley, Kent DA5 1PQ
Open: Mon-Fri 09.30-16.30
Sat 10.30-16.30
Sun closed

Harrow TIC
Gayton Library, Garden House
5 St John's Road, Harrow HA1 2EE
Open: Mon-Fri 09.00-17.00
Sat and Sun closed

Kingston TIC
Market Place, Kingston upon Thames KT1 1JS
Open: Mon-Sat 10.00-17.00
Sun closed

Lewisham TIC
Lewisham Library
19 Lewisham High Street SE13 6LG
Open: Mon 10.00-17.00
Tues-Sat 09.00-17.00
Sun closed

Swanley TIC
Swanley Library & Information Centre
Kent BR8 7AE
Open: Mon-Thurs 09.30-17.30
Fri 09.30-18.00
Sat 09.00-16.00
Sun closed

Twickenham TIC
Civic Centre
Twickenham TW1 3BZ
Open: Mon-Thurs 09.00-17.15
Fri 09.00-17.00
Sat and Sun closed

Travel Information Centres

Euston Railway Station
Opposite platform 10
Open: Mon-Fri 07.15-21.15
Sat 07.15-18.15
Sun & Public Holidays 08.15-18.15

Heathrow Airport
Heathrow Terminals 1,2,3 Tube Station
Open: Daily 07.15-21.00

King's Cross Tube Station
Western Ticket Hall near St Pancras
Open: Mon-Sat 07.15-21.15
Sun & Public Holidays 08.15-20.15

Liverpool Street Tube Station
Open: Mon-Sat 07.15-21.15
Sun & Public Holidays 08.15-20.15

Piccadilly Circus Tube Station
Open: Mon-Sat 07.15-21.15
Sun & Public Holidays 08.15-20.00

Victoria Railway Station
Opposite platform 6
Open: Mon-Sat 07.15-21.15
Sun & Public Holidays 08.15-20.15

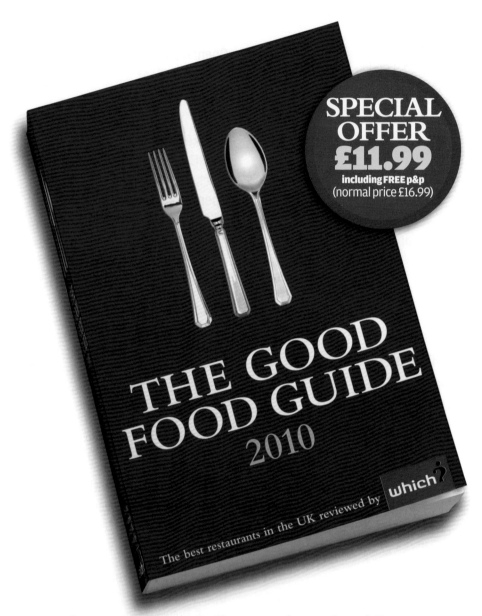

To order your copy of _The Good Food Guide 2010_ at the special offer price of £11.99 including FREE p&p (normal price £16.99), please call 01903 828557 and quote GFGOB10.

Offer is valid to 31 August 2010 (while stocks last).

ISBN: 978 1 84490 066 4 | 624 pages | Full colour, including maps for each region
The Good Food Guide is pleased to support the work of OpenBritain

Index of Accessible Sightseeing

Index – Where to stay by property name

H continued

R

S

T

V

W

Y

Index – Where to eat by property name

B continued

I continued

M continued

N

O

P

P continued

Q

R

S

T

Index of Display Advertisers

Published by: Tourism for All UK, c/o Vitalise, Shap Road Industrial Estate, Kendal LA9 6NT in partnership with RADAR and Shopmobility UK and supported by the London Development Agency and Visit London.

Chief Executive: Jennifer Littman

Chairman: Sir William Lawrence

Compilation, design, editorial, production and advertisement sales: Heritage House Group, Ketteringham Hall, Wymondham, Norfolk NR18 9RS
t 01603 813319

Publisher: Kate Kaegler

Production Manager: Sarah Phillips

Group Director: Kelvin Ladbrook

Cover design: Peter Moore Fuller, Woolf Design

Design/prepress: PDQ Digital Media Solutions Ltd, Bungay, Suffolk

Printing and binding:
Burlington Press, Cambridge.

Cover image:
Merlin Entertainments The London Eye

Page 2 image:
People on the Southbank, Tower Bridge in background.
visitlondonimages/britainonview/Pawel Libera

Photography credits:
ATOC (Andrew Molyneux / Giles Park); Britainonview (Pawel Libera / Alan Chandler / Juliet White / Jasmine Teer / Simon Winnall / Andrew Orchard / Damir Fabijanc); Transport for London.

WWW.OPENBRITAIN.NET